The Salem Witch Crisis

THE
SALEM WITCH
CRISIS

LARRY GRAGG

PRAEGER

New York
Westport, Connecticut
London

Library of Congress Cataloging-in-Publication Data

Gragg, Larry Dale, 1950–
    The Salem witch crisis / Larry Gragg.
       p.   cm.
    Includes bibliographical references and index.
    ISBN 0-275-94189-2 (alk. paper)
    1. Witchcraft—Massachusetts—Salem.   I. Title.
  BF1576.G73   1992
  133.4′3′097445—dc20   91-47099

British Library Cataloguing in Publication Data is available.

Library of Congress Catalog Card Number: 91-47099
ISBN: 0-275-94189-2

First published in 1992

Praeger Publishers, One Madison Avenue, New York, NY 10010
An imprint of Greenwood Publishing Group, Inc.

Printed in the United States of America

The paper used in this book complies with the Permanent
Paper Standard issued by the National Information Standards
Organization (Z39.48-1984).

10 9 8 7 6 5 4 3

For Doris and Julie

Contents

Preface

Three hundred years ago, the people in and around Salem, Massachu-setts, engaged in the most massive witch hunt in American history. Authorities arrested over 150 suspects from more than two dozen towns, juries convicted twenty-eight, and nineteen were hanged. Recent scholarship on this topic has been substantial. In the past two decades, studies emphasizing economic conflict, sexual hostility, religious division, challenges to the legal system, and exaggerated fears of witch cults have modified long-held notions about early American witchcraft. However, this revisionary work, with all its new insights, generally has not been written for the general reader. Instead, these tend to be specialized works based on the often arcane methodologies of the social sciences. While drawing on this valuable body of research, I have adopted a narrative style that presents the events in chronological order. Within that framework, I have focused on the impact that individuals' decisions had on the outcome of events. This is an old-fashioned approach, one based on the belief that history is first and foremost a good story.

As all specialists in this growing area of the colonial period of American history will quickly note, I am indebted to the work of a host of scholars, notably Paul Boyer, John Demos, Richard Gildrie, David Hall, Chadwick Hansen, Carol Karlsen, Lyle Koehler, David Thomas Konig, Stephen Nissenbaum, Richard Trask, and Richard Weisman. I hope readers will consult their often challenging, specialized studies to deepen their understanding of this engaging topic.

My research was made easier by the help I received at several libraries and archives. The staffs at the State Historical Society of Missouri, the Connecticut Historical Society, the Essex Institute, and the Danvers Archives were particularly helpful. The reference librarians at the University of Missouri-Rolla deserve special thanks for their patient handling of my numerous interlibrary loan requests.

The University of Missouri-Rolla supported the research for this project through a 1989–90 Weldon Spring Humanities Fellowship.

Several people assisted in the preparation of this book. Jack Ridley, Lawrence Christensen, and my wife, Doris, offered valuable suggestions at each stage of the manuscript's development. David Burwell provided crucial help in the final preparation of the manuscript. The staff at Praeger was always gracious and helpful, particularly editor Dan Eades and project editor Nina Neimark.

I have modernized the spelling and the most erratic punctuation in quotations. Whenever possible, I have used reprints of the original sources for the quotations used. Notably, I have drawn from two important collections edited by Paul Boyer and Stephen Nissenbaum: *Salem-Village Witchcraft: A Documentary Record of Local Conflict in Colonial New England* (Belmont, CA, 1972) and *The Salem Witchcraft Papers*, 3 vols. (New York, 1977). Also important for quotations in the book are the numerous essays and letters reprinted in George Lincoln Burr, ed., *Narratives of the Witchcraft Cases: 1648–1706* (originally published 1914; reprint: New York, 1975).

One

In the "Mists of Darkness": Occult Beliefs and Practices in Early New England

The people of the seventeenth century inhabited a mental world that few in this century would recognize. It often was a frightening place, one in which individuals suffered assaults from agents of the "invisible world."

One night late in November 1679, William and Elizabeth Morse of Newbury in Essex County, Massachusetts, thought they received a visitation. The sixty-five-year-old man and his wife heard a noise outside their house. When they stepped out to investigate, a hail of rocks and sticks forced them to retreat back inside. Over a two-month period, the Morses experienced dozens of other incidents that persuaded them that Satan had loosed unseen forces called poltergeists to invade their household. Before their frightening ordeal would end, Elizabeth and a man named Caleb Powell would be tried for practicing witchcraft, and the Morses's grandson, John Stiles, would suffer physically and emotionally from a host of afflictions.

After going to bed that first evening, Thursday, November 27, the Morses awoke at about midnight to the grunting of a large hog that had gotten into the house, even though William was certain he had locked the door before retiring. The following day, utensils hanging in the fireplace were repeatedly "thrown down." In addition, that night a large awl, a basket, and a brick came down the chimney numerous times. On Saturday, so many sticks and stones came down the chimney that the Morses had trouble simply dressing and eating their breakfast. Similar alarming incidents continued throughout the weekend, but on Monday afternoon the situation took an even more bizarre turn. As William described the scene:

[T]he pots hanging over the fire did dash so vehemently one against the other. We set down one that they might not dash to pieces. I saw the andiron leap into the pot and dance and leap out, and again leap in and dance and leap on a table and there abide, and my wife saw the andiron on the table. Also I saw the pot turn itself over and throw down all the water. Again we saw a tray with wool leap up and down and throw the wool out and so many times and saw nobody meddle with it.

Other extraordinary phenomena baffled Morse and his wife. He contended, for example, that "a chair standing in the house and not anybody near it did often bow towards me and so rise up again."[1] Even more frightening, the couple heard occasional voices. After putting out the lights one night, they were shocked to hear a voice sing out, "Revenge! Revenge! Sweet is revenge!" When the terrified Morses prayed to God for help, the voice responded, "Alas! Alas! me knock no more! me knock no more!" And all was quiet.[2]

Several neighbors also claimed to have seen moving and flying objects when they visited the Morses's home. Indeed, many of them testified later in court to the reality of the episodes. One of the visitors and a temporary resident of Newbury, Caleb Powell, dropped by often. Once, as he approached the house, Powell saw that the old man was at prayer, and as he waited for Morse to complete his meditation, he spied the grandson playing "tricks." Specifically, Powell said that he saw the boy toss a shoe at his grandfather's head. During a later visit, Powell told the couple that he believed that their grandson had caused their trouble. "Although he may not have done all," Powell admitted, "yet most of them, for this boy is a young rogue, a vile rogue, I have watched him and seen him do things as to come up and down." Powell offered to take the boy for a time and free them from their afflictions. Morse reluctantly permitted Powell to take young Stiles, and though he was gone only a day or two, the "troubles" ceased.[3]

Relieved that calm had returned to his household, Morse nonetheless worried that Powell had employed witchcraft to accomplish it. After all, the seaman had claimed to know "the working of spirits" and to have an "understanding in astrology and astronomy." On December 3, two days after allowing his grandson to go with Powell, Morse acted on his apprehensions and filed a formal complaint against Powell for "working with the devil to the molesting of William Morse and his family." After a hearing five days later, authorities took Powell into custody and scheduled a trial for the next meeting of the county court in March. Remarkably, on the day of the hearing, with John Stiles back in the household, the "disturbances" commenced again.[4]

William and Elizabeth once more had to endure incidents ranging from the mischievous to the frightening. At some of their meals, ashes from the hearth were tossed onto their food and clothing and into their eyes. Prior to one meal, "a chair flew about, and at last lighted on the table where victuals stood ready." Once, while Elizabeth was milking, cow dung was pitched into the pail. On another occasion, a ladder that Morse thought he had lost banged against the door late at night. Simply trying to sleep became an ordeal. At various times in December, William, while in bed, was hit in the stomach with a stone, was scratched and pinched, had his hair and beard pulled, and was hit with a "heavy pair of leather breeches." The most painful experience occurred while Morse slept with his wife and grandson. He suffered jabs from needles and sharpened sticks that caused his face and thigh to bleed. Twice while he was writing, candlesticks were thrown at Morse. As he prayed with the family, he was hit in the head by a broom. On another occasion, a fire shovel struck him in the face.[5]

By mid-December, however, the old couple experienced fewer and fewer misadventures. Instead, their grandson became the target of the unseen forces afflicting the household. He was "flung about" in such a violent manner that the Morses "feared that his brains would have been beaten out." They could not prevent the boy's "bedclothes flying off him" even though they slept with him. The boy seemed almost constantly endangered. On three occasions he had to be pulled out of the fireplace. Often, he complained of pains in his back, and at different times, the grandparents found a "three-tined fork," "an iron spindle," and "pins" stuck in the boy's back. Not only did he suffer physical afflictions but he also began to act strangely. He barked like a dog and clucked like a chicken. Finally, on December 26, John accused Caleb Powell of being responsible for his afflictions. After making the charge, the boy recovered, and things briefly returned to normal.[6]

This already strange case took a dramatic new direction on January 7. Local magistrate John Woodbridge began taking depositions, not to further implicate Caleb Powell but to gather evidence for charges of witchcraft against Elizabeth Morse! For a number of years, Elizabeth's neighbors had suspected that she might have dabbled in the occult. For example, Caleb Moody, a neighbor of the Morses for about twenty years, recalled in his deposition a sixteen-year-old incident. After an argument with Elizabeth, Moody found one of his "best hogs . . . dead in the yard, and no natural cause that I know of." Moody clearly implied that she had bewitched the swine. Another neighbor, Joshua Richardson, had a similar story. Five years earlier, Elizabeth had chastised him for driving his sheep into the Morse "cow house" without permission. Later the same day, all three of the animals got sick and "did foam at the mouth." One eventually died, and Richardson concluded that "they were bewitched." Other Newbury residents, given the six weeks of odd occurrences at the Morse home, also decided that Elizabeth was as responsible, if not more so, than Caleb Powell. One of the depositions even indicated that Powell had collected some of the evidence against her! As nearly a dozen citizens came forward on January 7, long-remembered rumors and gossip about Elizabeth Morse's evil magical powers became the basis for an indictment that was issued against her months later.[7]

On January 9, John Stiles disappeared for most of the day. He crawled home, claiming that Powell had taken and beaten him. Stiles went through a period of fainting often, and food "would forcibly fly out of his mouth," a phenomenon that the boy attributed to Powell. Stiles also began to eat peculiar objects. On January 19, he "swooned and coming to himself, he roared terribly, and did eat ashes, sticks, and rugyarn."[8] Gradually, the boy's afflictions occurred less frequently, but as that problem diminished, the Morses still had to face Elizabeth's formal indictment for witchcraft by the grand jury and her incarceration at the nearby Ipswich jail on March 6 to await trial in May.

Meanwhile, Caleb Powell had his day in court in late March. Several residents, including William Morse who submitted a lengthy deposition, testified that they had heard Powell claim to have occult powers. The judges, nonetheless, found insufficient evidence for a conviction. At the same time, they refused to grant Powell an unqualified acquittal:

Though this court cannot find any evident ground of proceeding farther against the said Powell, yet we determine that he hath given such ground of suspicion of his so dealing, that we cannot so acquit him, but that he justly deserves to bear his own shame and the costs of the prosecution of the complaint.[9]

Following the Powell trial, attention shifted again to Elizabeth Morse. In early May, the jailer at Ipswich transported her to Boston to be tried by the Court of Assistants, the colony's highest judicial authority. During the journey, she steadfastly proclaimed her innocence, telling the jailer that "she was as clear of the accusation as God in Heaven." After Elizabeth's arrival, the authorities ordered a group of women to examine her body. A simple assumption lay behind this "test." Individuals who had made a pact with the Devil often received an animal-like familiar spirit to do their bidding that they were obligated to nourish through a witch's teat. If a physical examination revealed a growth that was cold to the touch or insensitive to a pin prick, most judges considered that proof of the accused's affiliation with the Devil. Unfortunately for Elizabeth, the women found "teats . . . in her privates."[10] That physical evidence was presented on May 20, along with depositions from two dozen individuals. Some reaffirmed that Elizabeth had long had a reputation as a witch. Jane Sewall, for example, stated that many years ago William Morse had openly said to her that "his wife was accounted a witch." Morse attributed that to Elizabeth's healing powers as a midwife; nonetheless, he admitted to her unfavorable renown.[11]

A few witnesses contended that Elizabeth had the extraordinary power to determine the contents of a letter without having seen it and to know about incidents despite not being present when they occurred. John March's testimony suggested that Morse could understand such things because of her familiar spirits. March explained that in 1674 he and Daniel Greenleaf spent a night at John Wells's home. Shortly after going to bed:

We heard a great noise in the chamber. I looked up and saw several cats and rats at play together in the chamber, running one after another; the rats after the cats, and I was very much amazed at it; and a little while after I slung several things at them but could not strike them. The next morning, before we came out of the chamber I heard Goody Morse and my Dame Wells a talking together without the door. Several words they had which was very loud and I heard my Dame Wells call Goody Morse witch, and several such words, which I could not tell the meaning of, before I came down, and I came down my Dame Wells came in again. She asked me if I saw such things as before expressed. I asked her why she asked me. She told me that Goody Morse told her that I had seen cats and rats that night. Then Goody Wells told me that she asked her how she knew it. She told her that she heard so, though neither I nor Daniel Greenleaf who only knew it, had not been out of the chamber to tell anybody.

March concluded by telling the court that Goody Wells told him that she had seen creatures "like mice and rats" run into Elizabeth Morse's house and "under her coats."[12]

John Chase testified that the day he had given his initial testimony against Elizabeth he "was taken with the bloody flux," and it persisted until he "came to the court and charged her with it." Moreover, Chase suggested that Elizabeth was responsible for his wife being "troubled with sore breasts, that she have lost them both, and one of them rotted away."[13]

While such evidence might have demonstrated Elizabeth Morse's evil powers, perhaps most damaging to her case was Esther Wilson's testimony. Wilson explained that when she had stayed with her ill mother, the latter "would often cry out and complain that G[oodwife] Morse was a witch, and had bewitched her, and every time she came to see her she was the worse for her." Wilson's mother took a neighbor's suggestion and employed countermagic against Morse, nailing a horseshoe over the threshold. As long as the horseshoe remained there, Morse would not enter the house; rather "she would kneel down by the door and talk and discourse, but not go in." When another neighbor knocked the horseshoe off, saying it was "a piece of witchery," Morse willingly came in.[14]

The accumulated evidence resulted in a quick guilty verdict. On May 27, Governor Simon Bradstreet pronounced that Elizabeth Morse would be "hanged by the neck till she was dead." Less than a week later, the Court of Assistants granted Elizabeth a reprieve until its October session, apparently because there were not two witnesses to a number of the alleged incidents. On June 4, William petitioned them:

to grant her liberty, in the daytime to walk in the prison yard, and to the prison house, and that in the night she may have privilege of a chamber in the common jail, and be freed from the dungeon which is extreme close and hot in this season, and also liberty on the sabbath to go to meeting; he and his children giving security for her safe imprisonment.

If the court responded, there is no record of it. Yet given their leniency in Elizabeth's case, it is likely that they granted some of William's requests, making her summer incarceration a little less oppressive. In October, the court granted her another reprieve, a decision that stirred some controversy in the provincial government. The House of Deputies expressed surprise that Morse's sentence "is not executed. Her second reprieve seems to go beyond what the law will allow." Yet the deputies' complaint failed to prompt any action, and Elizabeth remained in jail.[15]

During the spring of 1681, William petitioned the court two more times on his wife's behalf. On May 14, he submitted a detailed rebuttal to the evidence offered in Elizabeth's trial. In some instances, Morse questioned the consistency of the witnesses' allegations. In response to Zachary Davis's claim that Elizabeth was responsible for his calf's death, Morse said that Davis's father "did profess it to us, that, he judged it a hand of God, and was far from blaming us." Further, Morse tried to prove that some of the witnesses had been encouraged to give false testimony. He specifically discussed the charge made by Susannah Goodwin who alleged that Elizabeth had bewitched her child. In his petition, Morse explained that when he and his wife confronted the Widow Goodwin with her charge, she broke into tears. She begged their forgiveness, saying that "it was others put her upon it, to say as she did." Strangely enough, Caleb Powell played a role in Goodwin's change of heart. Although a year earlier, he had apparently been helping collect evidence against Elizabeth, Powell, according to Susannah Goodwin, urged her "to say as she now saith." William also contended that he and his wife had been unaware of many of the incidents mentioned in the testimony against her. "This being twelve years ago," Morse wrote in rebuttal to John Mighill's charge that Elizabeth caused his loss of livestock, "did amaze us now to hear of it."[16]

William presented the other petition only four days later. This one, however, came from his wife. Having been in jail for over a year, Elizabeth had become impatient with all of the delays and appeals. She had even made some "passionate speeches" about "suffering wrongfully." Obviously tired, Elizabeth, in a plaintive tone, beseeched the court to resolve her case. According to her petition, she:

pleaded not guilty, and by the mercy of God and the goodness of the honored Governor, I am reprieved and brought to this law, and know not how to present my case, but humbly beg that my request may not be rejected, it being no more than your sentence upon my trial whether I shall live or die.

Provincial authorities, obviously moved by the old woman's condition, reacted quickly. Although the motion for a new trial was rejected, Elizabeth received another reprieve. Also, the Court of Assistants finally permitted her to go home, although they would not grant her an acquittal.[17]

After taking his wife home, William asked a number of neighboring ministers to meet with her. Eager for vindication in the eyes of her spiritual leaders, Elizabeth, according to one of the clergy, "pleaded her innocence as to that which was laid to her charge." Though "her discourse was very Christian," the visiting ministers concluded that it was not prudent for them "to pass any definitive sentence upon one under her circumstances, yet we inclined to the more charitable."[18]

It had been a frustrating, bewildering, and often terrifying eighteen months for this Newbury matron. She had endured what had appeared to be the actions of poltergeist in her home, the suspicions and accusations of her neighbors, a trial for witchcraft, and over a year of the horrid conditions in colonial jails. Although released, Elizabeth remained guilty in the eyes of the judicial authorities. Indeed, they had restricted her movement. She could not go "above sixteen rods [264 feet] from her own house and land at any time except to the meetinghouse."[19] While she had the sympathy of spiritual authorities, they too had refused to certify her innocence, and there is no evidence that she ever gained the confidence or sympathy of her neighbors. Elizabeth's only constant source of support had been her indefatigable husband, and he died two years later. Given these devastating circumstances, it is not surprising that "in her last sickness she was in much darkness and trouble of spirit." The widow Morse "sought her pardon and comfort from God in Christ," one minister explained, "and died so far as I understood, praying and resting upon God in Christ for salvation."[20]

The experiences of the Morses illustrate much about early American witchcraft beliefs. The elderly couple had automatically assumed that their difficulties had a supernatural explanation. Few of their contemporaries would have questioned such a conclusion, because the English on both sides of the Atlantic shared a wide array of occult beliefs. Floods, thunder, lightning, hailstorms, hurricanes, earthquakes, and comets were considered the harbingers of illness or destruction. Curses, spells, and the evil eye, most believed, could cause harm. Reports of strange dreams, visions, unseen voices, and prophecies circulated frequently.[21] In England, practitioners of magic, men and women who sought to manipulate supernatural powers, abounded. "Sorcerers are too common," Robert Burton wrote in 1621, "cunning men, wizards and white witches . . . in every village."[22] These specialists in the occult attracted clients from all levels of English society. Rich and poor alike consulted cunning folk to recover lost property, to discover a cure for illness, for help in finding missing family members or livestock, for advice in making personal and business decisions, or to identify witches.[23] In 1610, English Puritan minister William Perkins acknowledged the frequent resort of his countrymen to occult practitioners:

As the ministers of God do give resolution to the conscience, in matters doubtful and difficult; so the ministers of Satan, under the name of wise-men, and wise-women, are at hand, by his appointment, to resolve, direct and help ignorant and unsettled persons in cases of distraction, loss, or other outward calamities.[24]

New Englanders likewise used charms; engaged in fortunetelling, divination, and sorcery; carefully read almanacs for astronomical data essential to the practice of astrology; read about and pursued the mysteries of alchemy; and a few, like Caleb Powell, boasted about their knowledge of the occult. Boston clergyman Cotton Mather claimed that many colonists "would often cure hurts with spells, and practice detestable conjurations with sieves, and keys, and peas, and nails, and other implements, to learn the things for which they had a forbidden and impious curiosity." Through such experiments, he believed, "the minds of many had been so poisoned" that they began to study the more insidious practice of witchcraft.[25]

The fear that Mather expressed is best understood in the context of European developments from the late fifteenth through the mid-seventeenth centuries. Although the belief in witchcraft had been present for several centuries, religious and secular authorities in Catholic and Protestant regions alike in that era grew concerned about an organized cult of witches. In 1484, Pope Innocent VIII issued a bull condemning witchcraft as heresy, the exercise of supernatural powers obtained through a demonic pact. Two years later, with papal approval, Heinrich Kramer and Jacob Sprenger, Dominican inquisitors, published the *Malleus Maleficarum* (*The Hammer of Witches*), the first major treatise on witchcraft beliefs. A case-book manual for inquisitors, the *Malleus* went through over a dozen reprints by 1520. Other works on witchcraft followed, particularly after 1570.[26] By the early seventeenth century, they collectively offered a picture of a secret society of Devil-worshiping witches. Despite the efforts of writers like Margaret Murray, Montague Summers, and Jeffrey B. Russell to prove the existence of such cults, recent scholarship has demonstrated that no organized society of witches ever developed.[27]

However, in the century after the publication of the *Malleus*, governments across Europe made the practice of witchcraft a capital crime, and many permitted the use of judicial torture to obtain confessions.[28] Large witch hunts, however, did not automatically follow implementation of such laws. A combination of other factors usually were essential. Increases in prosecutions at times were associated with periods of economic distress or political and religious turmoil. Yet inflation, depression, poor harvests, rumors of war, or hostilities between Catholics and Protestants would not necessarily trigger a search for witches. The most likely locales of rigorous hunts were those that experienced some of the above conditions in conjunction with an intense fear of a powerful witch conspiracy. In all, about 110,000 were prosecuted, and about

60,000 of those were executed. The most extensive prosecutions took place in French- and German-speaking regions between 1550 and 1650. England, by contrast, had one of Europe's most restrained records of prosecution. In the British Isles, there were probably no more than about 5,000 trials, and more than half of those occurred in Scotland. More important, probably fewer than 500 were executed in England. In the most closely studied locale, Essex County, only about twenty-five percent of those convicted were executed. Restraint in the use of judicial coercion partly explains the comparatively low figures. Most crucial, however, was the focus of English trials. Judges displayed little concern for the discovery of an organized witch society. Rather, they sought to punish witches for the harm they caused, notably the injury or death of humans or animals or the destruction of property. In his study of Essex prosecutions, Alan MacFarlane found that over ninety percent of all indictments fell into this category.[29]

This emphasis upon the more mundane aspect of witch beliefs prevailed in New England as well. Ordinary people worried less about witches worshiping Satan than their dealing in *maleficium*, the use of magic to harm others. In short, their fundamental concern was with the threat a witch posed to their farm and family. Most of Elizabeth Morse's neighbors who testified against her recalled specific examples of her *maleficia*. They charged that she was responsible for the illness and death of hogs and sheep and that she had caused the physical ailments of at least two people. To combat these evil powers, many resorted to countercharms or countermagic. Students of folklore have identified several techniques that were employed. "For human sickness," Jacqueline Simpson found, "one should make a 'witch bottle' by filling a bottle with the victim's urine plus pins or thread, or boiling it."[30] This would force the witch to lift her spell because it would cause her pain. Esther Wilson's mother's use of a horseshoe above her threshold to keep Elizabeth Morse from entering her home was a variation on that approach.

Rejecting supernatural methods, colonial authorities, like those in Europe, chose instead to outlaw the practice of witchcraft. By 1647, all the New England colonies had incorporated the death penalty for convictions into their legal codes.[31] Caleb Powell and Elizabeth Morse were two of the approximately 100 individuals in New England accused of witchcraft prior to the Salem Village episode in 1692.[32] Most faced some sort of judicial proceeding, ranging from a preliminary examination to a full-scale trial. As both their cases illustrate, most judges in witchcraft trials were not eager to convict and execute the accused. They cautiously used evidence, especially specter evidence. This involved someone claiming to have seen the image, or specter, of the accused doing harm. To some legal authorities, such allegations were crucial. They reasoned that Satan could not use a person's specter without her permission. That judges were not in agreement on specter evidence is clear from the Morse case: "They were not satisfied that a specter doing mischief in her likeness, should be imputed to her person, as a ground of guilt."[33] The best measure of judicial restraint can be found in the proportion of accused who subsequently were convicted and executed. In the years prior to the Salem Village episode, there were only twenty convictions and sixteen executions. Between 1663 and 1692, courts convicted only four suspects and executed only one.[34]

Although biographical data about those accused of witchcraft is far from complete, a profile of the individuals most vulnerable to witchcraft accusations developed. Women comprised almost eighty percent of those accused, making gender the most significant characteristic. Moreover, approximately half of the males accused had direct involvement with accused women as friends, supporters, or kin.[35] There are no completely satisfactory explanations for the preponderance of women among the accused. They obviously lived in a male-dominated culture. Men held political and religious power, controlled most property, and were the acknowledged heads of households.[36] Such circumstances make it tempting to view the accused as women who challenged "prescribed gender arrangements."[37] This would make them the targets of a misogynist culture unwilling to tolerate females who were assertive, economically independent, or reluctant to defer to men; in short, individuals who had refused to accept their place in the traditional social order. There are, however, several problems with such an explanation. Little evidence exists that English culture in the seventeenth century experienced "generalized" conflict or hostility between the sexes on either side of the Atlantic.[38] In addition, although men filed most of the charges of witchcraft against women, many came from other women.[39] These might have been women who shared a distrust or dislike of nonconforming women. More likely, such considerations played little or no role in their charges; women accused other women because they sought to punish those causing harm in their community. Finally, according to one recent survey of seventeenth-century material, "no colonist ever explicitly said why he or she saw witches as women."[40] Perhaps the tendency to single out women reflected the seventeenth-century assumption that women were morally and intellectually inferior to men and as a consequence were less able to resist Satan. Clearly, William Perkins believed so. In

1608, he wrote, "The woman being the weaker sex, is sooner entangled by the devil's illusions with this damnable art than the man."[41]

Age and wealth were also significant factors in witchcraft accusations. The young seldom had to fear suspicion or formal charges. The overwhelming majority of the accused were over forty. Moreover, in the two decades preceding the Salem Village episode, women over sixty, like Elizabeth Morse, became particularly vulnerable.[42] While older women of all levels of New England society might be accused, a higher proportion came from the ranks of the poor, but not the very poor.[43]

Many of the accused witches shared unsavory reputations. Some were known for their contentious behavior.[44] For example, during Elizabeth Morse's trial, several witnesses testified to heated confrontations with her. Also, like Morse, the accused often revealed special healing powers. Jane Sewall recalled that midwife Elizabeth Morse had been instrumental in the delivery of a child after a particularly difficult labor. Contemporaries usually attributed such skills to some occult connection. Elizabeth Morse's renown was such that Margaret Mirack recalled her husband wondering if Elizabeth was "a witch, or a cunning woman."[45] It had become commonplace by the late seventeenth century for people to suspect spiteful, poor, older women of being witches. A witness of a witch hunt in Chelmsford, England, contended that villagers had come to suspect "every old woman with a wrinkled face, a furred brow, a hairy lip, a squint eye, a squeaking voice, or a scolding tongue, a skull cap on her head, a spindle in her hand, a dog or cat by her side." Cotton Mather would have agreed. He insisted that New Englanders found it easy "to traduce for, a witch, every old woman, whose temper with her visage is not eminently good."[46]

An extraordinarily detailed account of the possession of Elizabeth Knapp reveals one other significant dimension of seventeenth-century witchcraft beliefs. A maidservant in the home of pastor Samuel Willard of Groton, Massachusetts, Knapp began to act "in a strange and unwanted manner" with "sudden shrieks" and "extravagant laughter" in mid-October 1671. Over the next three months, Willard closely observed the sixteen-year-old and carefully recorded her "distemper."[47] Although he was not truly an objective observer, Willard nonetheless viewed the young woman's experiences with a critical eye. On October 30, just before going to bed, Elizabeth complained of pains in her legs and breast and felt that she was being strangled. Initially, those in the household did not know "what to make of it, whether she was in earnest or dissembled." The following day, she alternately wept and laughed and, according to skeptical Willard, made "many foolish and apish gestures."[48]

His attitude began to change after Elizabeth retired that evening. In the quiet of the night, she was "thrown down into the midst of the floor with violence" and thrashed about the house with such strength that the Willard family could barely keep her from hurling herself into the fireplace.[49] In all, Elizabeth suffered through thirty-four days of fits of varying degrees of intensity.[50] During some of those episodes, she could not speak. For several hours on November 15, for example, her tongue was "drawn into a semicircle up to the roof of her mouth, and not to be removed" even when several people tried prying it loose with their fingers. On other occasions, Elizabeth mumbled words like "money, money" or "sin and misery." She screamed and roared about "hellish torments." On November 27 and 28, she even "barked like a dog and bleated like a calf."[51]

One person could not control Elizabeth when she leaped and skipped about the house or when she swung sticks about menacingly. In December, she not only struck at but also spat on those who tried to calm her. Restraining her usually required the efforts of three to six adults. On November 5, a physician examined the troubled young woman and concluded that her "distemper" resulted largely from natural causes. The "foulness of her stomach and corruptness of her blood," he believed, had caused "fumes in her brain and strange fantasies." She took his prescribed medication for a week and convinced herself "that the Devil had left her." Yet the fits began anew. The physician returned on November 26 and changed his diagnosis. Now he attributed her problems to a "diabolical" source, and he advised "extraordinary fasting" rather than medicine. Willard, alone or in collaboration with other clergy and villagers, followed the advice and pursued a therapy of prayer and fasting but with only intermittent success. During those "intermissions" when she was lucid, Elizabeth discussed her trauma at length with Willard. Twice, on November 1 and December 4, she accused neighbors of causing her afflictions. In both cases, however, when the women were brought to the parsonage and prayed with Elizabeth, she withdrew her allegations. In the first instance, she did so after concluding that "Satan had deluded her."[52]

Elizabeth's discussions of her lengthy efforts to resist Satan's temptations startled Willard and the villagers who often crowded into the pastor's home. She recalled that Satan had first approached her when she was thirteen (on another occasion she thought she might have only been eleven) and had been particularly persistent since she had moved into the parsonage with the Willards. He had offered Elizabeth a covenant, and she was sorely tempted to accept because he had tantalized her with items that "suited her youthful fancy . . . money, silks, fine clothes, ease from labor, to show her the whole world, etc." She felt vulnerable to the enticements, she explained, because she had become discontented with her life.[53] On December 10, Elizabeth told several who had gathered at the parsonage:

. . . that her condition displeased her, her labor was burdensome to her, [and] she was neither content to be at home nor abroad; and [that she] had oftentimes strong persuasions to practice in witchcraft, had often wished the Devil would come to her at such and such times, and [had] resolved that if he would she would give herself up to him soul and body.[54]

In all her dealings with Satan, Elizabeth emphasized the deceit that he had employed. He had appeared to her in several guises. He had come to her "in the likeness of a little boy" and "in the habit of an old man." She even confessed to traveling with him when he took the "form of a black dog with eyes in his back." He had deceived her on a grander scale when he convinced her that the two women she had accused had harmed her when actually he had been her tormenter using "their likeness or resemblance."[55]

In confessions given to Willard over several weeks, Elizabeth offered a compelling picture of how this cunning creature had manipulated and coerced her into doing his bidding. He brought a book with the covenants others had signed in blood and urged, then demanded, that she add her name. After some resistance, Elizabeth said she had cut her finger, and he "caught the blood in his hand." He then took a sharp stick, dipped it in her blood "and put it into her hand and guided it, and she wrote her name with his help." The agreement stipulated that she would be faithful to Satan for one year, and in return he would serve her for six years and make her a witch. As part of her service, Satan told Elizabeth to murder some of her neighbors, her parents, and the Willard children. She resisted but when he commanded her to kill the Reverend Willard as he slept, she took a "bill-hook" and headed for the pastor's bedroom. Her deadly mission was foiled, however, when the pastor met her on the stairs. As Willard listened to Elizabeth's account, he distinctly recalled bumping into her on the staircase. He remembered "a strange frame in her countenance and saw she endeavored to hide something."[56]

Elizabeth not only failed to fulfill her part of the covenant but also began to question the wisdom of contracting with the Devil. She explained that shortly after she had signed the covenant, he had revealed the damned of hell to her and warned she would join them if she proved unfaithful. When Elizabeth asked him to show her heaven, he refused because to him it was "an ugly place," the home of "base rogues whom he hated." She worried that the Devil would not keep his promises, but equally troubling was the possibility that he might indeed make her a witch and she then might "be discovered and brought to a shameful end." Her growing doubts led to an effort to break the agreement. Elizabeth contended in early December that her resistance had angered the Devil who, as a consequence, had caused all her suffering since October.[57] Yet on several occasions during November and December, Elizabeth ascribed her misery to the "many sins" she had committed. In addition to attempting Willard's murder, she confessed to neglecting worship and disobeying her parents. Most troubling, however, was her renunciation of God and "giving herself up to the Devil." She felt that God was justly punishing her for the "unprofitable life she had led" and ultimately feared that it was too late for her to make peace with God.[58]

Though usually sympathetic, Willard had difficulty believing all that Elizabeth confided to him or that her fits were always genuine. In early November, she told him that the Devil had put "excuses into her mouth" and then admitted that she had "feigned and forced" her hysterical laughter.[59] On Sunday, December 10, Elizabeth sent for Willard to hurry home from the meetinghouse. When he arrived, she had a stunning new story—she had been lying. "Most of the apparitions she had spoken of were but fancies," she confessed, "as images represented in a dream." A puzzled Willard, not knowing which version of the young woman's experiences reflected reality, told Elizabeth that he could believe only what he had "good grounds to apprehend." Consequently, he demanded that she tell him honestly what had happened to her in the past two months. She promised to do so but desired all those who had observed her over the past several weeks be present "as they had heard so many lies and untruths, they might now hear the truth."[60] When the interested gathered, Elizabeth did not repeat her confession. Instead, she told them that the Devil had appeared to her several times and that she had been tempted to give in to his offer, but she had refused to covenant with him. Willard "declared a suspicion of the truth of the relation" but wished to speak with Knapp alone about his doubts. His first opportunity came the next day, and Willard explained that her stories were too filled with contradictions to be believed. Nonetheless, she stood by her account of the previous evening. "What to make of these things," the frustrated pastor admitted, "I at present know not, but am waiting till God (if He see meet) wind up the story and make a clear discovery."[61]

Unfortunately for Elizabeth, her violent, speechless fits returned shortly afterward, and on Sunday, December 17, her strange saga took its most peculiar turn. According to Willard, the Devil took possession of the young woman. As several witnesses watched in horror, Elizabeth's tongue was drawn out of her mouth "to an extraordinary length," and her body was contorted into "many amazing postures." They heard a strange voice from within her and sent someone to the meetinghouse for her father. When he arrived with a neighbor, the voice called them "rogues" and said they were foolish to have been listening to Willard—"a black rogue who told them nothing but a parcel of lies." When Willard reached the parsonage, he heard the "grum, low, yet audible" voice and was startled by the salutation, "Oh! you are a great rogue." After the always cautious minister regained his courage and composure, he asked for a light to determine if Elizabeth somehow dissembled, but he "observed not any of her organs to move" as the voice issued from her. The pastor, with villagers crowded about, then engaged in a debate with the voice:

He then again called me a great black rogue. I challenged him to make it appear [so]; but all the answer was "You tell the people a company of lies." I reflected on myself, and could not but magnify the goodness of God not to suffer Satan to bespatter the names of His people with those sins which He himself hath pardoned in the blood of Christ. I answered, "Satan, thou art a liar and a deceiver and God will vindicate His own truth one day." He answered nothing directly, but said, "I am not Satan; I am a pretty black boy [and] this is my pretty girl. I have been here a great while." I sat still and answered nothing to these expressions. But when he directed himself to me again—[saying] "Oh! you black rogue, I do not love you"—I replied, "Through God's grace I hate thee." He rejoined, "But you had better love me." These manner of expressions filled some of the company there present with great consternation. Others put on boldness to speak to him, at which I was displeased and advised them to see their call clear, fearing lest by his policy and [the] many apish expressions he used he might insinuate himself and raise in them a fearlessness of spirit of him. I no sooner turned my back to go to the fire but he called out again, "Where is that black rogue gone?" I, seeing little good to be done by discourse, and questioning many things in my mind concerning it, I desired the company to join in prayer unto God. When we went about that duty and were kneeled down, with a voice louder than before he cried out, "Hold your tongue, hold your tongue; get you gone, you black rogue; what are you going to do; you have nothing to do with me," etc. But through God's goodness he was silenced, and she lay quiet during the time of prayer; but as soon as it was ended [he] began afresh, using the former expressions—at which some ventured to speak to him, though I think imprudently. One told him [that] God had him in chains; he replied, "For all my chains, I can knock thee on the head when I please." He said he would carry her away that night, [and] another answered, "But God is stronger than thou." He presently rejoined, "That's a lie, I am stronger than God"—at which blasphemy I again advised them to be wary of speaking, counseled them to get serious persons to watch with her, and left her, commending her to God.[62]

Two days later, Elizabeth said that the Devil had entered her through her mouth on the second day of her possession and had been in her ever since. She could not explain, however, how he had spoken through her. Nonetheless, witnesses heard the voice again on December 22, and Elizabeth continued to suffer alternating periods of fits and melancholy until Willard's description of her struggle ended in mid-January.[63]

He closed the account with his assessment of Elizabeth Knapp's experiences. Because of the strength of her fits, Willard concluded that they had been genuine and had resulted from a diabolical cause. He could not, however, decide if she had truly entered into a covenant with the Devil. Her stories concerning her agreement had "been so contradictory" that he was left with "many doubts." The question that most engaged the clergyman was whether or not the Devil had actually possessed Elizabeth. Since some had expressed doubts, he felt compelled to offer arguments in the affirmative. The voice's "manner of expression," he pointed out, had involved no movement of any of her organs. Indeed, when the voice spoke, Elizabeth's "mouth was sometimes shut without opening, sometimes open without shutting or moving." Moreover, "the labial letters . . . B, M, P—which cannot be naturally expressed without motion of the lips . . . were uttered without any such motion." Willard also emphasized that "the reviling terms" used by the voice were not ones Elizabeth had "used before nor since" the possession. Finally, witnesses had noted that "when the voice spoke her throat was swelled formidably, as big at least as one's fist."[64]

Obviously, Willard's doubts about some of Elizabeth Knapp's actions did not extend to the question of her possession, and that was the aspect of witchcraft beliefs that most frightened many New Englanders. Most witnesses in possession cases were convinced that the Devil had taken control of the victims's body and caused hideous fits. Clergymen struggled not only to exorcise the demon but also to determine the identity of the witch or witches who may have assisted. The possessed often claimed that they could see the "specter" of those afflicting them. These accusations, though not in Elizabeth Knapp's case, usually led to prosecutions of those named. This presented judges, like those in the Elizabeth Morse case, with the dilemma of ruling on its admissibility in trials.

The people of Salem Village may have heard about Elizabeth Knapp's possession or may have had access to Increase Mather's brief mention of it in *An Essay for the Recording of Illustrious Providences,* published in 1684.[65] They more likely knew about the events involving Elizabeth and William Morse, since these took place in their county and she was jailed in nearby Ipswich. There were three other individuals from the immediate vicinity who faced witchcraft charges in the 1680s. In February 1680, as Elizabeth Morse awaited her trial, Bridget Oliver, a Salem widow, became a suspect. A slave named Juan, belonging to John Ingerson, supplied the evidence. He testified to some misadventures with animals a month earlier for which he held Oliver responsible. He had taken a team of horses and a sled into the woods to get a load of firewood. As he returned, the horses "started and snorted as if they were frightened," and they bolted into a nearby swamp. Since the animals, in the water "up to their bellies," had dragged the loaded sled with them, the slave could get them out only by releasing their harness. According to Juan, several neighbors who witnessed the incident said they had never seen "the like and they thought the horses were bewitched." The following week, he saw Bridget Oliver's "shape" sitting on a beam in the "hay-house." When he looked away to find something with which to strike her, the shape disappeared. That evening at dinner, the slave saw two black cats in the house, but since the Ingersons only had one, he asked, "How came two black cats here?" As he spoke, Juan felt three sharp pains in his side, which caused him to cry out, pains that lasted about half an hour. On the basis of the slave's allegation that she had used witchcraft, Oliver appeared before the Essex County Court on February 25. The judges felt the evidence sufficient to order her appearance at the next meeting of the Court of Assistants.[66]

Bridget was not particularly poor and operated a tavern; nonetheless, she was about forty and did display a characteristic of the "typical" witch. She had an apparently well-deserved reputation for her temper. Her marriage with Thomas Oliver had been notable for its frequent violent quarrels. In 1670, both were fined for fighting. A neighbor, Mary Roper, testified that several times she had been called to the Oliver household to listen to one or the other complain about his or her abusive spouse. Mary recalled seeing Bridget's face bloodied and bruised on more than one occasion and that Thomas had complained to her that Bridget "had given him several blows." Their relationship did not mellow with the passage of time. Eight years later, they were back in court for their vicious name calling. Specifically, Bridget, on the Sabbath, had called Thomas "many opprobrious names, as old rogue and old devil." The judges ordered the couple to stand back to back "in the public market place, both gagged, for about an hour, with a paper fastened to each of their foreheads upon which their offense should be fairly written."[67]

It is unclear how Bridget's case turned out; there is no evidence of an appearance by her at the Court of Assistants. The same is true of the ultimate disposition of Margaret Giffard's case. A month after Bridget Oliver appeared in the Essex County Court, Philip Reade filed a complaint against Giffard. Reade claimed to have evidence that she had been practicing witchcraft. The judges ordered her appearance at their next session to answer the charges and that Reade bring his evidence. Reade was there ready "to prosecute" Giffard, but she failed to appear. Since the court took no further action, it is likely that Reade dropped his plans to pursue the case. Margaret may well have been the innocent victim of a dispute between Reade and John Giffard, her husband. A month after he filed his complaint against Margaret, Reade sued John Giffard for slander. Although the evidence is sparse, it is likely that Reade's complaint against Margaret was a result of his dispute with John.[68]

The third case involved Rachel Clinton of Ipswich. A fifty-eight-year-old divorcée, Rachel was shunned in her village because of her poverty, ill temper, and the suspicions that she was a witch. In 1687, Thomas Knowlton filed a complaint against her. Knowlton said that he had discovered Clinton wandering through a neighbor's house looking for milk and meat. When Clinton saw him, Knowlton contended, she left "scolding and railing, calling me . . . 'hellhound' and 'whoremasterly rogue,' and said I was a limb of the devil." She then picked up a stone and threw it at him. Even though it barely touched his shoe, Knowlton said that his "great toe was in a great rage, as if the nail were held up by a pair of pincers." He also charged that Clinton was responsible for the extraordinary pains suffered by his daughter. Evidently, local authorities thought Knowlton's evidence inadequate to indict Clinton on witchcraft charges because no trial resulted.[69]

While none of these charges developed into full-scale trials of the accused, they served as vivid reminders of the intrusion of witchcraft into the daily lives of the people living in Essex County. One additional witchcraft episode captured the attention of county and provincial residents alike. In the fall of 1688, four children in the family of Boston mason John Goodwin began having fits. Their afflictions had begun shortly after one of them, Martha, had argued with a laundress. The laundress's mother, Goodwife Glover, had "bestowed very bad language" on Martha who began to suffer "strange fits, beyond those that attend epilepsy." Soon, the other three children were afflicted. Spurning suggestions that he employ countermagic, John Goodwin called in several physicians, and one, Thomas Oakes, concluded that "hellish witchcraft" had caused the children's afflictions. Because she had cursed at Martha and because of a suspicion, shared even by her late husband, that she was a witch, Glover was arrested on a complaint filed by Goodwin. At her trial, she confessed to practicing witchcraft. After a panel of physicians determined she was sane, Glover was found guilty and executed. Cotton Mather, who had cared for Martha Goodwin in his home, wrote an account of the episode. Published in 1689, *Memorable Providences, Relating to Witchcrafts and Possessions* apparently enjoyed wide circulation and was subsequently reprinted in London in 1691 and Edinburgh in 1697.[70]

By 1692 the people of Salem Village and the rest of New England had become familiar with a wide range of occult beliefs. They understood the powers of the Devil and that God chose, at times, to release this prince of evil on his chosen people. Their fears of witchcraft centered on the harm witches could cause the people and property dear to them. Should a disagreement with an older woman of low repute be followed by some mishap, most assumed that she was responsible and that she had employed *maleficia*. Some responded with countermagic, countercharms, or white magic, but others chose a more cautious approach. They called upon physicians, for example, if the afflictions seemed the result of illness. Yet medical specialists inevitably concluded that no physical explanation sufficed, that witchcraft had produced the suffering. Complaints to judicial authorities followed. Officials arrested and examined the suspects, and neighbors provided evidence of the accused's bad temper and attributed mishaps to their occult powers. The afflicted often charged that they had seen the "shape" of the suspect doing harm, and few would stand in their defense. Judges moved with great care at this point in the typical trial. They wanted to be sure before condemning someone for practicing witchcraft. Short of a confession, most of the accused escaped punishment in the 1670s and 1680s.

To the modern eye, much of the foregoing seems little short of absurd. It remains difficult to understand how the people of the seventeenth century could believe the things they said in court or in their depositions. Particularly hard to accept is the episode cited at the beginning of this chapter. What caused all the objects in the Morse household in Newbury, Massachusetts, to fly about and strike people? Certainly the grandson John Stiles must bear much of the responsibility. Caleb Powell's charge that Stiles was a "young rogue" seems accurate. When neighbors initially heard of the strange occurrences at the Morse home, young Stiles attributed their causation to malign influences. "I asked him what was the best news at their house," neighbor William Fanning recalled in a court deposition, "and he told me that there was several hundred of devils in the area, and they would be at their house by and by." Moreover, it is clear that the boy frequently threw things at people. When his grandfather took him to a neighbor's home, John "threw a great stone at a maid in the house." Most important, whenever Caleb Powell took the boy away or when a physician briefly took him into his home, the disturbances at the Morse home ceased. Coupled with Powell's claim that he saw the boy throw, among other things, a shoe at his grandfather, the evidence leads us to blame John Stiles for most of the problems.[71]

Yet the dancing andirons and moving chairs that William Morse graphically described cannot be attributed to Stiles because those objects moved, Morse contended, when no one was near them. The old man could have fantasized much of what he described. A nineteenth-century chronicler of this episode concluded that "some strange composition must have occupied the place in his head designed for brains." Without accepting that harsh assessment, we can still assume that a fanciful imagination played a role. Morse himself pointed out that some of the testimony against his wife could be ascribed to fantasy. He wrote of one witness's deposition, "he himself hath said he did not know but he was in a dream, and that unto several persons he hath so said."[72] Still, Morse was not known as an eccentric; rather, he had a more sober reputation as a "sincere and understanding Christian." If the phenomena he described were in his imagination, Morse nonetheless acted as if they were real. In the final analysis that is the crucial element. Humans act upon what they believe to be true, and in the seventeenth century, people believed fervently in the powers of witchcraft.

NOTES

1. *Records and Files of the Quarterly Courts of Essex County* (Salem, 1919), VII, 355–357.

2. Increase Mather, "An Essay for the Recording of Illustrious Providences," in George Lincoln Burr, ed., *Narratives of the Witchcraft Cases, 1648–1706* (New York, 1975), reprint, 30.

3. *Records of Essex County*, VII, 357–359.

4. Ibid., 355 and 357; and Mather, "Illustrious Providences," 31n.

5. Mather, "Illustrious Providences," 24–31.

6. Ibid.

7. Samuel G. Drake, *Annals of Witchcraft in New England* (New York, 1967), reprint, 263 and 262.

8. Mather, "Illustrious Providences," 29.

9. John Putnam Demos, *Entertaining Satan, Witchcraft and the Culture of Early New England* (New York, 1982), 135; and Drake, *Annals*, 143.

10. Drake, *Annals*, 280; and Demos, *Entertaining Satan*, 447.

11. Drake, *Annals*, 271–275, 281.

12. Ibid., 282–283.

13. Ibid., 280.

14. Ibid., 275–276.

15. John Noble, ed., *Records of the Court of Assistants of the Colony of the Massachusetts Bay, 1630–1692* (Boston, 1901), I, 159; Drake, *Annals*, 145–147; and Demos, *Entertaining Satan*, 136–137.

16. Drake, *Annals*, 148, 293–294n, 288n, and 268.

17. Ibid., 148–149; and John Hale, "A Modest Inquiry into the Nature of Witchcraft," in Burr, ed., *Witchcraft Cases*, 412.

18. Hale, "A Modest Inquiry," 412.

19. Noble, ed., *Records of Assistants*, I, 189–190.

20. Hale, "A Modest Inquiry," 412.

21. David D. Hall, "A World of Wonders: The Mentality of the Supernatural in Seventeenth-Century New England," in Hall and David Grayson Allen, eds., *Seventeenth-Century New England* (Boston, 1984), 249, 254, 255, 265, and 266; Hall, "Literacy, Religion, and the Plain Style," *New England Begins: The Seventeenth Century* (Boston, 1982), II, 108; and Mather, "Illustrious Providences," 13–14.

22. Alan MacFarlane, *Witchcraft in Tudor and Stuart England: A Regional and Comparative Study* (New York, 1970), 115.

23. Ibid., 120–122; and Jon Butler, "Magic, Astrology, and the Early American Religious Heritage, 1600–1760," *American Historical Review*, LXXXIV (April 1979), 320–321.

24. Butler, "Magic," 323.

25. Ibid., 325, 329, and 330; Lyle Koehler, *A Search for Power, The "Weaker Sex" in Seventeenth-Century New England* (Urbana, IL, 1980), 266 and 267; and Cotton Mather, *Magnalia Christi Americana*, edited by Kenneth Murdock (Cambridge, MA, 1977), 326.

26. Brian P. Levack, *The Witch-Hunt in Early Modern Europe* (London, 1987), 49–51; Geoffrey Parker, "The European Witchcraze Revisited," *History Today*, XXX (November 1980), 23–24; and Chadwick Hansen, *Witchcraft at Salem* (New York, 1969), 27.

27. The only evidence of their existence came from confessions that were often forced by judicial authorities; see Levack, *Witch-Hunt*, 12–13. Excellent

critiques of the notion of an organized witch society are Norman Cohn's "Was There Ever a Society of Witches?" *Encounter*, XLIII (December 1974), 26–41, and his *Europe's Inner Demons: An Inquiry Inspired by the Great Witch Hunt* (New York, 1975).

28. Levack, *Witch-Hunt*, 148–149. Besides the studies already cited, there are several outstanding works available on European witchcraft. Many of the authors of major books also contributed articles to special issues of *History Today*, which made their research available to a wider audience: Gustav Henningsen, "The Greatest Witch-Trial of All: Navarre, 1609–1614," *History Today*, XXX (November 1980), 36–39; Henningsen, *The Witches' Advocate, Basque Witchcraft and the Spanish Inquisition* (Reno, NV, 1980); Richard Kieckhefer, *European Witch Trials: Their Foundations in Popular and Learned Cultures, 1300–1500* (London, 1976); Joseph Klaits, *Servants of Satan: The Age of the Witch Hunts* (Bloomington, IN, 1985); Christina Larner, *Enemies of God: The Witch-Hunt in Scotland* (London, 1981); Larner, "Witch Beliefs and Witch-Hunting in England and Scotland," *History Today*, XXXI (February 1981), 32–36; H. C. Erik Midelfort, "Heartland of the Witchcraze: Central and Northern Europe," *History Today*, XXXI (February 1981), 27–31; Midelfort, *Witch Hunting in Southwestern Germany 1562–1684* (Stanford, 1972); William Monter, "French and Italian Witchcraft," *History Today*, XXX (November 1980), 31–35; Monter, *Witchcraft in France and Switzerland: The Borderlands During the Reformation* (Ithaca, NY, 1976); G. R. Quaife, *Godly Zeal and Furious Rage: The Witch in Early Modern Europe* (New York, 1987); Keith Thomas, *Religion and the Decline of Magic* (New York, 1971); and Russell Zguta, "Witchcraft Trials in Seventeenth-Century Russia," *American Historical Review*, LXXXII (December 1977), 1187–1207.

29. Levack, *Witch-Hunt*, 19, 20, and 207; Parker, "European Witchcraze," 23–24; Larner, "Witch Beliefs," 33; Butler, "Magic," 343; and MacFarlane, *Witchcraft*, 25.

30. Jacqueline Simpson, "Rural Folklore," in Jerome Blum, ed., *Our Forgotten Past, Seven Centuries of Life on the Land* (London, 1982), 163.

31. Frederick C. Drake, "Witchcraft in the American Colonies, 1647–1662," *American Quarterly*, XX (Winter 1968), 711.

32. Scholars do not agree on the precise number of cases. Frederick Drake contended that "there were over 95 incidents involving colonial people with witchcraft before 1692"; see ibid., 697. John Demos determined that there were ninety-three cases in New England excluding Salem, in the seventeenth century; see Demos, *Entertaining Satan*, 11. Lyle Koehler found that at least "103 persons were accused of familiarity with the Devil between 1638 and 1691"; see Koehler, *Search for Power*, 283. Carol Karlsen has compiled the longest list of accusations. She has argued that 155 people in New England through 1688 were accused of practicing witchcraft; see Carol F. Karlsen, *The Devil in the Shape of a Woman, Witchcraft in Colonial New England* (New York, 1987), 20, 29, and 34.

33. Hale, "A Modest Inquiry," 412.

34. Demos, *Entertaining Satan*, 402–409; and Karlsen, *Devil*, 24–29 and 34.

35. Karlsen, *Devil*, 47; and Demos, *Entertaining Satan*, 60.

36. Demos, *Entertaining Satan*, 63.

37. Karlsen, *Devil*, 119. Karlsen's work is the most sophisticated effort to advance this argument. Also, see Mary Nelson, "Why Witches Were Women," in Jo Freeman, ed., *Women: A Feminist Perspective*, 2d ed. (Palo Alto, CA, 1975), 451–468; and Ann Kibbey, "Mutations of the Supernatural: Witchcraft, Remarkable Providences, and the Power of Men," *American Quarterly*, XXXIV (September 1982), 125–148.

38. MacFarlane, *Witchcraft*, 160; and Demos, *Entertaining Satan*, 63.

39. Karlsen, *Devil*, 222; and Demos, *Entertaining Satan*, 64.

40. Karlsen, *Devil*, 153.

41. Antonia Fraser, *The Weaker Vessel* (New York, 1984), 2.

42. Demos, *Entertaining Satan*, 65–66.

43. Lack of sufficient financial data makes sound conclusions difficult; see ibid., 84–86. Karlsen raises questions about the poverty of the accused, *Devil*, 77–79.

44. Demos, *Entertaining Satan*, 79–93.

45. Drake, *Annals of Witchcraft*, 262, 263, 267, 268, 281, 283, 286, and 287.

46. Fraser, *Weaker Vessel*, 113; and Karlsen, *Devil*, 69.

47. Samuel Willard, "A Brief Account of a Strange and Unusual Providence of God Befallen to Elizabeth Knapp of Groton," in John Demos, ed., *Remarkable Providences* (New York, 1972), 358–371.

48. Ibid., 358.

49. Ibid., 358–359.

50. Demos, *Entertaining Satan*, 103–105.

51. Willard, "Brief Account," 361, 359, and 367.

52. Ibid., 362, 364, 367, 359, and 367.

53. Ibid., 359.

54. Ibid., 367.

55. Ibid., 364, 365, 367, and 361.

56. Ibid., 365 and 360.

57. Ibid., 365–366.

58. Ibid., 360, 361, 362, 363, and 366.

59. Ibid., 360.

60. Ibid., 366.

61. Ibid., 367.

62. Ibid., 367–369.

63. Ibid., 369–370.

64. Ibid., 370–371.

65. Burr, ed., *Witchcraft Cases*, 6.

66. *Records of Essex County*, VII, 329–330.

67. William B. Ardiff, "Bridget Bishop: Salem Witch," *Historical Collections of the Danvers Historical Society*, XLII (1964), 37–40; and Paul Boyer

and Stephen Nissenbaum, eds., *Salem-Village Witchcraft: A Documentary Record of Local Conflict in Colonial New England* (Belmont, CA, 1972), 155–156.

68. *Records of Essex County*, VII, 405, and VIII, 23.

69. For Clinton's background, see Demos, *Entertaining Satan*, 19–35. He reprinted the charges filed against her by Knowlton on 20–21.

70. Cotton Mather, "Memorable Providences Relating to Witchcrafts and Possessions," in Burr, ed., *Witchcraft Cases*, 93–131. There are several secondary accounts of the Goodwin case: Hansen, *Witchcraft*, 43–50; Demos, *Entertaining Satan*, 7–9; and David Levin, *Cotton Mather, The Young Life of the Lord's Remembrancer, 1663–1703* (Cambridge, MA, 1978), 147–157.

71. Drake, *Annals*, 266; and Increase Mather, "Illustrious Providences," 29.

72. Drake, *Annals*, 144 and 281.

Two

Strife in the Community: Life in Salem Village

The immigrants to New England, who had brought occult beliefs with them, sought to create a society of closely knit Christian villages with a strong sense of communal responsibility. They had concluded that the spirit of individualism was ascendant in England, that social and economic disorder were triumphant. Depressions, enclosures, and escalating unemployment appeared to be the norm in the increasingly capitalist nation.[1] The devout among the immigrants to the Massachusetts Bay colony shared John Winthrop's vision of a newer, better place. The leader of the first large contingent of Puritan migrants, Winthrop eloquently called upon his followers in 1630 to:

be knit together in this work as one man. We must entertain each other in brotherly affection. We must be willing to abridge our selves of our superfluities, for the supply of others necessities. We must uphold a familiar commerce together in all meekness, gentleness, patience and liberality. We must delight in each other, make others conditions our own, rejoice together, mourn together, labor, and suffer together, always having before our eyes our commission and community in the work, our community as members of the same body. . . . For we must consider that we shall be as a city upon a hill, the eyes of all people are upon us.[2]

Inspired by the belief that they were on a mission for God to preserve the true church, these committed immigrants eagerly pursued the task of establishing a Christian utopia. God, they believed, had entered into a covenant with man to save his predestined "elect." These "visible saints," the founding generation hoped, would enter into church covenants where they could worship God without the "popish remnants" of the Roman Catholic and Anglican churches—the episcopal structure of church government, the priestly vestments, the kneeling at communion, and the signing of the cross among others. Most New England congregations developed procedures to evaluate all applicants for membership in the church for signs of their "elect" status. This exclusivity promised the assurance that when a person worshiped with one of the "elect," he or she did so with an individual who could not fall from God's grace.[3]

While these early settlers anguished over their place in the cosmos, they also struggled to replicate the village life familiar to them in England. For many, if not most, that meant some version of the open field system of agriculture. Farmers in this type of settlement tilled their lots in the outlying countryside yet resided in a village center. Cooperation became an inescapable part of their work day, since few, if any, of the individual lots were enclosed by fences. The Massachusetts Bay colony distributed the province's land in a manner calculated to encourage such nuclear villages. The government granted land to groups of settlers, rather than to individuals, who organized towns. They, in turn, distributed it to families. What better procedure to bring together the "elect" on a daily basis. Such an approach did not preclude the development of closed field villages. Some settlers from the colony's earliest years consolidated their holdings in one farmstead where they lived rather than in a village center. Over time, that is what happened to most New England villages. Regardless of the type of village, life in these early communities assumed a remarkable uniformity.[4]

As most had in their homeland, New Englanders lived on a small scale, and unlike their high hopes of religious glory, with low expectations for their economic futures. They understood that their limited material fortunes often depended upon the vicissitudes of changing weather patterns. "Like agricultural folk everywhere," John Demos has demonstrated, "the New Englanders were obliged to attend closely to the day-by-day sequence of rain and sun and wind, of warmth and cold."[5] While most were farm families struggling to move beyond a bare subsistence, invariably there were a few, along with some artisans and merchants, connecting them to the larger world of transatlantic commerce.[6] Ironically, as their economic horizons slowly expanded, farmers found it increasingly difficult to participate in a market economy because of growing population pressure on their land. Salem Village certainly was no different. In 1660, farmers owned an average of almost 250 acres, but by 1690, the average had slipped to 124. This overcrowding led to an increase in the number of landless men and to a migration out of the village.[7] Darrett Rutman has captured the general evolution of these small-scale settlements:

Every place proceeded from a period of jostling when relative strangers were attempting to establish themselves vis-à-vis both the resources available (principally land) and each other, toward accommodation, a time of dense kinship and friendship ties, established modes of cooperation in the manipulation of resources, and the orderly mobility of most of the young as they moved out from a family of origin into a regional agricultural economy.[8]

The farmers of Salem Village labored under an additional obstacle because they were under the control of one of New England's oldest towns, Salem. Roger Conant and his followers had located the town on the north shore of Massachusetts Bay in 1626. Like Boston, down the coast, Salem quickly became an important commercial center because of its fine deep harbor. A growing number of merchants, including William Browne, George Corwin, and Walter Price, developed a commercial network beyond the coastal trade to ports as far away as England, Spain, West Africa, and the West Indies.[9] By mid–century, the town had perhaps 800 residents, many of whom were merchants, shipwrights, carpenters, or were in trades related to shipping and commerce. Samuel Maverick described Salem as "very commodious for fishing, and many vessels have built there and (except Boston) it hath as much trade as any place in New England both inland and abroad."[10]

Not all in Salem, however, depended on commerce for their livelihood. By 1660, dozens of families had established farms in the interior, some more than ten miles from the shipyards, wharves, and warehouses of the harbor. Known variously as the "Salem farms" or "Salem Village," the area remained the domain of small farmers throughout the seventeenth century. The people of the village led lives increasingly distinct from their neighbors nearer to the coast. Villagers moved about less, and more often they belonged to the church, but they paid for their greater stability in material and political terms. With commercial enterprise generating most of the new wealth in the area, village farmers became the poorer cousins of the Salem merchants. By the 1680s, the probated estates of the town's merchants were almost ten times as valuable as those of the farmers'. Moreover, merchants wrested control of town politics from the farmers. Once dominant in local government, farmers, by the latter decades of the century, rarely won elections as town selectmen or as deputies to the provincial General Court.[11] As Richard Gildrie has shown, the "physical separation of the farming population from their fellow townsmen exacerbated their sense of being left out as the town developed economically. It severely challenged their sense of unity and identity with the whole community."12

New England towns, Salem included, often permitted outlying or dissident sections to separate and form independent communities. Salem had granted autonomy to Wenham, Manchester, Marblehead, and Beverly between 1643 and 1667, but resisted when the farmers of Salem Village sought the same status. In the 1660s, the villagers took their first steps toward a separation when they requested their own minister and release from participation in the town watch. In repeated petitions to the Salem church, the county court, and the General Court in Boston, the villagers emphasized their isolation, the "distance from the meeting house," and "the remoteness of our habitations from the town." The General Court, in 1667, rewarded their persistence by exempting from the watch "all farmers dwelling above four miles from the meeting-house." Five years later, the Salem town meeting grudgingly permitted the villagers the "liberty to a minister by themselves." This, however, was a limited concession. Salem leaders had created Salem Village parish, not an independent covenanted congregation. The villagers could gather to listen to sermons but maintained membership in neighboring churches and had to return to them to receive the communion sacrament. The dissatisfied villagers persisted, and Salem leaders eventually grew tired of the struggle and permitted Salem Village its own church in 1689. Yet they remained steadfast in their refusal to grant full autonomy to their neighbors. Having already yielded so much of their original township in Essex County, town leaders felt they could not "spare any more without much straightening themselves." Since the village included the "best part" of the remaining lands, its loss would seriously erode Salem's tax base.13

In their ongoing struggle to gain control of their destiny, the villagers seldom displayed unity. Outsiders and villagers alike remarked on the viciousness of their internal bickering. For example, when the villagers split over whether to seek ordination for their third minister, Deodat Lawson, a panel of five Salem arbitrators were struck by the level of rancor in the dispute. "To our grief," they noted, "we observe such uncharitable expressions and uncomely reflections tossed to and fro as look like the effects of settled prejudice and resolved animosity." Villager Jeremiah Watts similarly described the dissension in a 1682 letter to the village's second minister, George Burroughs. "This village is aiming to make it a town," he wrote, "which is all very necessary work. But how can this be accomplished in a way of God when brother is against brother and neighbors against neighbors, all quarreling and smiting one another."[14]

Religious issues provoked the most serious divisions in the village. In 1666, when six farmers first sought to have a minister for the village, they faced opposition not only from the Salem church but also from five of their "neighbors and brethren thereabouts desiring that they might not be engaged in that design."[15] The religious turmoil persisted for decades and drove away the village's first three clergymen. James Bayley, a young Harvard graduate, became the first Salem Village minister in 1672. After seven years of apparent calm, Bayley wrote a letter to the villagers describing the "uncomfortable divisions and contentions fallen out amongst us here." A flurry of letters and petitions followed that revealed several charges against Bayley. There was disagreement over whether he had assumed his position by "invitation of a few" or by "a general consent and vote of the inhabitants." Some contended that he was unqualified for the position, or that he was unorthodox in his sermons, or that he neglected family prayers. Despite majority support in the village and the General Court's conclusion that he was "orthodox and competently able and of a blameless and self-denying conversation," Bayley left in 1680. His opponents, though defeated, had been zealous, and consequently, he saw no "hope for my future comfortable living amongst you in that work of the ministry in this place."[16]

Bayley's successor, George Burroughs, another Harvard graduate, came to Salem Village after preaching in Falmouth, Maine, and living in Salisbury, Massachusetts. Clearly aware of Bayley's difficulties, Burroughs negotiated a contract that stipulated "that in case any difference should arise in time to come, that we engage on both sides to submit to counsel for a peaceable issue." Burroughs correctly anticipated problems. Because several inhabitants evaded the tax collector, the village failed to pay his agreed-upon salary. His need became particularly acute when his wife died in 1681. That tragedy forced him to borrow money to cover her funeral expenses as well as to maintain his household. As he struggled with his finances, Burroughs received a letter of rebuke from Jeremiah Watts who had also opposed Bayley. Watts included Burroughs among those arrogant ministers who in their "pulpit preaching . . . deliver what they please and none must object." He also criticized Burroughs for not doing enough to heal the differences in the village and unite the people in their campaign for religious and secular autonomy. Although the courts admonished Watts for "speaking scandalously of the ministry, and writing offensively against . . . the leaders of churches in this place," Burroughs concluded, as Bayley had before him, that he had no future as a minister in Salem Village. He quit preaching in March 1683 and returned to Maine.[17]

The villagers stumbled through over a year of interim preaching and negotiations with Deodat Lawson before he finally accepted the position in late 1684. Born in England, educated at Cambridge, and a minister on Martha's Vineyard in the 1670s, Lawson came to the village from Boston. During his four-year stay, Lawson found himself in the middle of a bitter campaign to gain an independent congregation. The particulars of the fight are unclear, but the inability of the two groups involved to compromise is not. At an impasse in 1687, they appealed to five Salem leaders—Bartholomew Gedney, John Hathorne, William Brown, Jr., and ministers John Higginson and Nicholas Noyes. The whole affair, in the arbitrators' judgment, "had not been so inoffensively managed as might have been." Struck by the willfulness displayed by both sides, these Salem leaders advised their neighbors to "desist at present from urging the ordination of the Reverend Mr. Lawson till your spirits are better quieted and composed."[18] Clearly certain that that would not happen, Lawson departed within a year of the arbitrators' recommendation that his ordination be postponed.

The villagers had found each minister flawed in some way. One they deemed guilty of doctrinal error, the second failed to provide proper leadership, and the third let himself become the tool of a particular faction. Rather than a profound disagreement over reformed doctrine or religious style, the bitter episodes involving the ministers reveal a different kind of dilemma. As with a number of other locales in late seventeenth-century New England, Salem Village discovered the resolution of conflict to be increasingly difficult. Early villagers had sought to settle differences through mediation. Seldom did they seek the aid of outside authorities, and division only occasionally endured; if it did, exclusion of the most offensive party usually solved the problem. As in Dedham, factions attempted to abide by the admonition to "live together in a way of neighborly love and do each other as they would have the other do themselves."[19]

Over time, as controversies escalated over land distribution, location of meetinghouses, and separatist movements within villages, New Englanders turned ever more to outside authorities to resolve conflict. Between 1672 and 1692 in Essex County alone, the county court "had to end forty-five disputes after arbitration had been tried unsuccessfully."[20] Complicating matters, Salem Village lacked the traditional governmental institution of New England communities—the town meeting. The village "inhabitants" could gather to discuss minor issues like maintenance of the meetinghouse or to determine the location of roads, but they could not decide substantial issues. Instead of a board of selectmen, they had only a rate committee that did little more than assess taxes to support their ministry.[21] Beyond this serious institutional weakness and the ineffectiveness of arbitration, the location of their homes, "scattered and remote one from another," made cooperation difficult.[22] The scattered settlement pattern limited daily face-to-face contacts and diminished opportunities for collective action. Because of these factors, Salem Village fell far short of the founding generation's hope of communities laboring with a common purpose.

At times, the religious discord in the village also reflected a conflict between its two leading families, the Putnams and the Porters. In a way, the lives of Thomas, Nathaniel, and John Putnam paralleled those of Joseph, Benjamin, and Israel Porter. Their fathers, John Putnam and John Porter, arrived in Salem in the 1640s. When these two patriarchs died, Putnam in 1662 and Porter in 1676, they left more than substantial acreage to their offspring—they bequeathed a tradition of political leadership. Both men, in addition to many other local and provincial posts, served several terms as Salem selectmen. Through marriage to other prominent Salem families, the sons extended their clans' networks of power. The differences between the two families, however, were more important than the similarities. The Porters owned land primarily on the east side of the village, nearer to the hectic pace of the harbor. While they farmed and leased land to tenants, the Porters also had commercial connections; they held waterfront property and operated a sawmill. Putnam land was on the opposite side of the village. Their soil was not as good as the Porters's, and their locale afforded them less access to markets.

Over time, the Porters lost interest in participating in village politics. Israel and Joseph served only one year each on the village rate committee between 1670 and 1692. Instead, they sought election to the Salem board of selectmen. Israel, alone, served twelve terms between 1680 and 1695. While the Porters identified ever more with the interests of commercial Salem, the Putnams became the leaders of the "small farmer faction" in the village. Seldom able to win election as selectmen after 1670, the Putnams concentrated on controlling the village rate committee. From that position, although a relatively powerless one, they often took the lead in the village separatist campaign.[23]

While division between the families predominated, there were instances of cooperation. The 1667 petition to the General Court requesting release of villagers from the town watch included the names of Porters and Putnams. Twelve years later, Joseph Porter joined with Thomas and John Putnam in support of the Reverend Bayley. Most surprising, Porters even supported the Putnams in a petition in 1690 to Salem leaders to obtain township status.[24] The split would become most sharply drawn in the aftermath of the witch trials when the Porters and their supporters attempted to oust Samuel Parris from the pulpit over the determined resistance of the Putnam clan.

The villagers clearly understood the deleterious effect of religious discord on their community. In 1695, some of the supporters of Samuel Parris admitted, "We have had three ministers removed already, and by every removal our differences have been rather aggravated."[25] An examination of the Parris years in Salem Village illustrates how even these concerned villagers understated the damage done.

Born in London in 1653, Samuel Parris moved with his family to Barbados in the 1660s where both his uncle and father had prospered as sugar planters and merchants. He attended Harvard College in the early 1670s but returned to Barbados prior to graduating to serve as executor of his father's estate. He spent eight years as a merchant in the island's commercial center, Bridgetown, making a comfortable living on income from the lease of a plantation left to him by his father and his own efforts as a sugar broker. Following a devastating hurricane and a sustained drop in world sugar prices, he sold the plantation and moved to Boston in 1680. There Parris struggled to compete with the merchant elite of the provincial capital. Although he achieved modest success, he decided again, in 1688, to switch careers. That fall Parris began negotiations with a committee from Salem Village who was seeking a successor to the recently departed Deodat Lawson.[26]

On November 25, ten days after negotiations began, Parris apparently gave the congregation an acceptable sample sermon, and they voted to offer him the position. He refused to give them a definite answer. Rather, this cautious man, aware of the difficulties his predecessors had faced, extended the negotiations well into the spring of 1689. After discussing the job with three different committees and attending a stormy village meeting, Parris finally accepted the post during the summer. Upon taking the Salem Village job, Parris, ever concerned with providing for the economic security of his family, sought ownership of the parsonage. He found the Putnams, eager for allies in their separatist efforts, receptive to his overtures. Nathaniel and John Putnam in particular took the lead in the effort. In an October village meeting, they were among those in attendance who voted to give Parris "our ministry house and barn and two acres of land next adjoining to the house." The farmers did this after voting to overturn a 1681 village decision to make it unlawful "to convey the houses or lands" of the ministry to any individual. Nathaniel and John Putnam headed the committee appointed to make the conveyance of the property to their new pastor. From this beginning, Parris retained the support of the Putnams throughout his eight years in the village.[27]

During the lengthy negotiations between Parris and the village, the Salem church, most likely tired of dealing with the disputatious farmers, decided to permit them to have an independent covenanted congregation.[28] The separatists in the village realized the dream of their own church on November 19 when neighboring clergymen gathered to ordain Samuel Parris. "Learn ye of this place (this village)," Parris told the new congregation, that "God hath graciously brought you to a good day this day." Parris offered a positive message. While the villagers had suffered through decades of controversy and many had been negligent in regularly missing the communion sacrament, he proclaimed the dawn of a new era. Reform, however, would take an extraordinary effort. Parris acknowledged that much of the burden for change belonged to him. His sermons and behavior must be an example to all. Yet he gave the congregation the greatest charge. They must treat him as an "ambassador of Christ Jesus" and abide by his direction. Most important, the villagers had to change their ways. Their shoddy treatment of men of God and their quarreling must cease: "And not by unchristian like behavior to myself, or one another, or other Churches of God, or any whither within or without, or to God, or man to add to my burden, and to make my life among you grievous, and my labor among you unprofitable."[29]

Following the sermon, twenty-seven villagers entered into a covenant that drew upon the cooperative Christian spirit of New England's founding generation. Acknowledging their "great unfitness" for the task at hand and deploring their "miscarriages" of the recent past, they, nonetheless, pledged to "give up ourselves one unto another in the Lord." Unfortunately for the future peace of the village, the Porters and Putnams could not seize the opportunity and join together in this new religious venture. While eleven of the Putnam clan joined, no Porters chose to become members.[30]

Still, Samuel Parris appeared to have accurately predicted a better day for the religious life of Salem Village. In the year following his ordination, the membership of the congregation doubled despite Parris's insistence upon a rigorous membership procedure. Many other congregations admitted individuals who simply displayed familiarity with

Christian principles and led an upright life; Parris's approach reflected a return to the concern of earlier generations for a congregation truly of God's "elect."[31] Applicants not only had to explain a work of "faith and repentance wrought in their souls" but also needed testimony on their behalf "from the brethren."[32] Parris similarly charted a conservative course on baptism policy. By 1690, most Massachusetts congregations allowed the children of baptized parents to receive the sacrament even if their parents had failed to meet the test of full membership. Parris convinced his new congregation to revive the approach of the 1648 Cambridge Assembly, which restricted baptism to the children of the "elect."[33] In early 1690, with some dissenting votes, Parris succeeded in limiting baptism to children who had at least one parent in "full communion and the child religiously educated and free from open vices, and not exceeding the age of twelve years." Yet within only a year, fifty-one received the baptism sacrament.[34]

In addition to quickly establishing these crucial procedures, Parris set about fulfilling numerous pastoral duties. He counseled parents on the proper religious instruction of their children, advised villagers who sought baptism or membership in the congregation, disciplined those guilty of wayward behavior, and performed marriages.[35] Parris also sought to comfort grieving families. For example, he attended the Sheldon family when their ten-year-old son Nathaniel died in November 1689. Well on a Monday, the youngster became ill on Tuesday, "distracted on Thursday, and so continued till Friday he died."[36] Unfortunately, Parris could not always make it to a home in time. Twenty-seven-year-old Samuel Fuller died on the first day of 1690, thirty minutes before Parris's arrival. The minister even offered comfort to those in the village whom he considered sinful, like Samuel Wilkins. Though "a very naughty man," Parris observed, Wilkins "died very hopefully."[37] In all these episodes of emotional pain, Parris cautioned families to recall the words of his December 1, 1689 sermon to "be moderate in our griefs, in our sorrows."[38]

Preaching the gospel took precedence over these pastoral duties. In his sermons, Samuel Parris gave his ever larger congregation an orthodox version of the reformed faith. Despite man's evil nature, Parris explained, God chose some for eternal salvation. Through close attention to his sermons, a rigorous and sustained examination of their own lives, and a careful study of scripture, the villagers would learn whether they had been chosen as one of the "elect."[39] Those who developed a sense of assurance and gained entry into the congregation would form a "pure church." "Christ," he said, "gathers a church by separating of the elect from the rest of mankind as His peculiar flock." This notion of a sanctuary of God's chosen certainly gave comfort to those who met the rigorous baptism and membership requirements. More important, Parris assured them that the "elect" could not fall away. Their haven would be under constant assault from "the grand enemy of the church," Satan and his assistants who were in every village.[40]

Despite Parris's efforts and his congregation's generally favorable response to him, signs of trouble appeared early in his tenure. After the initial year of enthusiasm, growth in membership slowed dramatically. In Parris's second year, only seven individuals joined the congregation. In the following twelve months, because of growing dissatisfaction with his ministry and the witchcraft crisis, no one joined.[41] Those who attended, from the minister's perspective, paid too little attention to his sermons. "Some sit before the preacher," he complained in December 1689, "as senseless as the seats they sit on, pillars they lean on, dead bodies they sometimes tread on." More troubling to him than their indifference was the congregation's increasing absence from worship especially on communion Sundays. "It is at His table," he said in February 1692, "where some of us have been this day, & more should come."[42]

No doubt some stayed away because of the deteriorating condition of the meetinghouse. Once Salem had approved their hiring of a minister in 1672, the villagers had voted to build a meetinghouse. With less than 1,000 square feet of space, the simple wooden structure could accommodate few villagers even with the addition of galleries to both ends in 1685. By the time of Parris's arrival, the building displayed signs of serious disrepair. There had been occasional attempts at improvements; in 1684, the villagers had agreed to add six casement windows and a canopy over the pulpit, but for several years the only expenditures had been to pay someone to sweep the meetinghouse.[43] Parris may have prevailed upon the villagers to spend more because on two occasions in 1690 and 1691, the clerk of the village meeting noted an intent to "repair our meetinghouse and keep it decent."[44] There was, however, no money allocated to realize this intention. In a December 1692 petition to the General Court, the church described the consequences of years of neglect: "By reason of broken windows, stopped-up, some of them, by boards or otherwise, and others wide open, it is sometimes so cold that it makes it uncomfortable, and sometimes so dark that it is almost unuseful."[45] To make matters worse, Parris was appalled at the service provided for communion. In December 1690, he called upon the congregation to furnish the table properly, there being only two pewter tankards available.[46]

Samuel Parris's personal situation mirrored the deteriorating conditions of the meetinghouse in 1690 and 1691. Like his predecessors, Parris did not receive his full pay. After only one year, almost a quarter of the taxes assessed for his salary remained uncollected. When constable Edward Bishop pressured delinquent taxpayers, some paid, but as late as 1694 the village still owed him money for his first two years.[47] There was more involved here than mere tax dodging. Parris noted an increasingly louder chorus of complaints about his ministry. Some criticized the process used to select him, saying they had not "joined with the people in calling or agreeing with Mr. Parris."[48] Many who disliked the Putnam-engineered transfer of the parsonage to Parris took action in fall 1691. In October, an anti-Parris group won election to the village rate committee.

Controlled by Joseph Porter and men linked to him by family and interest, this committee set the tax rate for Parris's salary and had responsibility for its collection.[49] They called a meeting for December 1, 1691, to discuss, among other things, "wherein our right in the ministry house and land seems to be impaired and made void."[50] It is unclear if that meeting took place, but simply putting that item on the agenda indicates the depth of feeling some in the village had on the issue of the parsonage.

Villagers also complained that Parris appeared too concerned with making money. In addition to his salary, he received income from property in both Boston and Barbados. Further, he bought, received, or co-owned almost twenty acres in Salem Village beyond the acreage belonging to the parsonage. Certainly some in the congregation cynically recalled from one of his early sermons that a clergyman should not take a job for "his own private profit."[51] Parris had heard enough by the spring of 1690 to scold the congregation. They should avoid "reviling & reproaching . . . poor ministers, whose desire is your best welfare & whose endeavor is to be found faithful."[52]

Parris's problems became particularly acute in the late fall of 1691. A year earlier, he had relinquished his firewood stipend and had become dependent on a voluntary supply from the villagers. In October 1691, he revealed to the church members that few had brought him any wood, and on November 18, he complained that he "had scarce wood enough to burn till tomorrow." It was two weeks later, as he and his family shivered in the parsonage, that Parris learned that the village rate committee had decided against levying a tax for his 1692 salary.[53]

With no prospects for pay, no firewood for the winter, and the likelihood that he would lose title to the parsonage, Samuel Parris went on the offensive from the pulpit. In January and February 1692, he described the efforts to oust him as part of an assault on the congregation. His opponents were "wicked and reprobate men (the assistants of Satan)." "Christ having begun a new work," Parris said of the two-year-old congregation, "it is the main drift of the Devil to pull it all down." He skillfully linked his fate with that of the Salem Village church. The congregation must share in his personal struggle. They, like he and his family certainly did, could expect the situation to worsen. Despair seemed to be their plight as God's chosen. "It is a woeful piece of our corruption in our evil time," Parris noted in February, "when the wicked prosper, & the godly party meet with vexations by & by to cry down divine Providence, as if God had forsaken the earth."[54]

Parris's pessimistic appraisal was in part due to circumstances beyond his struggle with village opponents. By the early years of the 1690s, there had developed in Massachusetts Bay a general sense of an emerging crisis. The signs of it seemed to be all around. No one knew what kind of government the Crown planned to impose upon them in the wake of the overthrow of the Dominion government. Imperial officials, notably the Lords of Trade, long had sought to void the Massachusetts Bay charter to centralize administration of the empire. They had substantial support among English merchants who lost money because of repeated violations of imperial trade regulations by New Englanders. After years of legal maneuvering, the Court of Chancery granted the centralizers their wish in 1684 by voiding the Massachusetts Bay charter. This permitted Charles II to create a new administrative unit called the Dominion of New England that included all the New England colonies and New York. Following Charles's death, his brother, James II, appointed a royal governor for the Dominion, Sir Edmund Andros. Armed with broad authority, Andros arrived in Boston in 1686. Ruling with the aid of an appointed council rather than an elected legislature, he levied new taxes, enforced imperial trade regulations, and raised questions about the validity of land titles granted to towns and individuals under the old charter. Most serious to those hopeful of retaining the congregational form of worship, Andros forced Boston officials to permit Church of England services. In 1689, upon learning of the coup that forced James II to flee to the continent, New Englanders eagerly overthrew the Andros regime. The restoration of the old charter government was an interim move until the new king, William III, decided upon a permanent structure. Until then, troubling questions remained about the security of land titles and the status of the Church of England in Massachusetts.[55]

Other developments contributed to the malaise. Warfare on the northeastern frontier with Indians and their French allies persisted, bringing a flow of refugees into the Salem area and dramatically higher taxes for all in the province. For Salem Village, the frontier fighting also meant the periodic loss of the labor of some of its young men when they were most needed in the fields. In the spring of 1690, for example, Salem merchant and militia recruiter Bartholomew Gedney found the village farmers reluctant to leave their fields to go fight Indians, but he did persuade some "stout young men" to take up arms.[56] A much greater loss to the village was the occasional death of some of these young men, as in the summer of 1691 when four died in the fighting.[57] Persistent rumors (one as recent as fall 1691) that French soldiers or Indians had been seen in the vicinity kept the villagers on edge.[58] Weather problems added to the unease in this village, which was so dependent on agriculture. In the summer of 1691, the region suffered through a serious drought, only to be followed by damaging floods in February and March 1692.[59]

Despite the bleak prospects for their collective situation, Parris told his congregation not "to be offended at the present low condition of the church in the midst of its enemies."[60] He promised ultimate vindication for the "elect." They, and he, would overcome the challenges facing them and emerge triumphant because God was with them. "The Church may meet with storms," he explained on February 14, "but it shall never sink. For Christ sits not idle in the Heavens, but takes most faithful care of his little ship (the Church) bound for the port of Heaven, laden with many precious gems & jewels, a treasure purchased by his own inestimable blood."[61]

Perhaps Parris sought to comfort himself as well as the congregation with those words. It is hard to imagine a more difficult position for a clergyman than the one he faced. He labored in a village divided by factional strife, one vainly seeking greater independence from Salem. As Parris attempted to transform his personal struggle into one with cosmic consequences, the villagers turned again to the mundane task of seeking an exemption from taxes to maintain the roads in Salem.[62] Even if there appeared to be some cooperation between the village's leading families in this effort—Joseph Porter served with Nathaniel and John Putnam on the committee to negotiate with town officials—there was no evidence that they were ready to work together to lighten Parris's burden. While the Putnams, Porters, and Parris worried about the affairs of everyday life, there emerged an even greater crisis. Just as Parris assured the congregation that their situation would improve, the scourge of witchcraft appeared in his household, a terror that would engulf not only the village but also much of the province of Massachusetts Bay in 1692.

NOTES

1. See Carl Bridenbaugh, *Vexed and Troubled Englishmen, 1590–1642* (New York, 1967), 355–393.

2. Edmund S. Morgan, ed., *The Founding of Massachusetts, Historians and the Sources* (Indianapolis, 1964), 203.

3. There is an enormous body of literature on Puritan thought. An excellent place to begin is Perry Miller's *The New England Mind: The Seventeenth Century* (New York, 1939). Also helpful is his collection of essays entitled *Errand into the Wilderness* (Cambridge, MA, 1956). Francis J. Bremer offers a useful summary of Puritan thought in *The Puritan Experiment* (New York, 1976). John Winthrop's particular perspective on the Puritan mission is ably described by Edmund S. Morgan in his classic biography, *The Puritan Dilemma, The Story of John Winthrop* (New York, 1958).

4. This and the following paragraphs were drawn largely from Darrett B. Rutman, "Assessing the Little Communities of Early America," *William and Mary Quarterly*, 3d Ser., XLIII (April 1986), 163–178; Rutman, *The Morning of America* (Boston, 1971), 35–74; T. H. Breen and Stephen Foster, "The Puritans Greatest Achievement: A Study of Social Cohesion in Seventeenth-Century Massachusetts," *Journal of American History*, LX (June 1973), 5–22; and James A. Henretta, "Families and Farms: Mentalite in Pre-Industrial America," *William and Mary Quarterly*, 3d Ser., XXXV (January 1978), 3–32.

5. John Demos, *Entertaining Satan, Witchcraft and the Culture of Early New England* (New York, 1982), 373.

6. Even those who turned to this commerce often did so with caution. See Larry Gragg, "An Ambiguous Response to the Market: The Early New England-Barbados Trade," *Historical Journal of Massachusetts*, XVII (Summer 1989), 177–200.

7. Paul Boyer and Stephen Nissenbaum, *Salem Possessed: The Social Origins of Witchcraft* (Cambridge, MA, 1974), 89–91.

8. Rutman, "Assessing the Little Communities," 173.

9. Besides the work of Boyer and Nissenbaum, there are several books on seventeenth-century Salem. The most recent are James Duncan Phillips, *Salem in the Seventeenth Century* (Boston, 1933); Richard P. Gildrie, *Salem, Massachusetts, 1626–1683, A Covenant Community* (Charlottesville, VA, 1975); and Christine Alice Young, *From 'Good Order' to Glorious Revolution, Salem, Massachusetts, 1628–1689* (Ann Arbor, MI, 1980).

10. Phillips, *Salem*, 172. The Maverick quote is in Gildrie, *Salem, 1626–1683*, 107.

11. Ibid., 157, 158, and 167; Donald W. Koch, "Income Distribution and Political Structure in Seventeenth-Century Salem, Massachusetts," *Essex Institute Historical Collections*, CV (January 1969), 53–56; Manfred Jonas, "The Wills of the Early Settlers of Essex County, Massachusetts," *Essex Institute Historical Collections*, XCVI (July 1960), 231; Gildrie, "Salem Society and Politics in the 1680s," *Essex Institute Historical Collections*, CXIV (October 1978), 190, 198, and 199; Boyer and Nissenbaum, *Salem Possessed*, 87; and Young, *From 'Good Order,'* 69.

12. Gildrie, *Salem, 1626–1683*, 122.

13. Richard D. Pierce, ed., *The Records of the First Church in Salem, Massachusetts, 1629–1736* (Salem, 1974), 109; Boyer and Nissenbaum, eds., *Salem-Village Witchcraft: A Documentary Record of Local Conflict in Colonial New England* (Belmont, CA, 1972), 230, 231, and 234; and *Town Records of Salem, Massachusetts*, 3 vols. (Salem, 1913–1934), II, 272.

14. Boyer and Nissenbaum, eds., *Salem-Village Witchcraft*, 344 and 171.

15. Pierce, ed., *Records of First Church in Salem*, 110.

16. The documents in the Bayley controversy are in Boyer and Nissenbaum, eds., *Salem-Village Witchcraft*, 240–255.

17. A sketch of Burroughs's life is in John L. Sibley, *Biographical Sketches of Graduates of Harvard University* (Cambridge, MA, 1881), II, 323–334. Watts's letter is in Boyer and Nissenbaum, eds., *Salem-Village Witchcraft*, 170–171.

18. The Salem arbitrators' advice is in Boyer and Nissenbaum, eds., *Salem-Village Witchcraft*, 344.

19. T. H. Breen, "War, Taxes, and Political Brokers: The Ordeal of Massachusetts Bay, 1675–1692," *Puritans and Adventurers, Change and Persistence in Early America* (New York, 1980), 85.

20. David Thomas Konig, *Law and Society in Puritan Massachusetts, Essex County, 1629–1692* (Chapel Hill, NC, 1979), 108.

21. For examples, see Boyer and Nissenbaum, eds., *Salem-Village Witchcraft*, 313–372.

22. Ibid., 231.

23. The best account of the Porters and the Putnams is in Boyer and Nissenbaum, *Salem Possessed*, 110–132.

24. Boyer and Nissenbaum, eds., *Salem-Village Witchcraft*, 229–231, 243–244, and 237.

25. Ibid., 262.

26. For Parris's life prior to Salem Village, see Larry Gragg, *A Quest for Security, The Life of Samuel Parris, 1653–1720* (Westport, CT, 1990), 1–35.

27. Ibid., 39–49.

28. Unfortunately, Salem church records do not address this question until November 1689, Pierce, ed., *Records of Church in Salem*, 169–170.

29. Parris, Sermon Book, 12, 14, and 15. Parris's sermon book is located in the Connecticut Historical Society. I have used a microfilm copy of the book.

30. Boyer and Nissenbaum, eds., *Salem-Village Witchcraft*, 268–269.

31. J. William T. Youngs, Jr., *God's Messengers, Religious Leadership in Colonial New England, 1700–1750* (Baltimore, 1976), 82.

32. Boyer and Nissenbaum, eds., *Salem-Village Witchcraft*, 270. The membership is in Ibid., 269–276.

33. The best account of this question is that of Robert C. Pope, *The Half-Way Covenant* (Princeton, 1969).

34. Boyer and Nissenbaum, eds., *Salem-Village Witchcraft*, 271; and *Essex Institute Historical Collections*, XVI (July 1879), 235.

35. Gragg, *A Quest for Security*, 55–76; and "Persons Married by Sam. Parris," Salem Village Parish Records, 1670–1735, Reel 876,096, Genealogical Library, Salt Lake City.

36. *New England Historical and Genealogical Register*, XXXVI (April 1882), 187–189.

37. Ibid., 188.

38. Parris, Sermon Book, 28.

39. Gragg, *A Quest for Security*, 55–76.

40. Parris, Sermon Book, January 3, 1692, 136.

41. Boyer and Nissenbaum, eds., *Salem-Village Witchcraft*, 269–291.

42. Parris, Sermon Book, December 1, 1689, 22; and February 14, 1692, 143.

43. Boyer and Nissenbaum, eds., *Salem-Village Witchcraft*, 314, 332, 333, and 346.

44. Ibid., 351 and 355.

45. Ibid., 255.

46. Ibid., 273.

47. Ibid., 350–351.

48. Ibid., 265.

49. Paul Boyer and Stephen Nissenbaum have an excellent description of the links in the Porter and Putnam clans; see Boyer and Nissenbaum, eds., *Salem Possessed*, 110–132.

50. Boyer and Nissenbaum, eds., *Salem-Village Witchcraft*, 356.

51. Parris, Sermon Book, November 24, 1689, 19.

52. Ibid., May 25, 1690, 65.

53. Boyer and Nissenbaum, eds., *Salem-Village Witchcraft*, 348, 276, 277, and 356.

54. Parris, Sermon Book, January 3, 1692, 138–139; and February 14, 1692, 139.

55. Benjamin W. Labaree, *Colonial Massachusetts, A History* (Millwood, NY, 1979), 113–119. For a more complete treatment of these changes in the Bay colony's relationship to the empire, see Viola F. Barnes, *The Dominion of New England* (New Haven, 1923); Richard R. Johnson, *Adjustment to Empire:*

The New England Colonies in the Era of the Glorious Revolution, 1675–1715 (New Brunswick, NJ, 1981), and David S. Lovejoy, *The Glorious Revolution in America* (New York, 1972).

56. James Kenses, "Some Unexplored Relationships of Essex County Witchcraft to the Indian Wars of 1675 and 1689," *Essex Institute Historical Collections*, CXX (July 1984), 187.

57. *New England Historical and Genealogical Register*, XXXVI (April 1882), 188.

58. Breen, "War, Taxes, and Political Brokers," 105.

59. G. B. Warden, *Boston, 1689–1776* (Boston, 1970), 13; and Demos, *Entertaining Satan*, 523 n.27.

60. Parris, Sermon Book, February 14, 1692, 144.

61. Ibid., 140.

62. Boyer and Nissenbaum, eds., *Salem-Village Witchcraft*, 356–357.

Three

"The Devil Hath Been Raised Amongst Us"

In 1692, according to Cotton Mather, some of New England's youth were "led away with little sorceries."[1] Two of these children lived in the household of the Reverend Samuel Parris. His nine-year-old daughter Elizabeth and eleven-year-old niece Abigail Williams began to dabble with the occult in the cold days of January. In the darkness of the poorly lit two-story Salem Village parsonage, the two girls apparently sought to divine what their husbands would be like.[2] A neighboring clergyman understood that they employed "an egg and a glass," like a crystal ball, "in a vain curiosity to know their future condition," an act he condemned because they had "tampered with the Devil's tools."[3] Whatever Elizabeth and Abigail thought they had learned, their experiments frightened them, and they began to act in peculiar and disturbing ways. John Hale, a minister from nearby Beverly, described their "distempers":

These children were bitten and pinched by invisible agents. Their arms, necks, and backs turned this way and that way, and returned back again, so as it was impossible for them to do of themselves, and beyond the power of any epileptic fits, or natural disease to effect. Sometimes they were taken dumb, their mouths stopped, their throats choked, their limbs wracked and tormented so as might move an heart of stone, to sympathize with them, with bowels of compassion for them.[4]

Not only could Parris not end their torments but others in the neighborhood began to suffer similar afflictions. Following the prudent course others had taken in similar circumstances, Parris brought several physicians to the parsonage, none of whom could explain the cause of the girls' behavior. The last one consulted, most likely William Griggs, a recent arrival to the village, advised that they suffered from no physical cause, meaning "they were under an Evil Hand." When word of his diagnosis spread through the neighborhood, the villagers quickly concluded that someone was using the powers of witchcraft to harm the girls. Believing that he was now dealing with a spiritual rather than a medical problem, Parris called upon "some worthy gentlemen of Salem, and some neighbor ministers to consult together at his house."[5]

Notable among the group was John Hale, a man of considerable experience with witchcraft cases. A graduate of Harvard College and pastor at Beverly since 1665, Hale, like many clergymen and judges of his time, had developed an attitude of restraint in dealing with matters of the "invisible world."[6] In 1648, when he was only twelve, he had gone with a group of neighbors to visit convicted witch Margaret Jones of Charlestown on the day of her execution in Boston. He recalled that they had advised her "to confession and repentance." When Jones declared herself "innocent," one neighbor "prayed her to consider if God did not bring this punishment upon her for some other crime, and asked, if she had not been guilty of stealing many years ago." Jones admitted the theft but said she had repented the crime and reiterated that she was "wholly free" of the witchcraft charge. What had obviously impressed the young Hale was the woman's adamant claims of innocence.[7] That early episode had contributed to his tendency not only to act cautiously but also, on occasion, to be charitable to those accused of witchcraft.

Not long after taking the ministerial position at Beverly, he learned that a woman in the village, Dorcas Hoar, had developed a reputation as a fortuneteller. In 1670, she had confessed to him that she "had borrowed a book of palmistry." After chastising her, Hale believed that she had renounced "all such practices." Consequently, he "had great charity for her several years." Eight years later, however, one of Hale's servants and some of Hoar's children were suspected of stealing from the minister's house. When he questioned his twelve-year-old daughter Rebecca if she knew of the thefts, she admitted she did but feared Goody Hoar's powers to "raise the Devil to kill her, or bewitch her." Despite Rebecca's apprehension and Hoar's reputation, Hale did not attribute to her his daughter's death shortly after this episode.[8] In 1680, Hale was among the group of ministers who visited with Elizabeth Morse following her reprieve from execution for practicing witchcraft. He was moved, as he had been when he saw Margaret Jones over thirty years earlier, by the woman's claims of innocence.[9]

Hale was drawn into a fourth case in 1687. Christian Trask, a communicant in the Beverly church, asked Hale to forbid Bridget Bishop "the Lords Supper in our church till she had given her the said Trask satisfaction for some offenses that were against her." Bishop, the former Bridget Oliver suspected of witchcraft in 1680, and her husband, Edward, lived less than one half mile from the Trasks and, according to Christian, Bridget "did entertain people in her house at unseasonable hours in the night to keep drinking and playing at shovel-board whereby discord did arise in other families and young people were in danger to be corrupted."[10] On one occasion, Trask had gone to Bishop's house, seized the game pieces from the players, tossed them into the fire, and "reproved the said Bishop for promoting such disorders." Hale moved to stop the late-night entertaining but soon learned that Trask had become "distracted." Her husband explained that Christian had begun to suffer the night after she had registered her complaint against Bishop. Hale fasted and prayed often with Trask, but she regained "the use of her reason" only temporarily and then alternated between "rational" and "distracted" periods. About a month later, she was found with her windpipe and jugular vein cut and a short pair of scissors nearby. Hale doubted that Christian could have committed suicide. It seemed that she would have needed a larger pair of scissors "to mangle herself so." Rather than self-inflicted wounds, "some extraordinary work of the Devil or witchcraft" must have been involved. Lending credence to such speculation, Hale believed, was Trask's "strong suspicion that she had been bewitched" by Bridget Bishop. Still, he was unwilling to attribute the death of the tormented woman to Bishop. Indeed, he later admitted that he was "hoping better of said Goody Bishop at that time."

Hale clearly had much to offer the troubled Samuel Parris: a concern for the afflicted, a predilection to act deliberately, and a desire to determine the truth. Once he and the other ministers had visited the Parris household and "had inquired diligently into the sufferings of the afflicted," they "concluded they were preternatural, and feared the hand of Satan was in them." Hale's influence is evident in their advice to the Salem Village pastor. "He should sit still," they cautioned, "and wait upon the Providence of God to see what time might discover; and to be much in prayer for the discovery of what was yet secret."[11]

It is not clear how quickly and widely the afflictions spread from the parsonage through the village. Apparently, Thomas Putnam's daughter Ann and his maid, Mercy Lewis; John Proctor's servant Mary Warren; Dr. Grigg's niece and maid Elizabeth Hubbard; and Mary, the daughter of Parris's neighbor Jonathan Walcott were also afflicted by late February.[12] After discussing with neighbors the plight of these girls and young women (they ranged in age from twelve to twenty), Mary Walcott's aunt, Mary Sibley, decided to try some white magic to counter the evil powers assaulting the village. On February 25, she prevailed upon Parris's slaves, Tituba and John Indian, to make a witch cake. They took some of the girls' urine, mixed it with rye meal, baked it, and fed it to a dog (evidently assuming that the animal was a familiar) as a means "to find out the witch."[13]

Sibley's experiment did not cure the girls but it did prompt them to make their first accusations. They "cried out of the Indian woman, named Tituba, that she did pinch, prick, and grievously torment them, and that they saw her here and there, where nobody else could. Yea, they could tell where she was, and what she did, when out of their human sight." When questioned about these charges, Tituba confessed only to helping make the witch cake. She explained that her former mistress in Barbados had been a witch "and had taught her some means to be used for the discovery of a witch and for the prevention of being bewitched." Tituba refused, however, to admit that she was a witch.[14]

Four of the afflicted, Abigail Williams, Elizabeth Parris, Ann Putnam, and Elizabeth Hubbard, continued to have "fits," and they "cried out" against not only Tituba but also Sarah Good and Sarah Osborne. They charged that the three women "or specters in their shapes did grievously torment them."[15] At this point, perhaps after consultation with Reverend Parris, Joseph Hutchinson, Thomas Putnam, Edward Putnam, and Thomas Preston took action against the accused. They all lived close to the parsonage—the center of the afflictions. Moreover, all of these men were prominent in the village, "yeomen" accustomed to assuming leadership roles.[16] On February 29, they filed complaints against the three women with Salem magistrates Jonathan Corwin and John Hathorne. As assistants, members of the upper house of the Massachusetts legislature, Corwin and Hathorne issued warrants for the arrest of the women. They instructed constables George Locker and Joseph Herrick to take Good, Osborne, and Tituba to Nathaniel Ingersoll's ordinary by ten o'clock the next day to be questioned. They also ordered that the four afflicted females "or any other person or persons that can give evidence" be compelled to appear. Herrick even searched for physical evidence of the accused's witchcraft practices, "images and such like," though to no avail.[17]

Villagers, frightened yet curious, gathered to hear what the magistrates could learn about the role these women had played in the outbreak of evil in their midst. Sarah Good, the first to be examined, faced a hopeless situation. Her neighbors had come to view her as an incorrigible, disagreeable beggar woman given to cursing those who rejected her appeals for help. She had suffered through one economic reversal after another throughout her adult life. In her late teens, Sarah had lost an inheritance when her mother remarried following the death of her father, John Solart. When Sarah's first husband, Daniel Poole, died, he left her with little property but with several debts to pay. In 1686, when she and her second husband, William Good, could not pay their creditors, he went to jail and they lost what little property they had. They were unable to recover from this setback. In 1689, they did not have enough property to appear on the village tax list. Samuel and Mary Abbey took the destitute couple into their home but, according to the Abbeys, Sarah was "so turbulent a spirit, spiteful and so maliciously bent" that the Abbeys turned them out. In the subsequent years, the Goods survived by begging from neighbors in the village, and Sarah often mumbled something when she walked away from those who rejected her appeals.[18]

John Hathorne, who consistently took the lead in the questioning, asked Sarah Good about her behavior when turned down. "Why did you go away muttering from Mr. Parris his house?" he asked. "I did not mutter," Good replied, "but I thanked him for what he gave my child." Hathorne persisted, "What is it that you say when you go muttering away from person's houses?" In the exchange that followed, Good struggled with her answers:

If I must tell I will tell.

Do tell us then.

If I must tell I will tell, it is the commandments. I may say my commandments I hope.

What commandment is it?

If I must tell you I will tell, it is a psalm.

What psalm?

After a long time she muttered some part of a psalm.

Hathorne not only wished to confirm Good's reputation as a scolding troll but he also wanted the afflicted to affirm that she had hurt them. When Hathorne told them "to look upon her," they all "positively accused her of hurting them sundry times within this two months and also that morning." When she denied harming any of them, or even being near their homes, they accused her again, this time "face to face." Upon making these charges, Elizabeth Parris, Abigail Williams, Ann Putnam, and Elizabeth Hubbard were "dreadfully tortured and tormented for a short space of time." In the noise and confusion of their suffering, Hathorne pressed Good to confess: "Do you not see now what you have done, why do you not tell us the truth, why do you thus torment these poor children?" Good reaffirmed her innocence, tried to shift the blame first to both of the other accused women, and then specifically claimed that it was Sarah Osborne who pinched and afflicted the children.[19]

Sarah Good's effort to implicate others to save herself was doomed. She had no one to offer testimony on her behalf. Even her family turned against her. Six-year-old Dorcas claimed that her mother had three familiars—"three birds, one black, one yellow, and that these birds hurt the children and afflicted persons."[20] Her husband admitted that he thought Sarah was a witch or likely to become one. When Hathorne "asked him his reason why he said so of her whether he had seen any thing by her," William tearfully admitted that "her bad carriage" had convinced him that she was (in an unfortunate choice of words) "an enemy to all good." A few days later, William worsened Sarah's plight when he claimed that on the night before her examination he had seen a witch's teat "a little below her right shoulder which he never saw before."[21]

Moreover, Sarah's examination, for some, triggered memories of hostile confrontations with her, encounters that they described in depositions taken later in the year. In the two years after they forced Sarah and her family to leave their home, Samuel and Mary Abbey lost seventeen head of cattle, along with some sheep and hogs. The cattle, the Abbeys explained, died in "an unusual manner." Even though they would eat, they suffered from a "drooping condition" before dying. The Abbeys believed it was due to the witchcraft practiced against them by Sarah Good.[22] Sarah and Thomas Gadge recalled a similar experience. In 1689, Sarah Good approached the Gadge home, but Sarah would not let her enter because she feared that Good had been exposed to smallpox. Rebuffed, Gadge recalled, Sarah Good "fell to muttering and scolding extremely," and she told Gadge "she should give her something." The following morning, one of the Gadges's cows "died in a sudden, terrible and strange, unusual manner." When her husband and some neighbors performed an autopsy on the animal, they could "find no natural cause of said cow's death" and concluded it had been due to witchcraft.[23] Twenty-one-year-old Henry Herrick likewise recalled such an episode. Two years earlier, Sarah Good had asked his father, Zachariah, for lodging. When he refused, Herrick remembered, "She went away grumbling and my father bid us to follow her and see that she went away clear, lest she should lie in the barn: and by smoking of her pipe should fire the barn." When young Herrick, along with twelve-year-old Jonathan Batchelor, saw her dawdling near the barn, they ordered her to leave, "to which she replied that then it should cost his father" his best cows. During the next couple of weeks, according to Batchelor, several of the cattle were "set loose in a strange manner."[24]

Finally, Sarah had encountered an interrogator in John Hathorne, who believed from the beginning that she had made a contract with the Devil from whom she had gained the power to torment the afflicted. She was also at the mercy of a clerk who characterized all her responses in a singularly negative fashion. Ezekiel Cheever took care to record that "her answers were in a very wicked, spiteful manner reflecting and retorting against the authority with base and abusive words and many lies."[25]

Sarah Osborne fared no better in her examination. Although financially comfortable, she was regarded scarcely better than Sarah Good.[26] For several years, Osborne had been involved in a nasty dispute with her sons over land left to them by her first husband, Robert Prince, who died in 1674. It was also widely believed in the village that she had lived with her second husband, an immigrant indentured servant named Alexander Osborne, before their marriage. Worse, Osborne had not attended worship in over a year.[27] As with Good, Hathorne presumed Osborne to be guilty: "What evil spirit have you familiarity with?" "Have you made no contract with the Devil?" "Why do you hurt these children?" Likewise, the afflicted "accused her face to face" and promptly were "hurt, afflicted and tortured very much" even when the constables moved Osborne far from them. During her brief examination, Osborne denied harming the afflicted, making a contract with the Devil, or even seeing Sarah Good for two years, and even then "only how do you do or so, I did not know her by name."[28]

Osborne also raised an issue that had troubled judges, clergymen, and laymen before and would continue to perplex them throughout the trials in 1692. The afflicted and those who filed depositions consistently contended that they had witnessed the accused's specter doing harm. Osborne testified that she was unaware "that the Devil goes about in my likeness to do any hurt." Her statement resurrected the dilemma: If the Devil used an individual's specter without her knowledge, could that be considered admissible evidence? For the moment, Hathorne revealed less interest in that question than in Osborne's admission of an encounter with the occult. The afflicted had overheard her say "that she was more like to be bewitched than that she was a witch." When Hathorne asked her to explain her claim, "she answered that she was frighted one time in her sleep and either saw or dreamed that she saw a thing like an Indian all black which did pinch her in her neck and pulled her by the back part of her head to the fore of the house." Sarah said that she never actually saw the Devil but admitted that she had heard a voice, one that instructed her to "go no more to meeting." She refused to comply and went "the next Sabbath day." Hathorne seized the opportunity to catch Osborne in an admission of acquiescence with evil. "Why," he asked, "did you yield thus far to the Devil as never to go to meeting since?" Her weak response that ended her examination was that she had been too ill to attend.[29]

Where Sarah Good had denied knowledge of the Devil and Sarah Osborne had made only a grudging admission of contact with the occult, Tituba provided a richly textured story of witchcraft in Salem Village. Her responses reflected many of the familiar images from the lore of occult beliefs. Her examination extended well into the afternoon and no doubt held the villagers in rapt attention.[30] Tituba explained that when the afflicted began to suffer, the Devil appeared to her as a man just as she was going to sleep and informed her that "he would kill the children," and if she would not serve him, he would kill her also. She said he wore "black clothes sometimes, sometimes serge coat of other color, a tall man with white hair." Four times he appeared as a black dog and once as a hog. In addition, she claimed that she had seen several familiars. Sarah Good had "a little yellow bird"; indeed, she saw "the bird suck Good between the forefinger and long finger upon the right hand." Good also had a cat, and Tituba said that Sarah had sent a wolf to harm Elizabeth Hubbard. Tituba did not know what to call Sarah Osborne's familiars, but "one of them hath wings and two legs and a head like a woman" and the other one was "a thing all over hairy, all the face hairy and a long nose." This second familiar had two legs, was about two or three feet high, and walked "upright like a man."

Tituba maintained that there were four other witches active in the village—Good, Osborne, and two women she did not know from Boston. She explained that on occasion they traveled together to perform their evil deeds. "I ride upon a stick or pole and Good and Osborne behind me we ride taking hold of one another." Tituba had agreed to serve the Devil partly because of his threats but also because he had promised her "pretty things" and a familiar. Most significant, Tituba admitted that she and the other accused had harmed the afflicted, although they had to "pull me and haul me to pinch the children." She admitted that she had pinched Elizabeth Parris, Abigail Williams, and Elizabeth Hubbard. The other witches also made her go to Thomas Putnam's home the night before and instructed her to cut off the arm of Ann Putnam, Jr. Those who had witnessed Ann's afflictions confirmed that the twelve-year-old "did complain of a knife."

Surely most distressing to the Reverend Parris were Tituba's revelations about the occult happenings in the parsonage. The upright, hairy familiar belonging to Sarah Osborne once "stood before the fire in Mr. Parris's hall." The Devil himself appeared to her in the lean-to, and the four witches bothered her while she was cleaning the house. Osborne, Good, and a man even had the audacity to come "to her last night when her master was at prayer and would not let her hear and she could not hear a good while." By the end of her examination, all the children were stricken, especially Elizabeth Hubbard, who was "in an extreme fit." Hathorne demanded to know who caused the harm, but Tituba said that the other witches blinded her, and she was "taken dumb."

Although Tituba had given detailed responses to their questions, Hathorne and Corwin wanted clarification of her testimony. Specifically, how had she contracted with the Devil and who were the unnamed witches? They decided to examine the slave again the following day. Tituba explained that in mid–January, just before Abigail Williams became ill, a man came to her contending that he was God and promised that if she would serve him for six years, he would give her "many fine things." She would not elaborate except to mention a promise of a creature, "a little bird something like green and white." Unconvinced that she was addressing the deity, Tituba wanted to consult the Reverend Parris in his study and "would have gone up but he stopped me and would not let me." To appease him, she said that she believed him to be God, and five nights later he convened a meeting with the four other witches in the parsonage. Just before evening prayer, with Parris in the next room, Tituba "saw them all stand in the corner, all four of them, and the man stand behind me and take hold of me to make me stand in the hall." They made her pinch Elizabeth, which caused Tituba much grief, because she "loved Betty" and Abigail. The man then instructed her to go into prayer, and if Parris read from the Bible and asked her what she recalled, she was to say that she could remember nothing. When the Devil had her sign his book two days after this episode, Tituba saw Good's and Osborne's names. In addition, there were seven more names that she could not see, though the Devil told her the others were from Boston and Salem Village. Tituba then claimed that on the first day of examinations, Sarah Good admitted to her that she had signed. Sarah Osborne, however, "would not tell she was cross to me." The Devil also visited her the same day and warned her that if she admitted her experiences with him, he would cut her head off.[31]

It remains difficult to explain Tituba's extraordinary testimony. Unlike Good and Osborne, perhaps she sought only to please her listeners and willingly followed wherever John Hathorne's questions led her. On the other hand, she may have done so out of fear of her master. The author of one contemporary account contended that Tituba said afterward that Parris beat her until she confessed and named her "sister-witches."[32] Given the vivid imagery in her testimony, Chadwick Hansen has suggested a third possibility. Tituba, like others later in the year, may have been describing hallucinations resulting from her occult experiences as a fortuneteller.[33] Whatever the reasons for it, Tituba's testimony caused Hathorne and Corwin to question her again on March 3 and 5, along with Sarah Osborne on the former day and Sarah Good on the latter. Because Tituba reaffirmed her earlier testimony, the two magistrates concluded that sufficient evidence had been produced to merit trials for the three, and they sent them to a jail in Boston.[34]

Other than Tituba's elaborate testimony, however, this episode of witchcraft was hardly an unusual one. The accused fit the profile of those most often suspected of occult crimes, particularly Sarah Good. Her life strikingly resembled the portrait drawn by historians of women in sixteenth- and seventeenth-century English culture most at risk.[35] As Robert Calef explained in his 1700 account of the witchcraft outbreak, the accused were an Indian woman who confessed and "Sarah Good, who had long been counted a melancholy or distracted woman, and one Osborne, an old bed-rid woman; which two were persons so ill thought of, that the accusation was the more readily believed."[36] The beginning, Salem pastor John Higginson accurately observed in 1702, "was small, and looked on at first as an ordinary case which had fallen out before at several times in other places, and would be quickly over."[37]

Yet this one was not like previous cases. Even though authorities had arrested, examined, and incarcerated the accused witches, the suffering of the afflicted continued. The Reverend Parris conducted a series of private fasts, but they had no positive impact, even after he invited several area ministers to join him on March 11. While the clergymen prayed, the afflicted remained calm, but they "would act and speak strangely" once the prayers ended. Abigail Williams in particular "would sometimes seem to be in a convulsion fit, her limbs being twisted several ways, and very stiff, but presently her fit would be over."[38] Parris revealed his growing concern over his daughter by sending her to the home of a Salem friend, Stephen Sewall. There the child continued to experience "sore fits," so much so that Sewall and his wife worried that she would not recover. The examination of Tituba, which the youngster had been forced to attend, had a profound effect on her. Elizabeth became consumed with the image of a devil constantly enjoining her to renounce her faith. She explained to Sewall's wife that "the great black man came to her and told her, if she would be ruled by him, she should have whatsoever she desired, and go to a Golden City." Eventually, Elizabeth recovered because the Sewalls convinced her that Satan was a liar and because her stay with them isolated her from the growing epidemic of witchcraft accusations, a circumstance denied the others afflicted.[39]

While community leaders sought to ease the suffering of the afflicted and contain the crisis, ever more villagers reported experiences with the occult. After the first day of examinations, constable Joseph Herrick placed Sarah Good in custody at his home and posted a guard of three men. In the morning, however, the men reported that Good had been gone much of the night even though they had kept her barelegged and barefooted. That same night, while Samuel Sibley was at William Grigg's home, the doctor's niece, Elizabeth Hubbard, cried out that Sarah Good was pinching and pricking her. When the young woman told Sibley that Good "with all her naked breast and barefooted barelegged" was standing on a table near him, he swung his staff in that direction and, according to Hubbard, he struck the specter. Informed of the nocturnal excitement, constable Herrick examined the accused witch and testified that one of Good's arms was bloody from the elbow to the wrist, confirming Hubbard's claim. Herrick distinctly recalled that "the night before" there had been "no signs of blood."[40]

Sarah Good's was not the only specter threatening the community. Early in the evening of March 1, as William Allen and John Hughes were walking through the village, they heard an unusual noise ahead of them. As the two men got closer, they saw a strange beast, but before they could get near it, "the said beast vanished away." In its place were three women who also "flew" from them. The women escaped not in "the manner of other women but swiftly vanished away out of our sight which women we took to be Sarah Good, Sarah Osborne, and Tituba." The following night, the men claimed they were visited by specters in their bed chambers. According to Allen, after he retired for the night, "Sarah Good visibly appeared" with an unusual light and sat on his foot. When Allen tried to kick Good, both her specter and the light vanished. John Hughes likewise saw a "great light." Awakened by the light, he rose up in bed and, even though he had locked the door to the room, Hughes saw "a large gray cat at his bed's foot."[41]

Certainly, wherever villagers gathered in early March, they discussed these visions, the continued fits of the afflicted, the inability of secular and religious leaders to end the crisis, and the seven unnamed witches mentioned by Tituba. On March 11, twelve-year-old Ann Putnam finally identified one of them. She complained that Martha Corey "did often appear to her and torture her by pinching and other ways."[42] The wife of Salem farmer Giles Corey, Martha was an unlikely witchcraft suspect. Even though she had had an illegitimate mulatto child several years earlier, Martha had sufficient standing in the community to gain membership in the village congregation in 1690.[43] Because she was "in church covenant with us," Edward Putnam, Ann's uncle and sometimes deacon in the church, along with Ezekiel Cheever, clerk in the initial examinations, took it upon themselves to visit Corey and listen to what she had to say about the charges. Unsure that the afflicted child had accurately named her tormentor, Putnam and Cheever devised a scheme to test her reliability. On the morning of March 12, they went to Thomas Putnam's house to see if a specter still assaulted Ann. The two men wanted her "to take good notice of what clothes" the specter wore so they "might see whether she was not mistaken in the person." Once the men had explained their plan to her, Ann said that Corey appeared, blinded her, and said "she should see no more before it was night." Consequently, Ann said she would be unable to help Putnam and Cheever.[44]

The news of Ann's charges and the mission of the two men spread quickly throughout the village. That was clear from their reception at Corey's home. "I know what you are come for," she said with a smile, "you are come to talk with me about being a witch but I am none. I cannot help peoples' talking of me." Martha then asked the men if Ann Putnam had been able to tell them what she was wearing. When they did not reply, she repeated her question "with very great eagerness." As they admitted that Ann could not describe the clothing because a specter had blinded her, Corey offered no response. Rather, according to Cheever and Putnam, she "seemed to smile at it as if she had showed us a pretty trick." The men pointed out that the charges leveled against her dishonored God and the church since she was a member. Corey displayed little concern since "she had made a profession of Christ and rejoiced to go and hear the word of God and the like." She was more interested in ending the gossip about her connection to witchcraft. In contrast to people like her, Corey reminded them, the Devil made covenants with "idle slothful persons." After "much discourse" with the confident matron, Putnam and Cheever returned to Ann to discover that Martha Corey's specter had appeared to her in their absence but had done no harm.

Martha Corey had confronted the accusations against her convinced that the villagers would not believe that persons in her station of life, spiritually and financially secure, could be associated with witchcraft. Yet another of the afflicted, Abigail Williams, cried out against her on March 14.[45] On the same day, apparently in an effort to prevent further accusations, Corey went to Thomas Putnam's home to assure his daughter that she had not harmed her. Unfortunately for Corey, her gesture only worsened the situation. As soon as Corey stepped inside the house, Ann fell to the floor in a fit. She complained of being choked and blinded, and her "feet and hands twisted in a most grievous manner and told Martha Corey to her face that she did it." Ann also said that she saw Corey nourishing her familiar, a yellow bird, between her middle and forefinger. Edward Putnam, who was also present, added that Corey invited Ann to approach her and examine the bird if she believed one was there. Then, according to Putnam, "Martha Corey put one of her fingers in the place where Ann had said she saw the bird and seemed to give a hard rub," an act that not only blinded the child but also caused her to collapse again. When Ann regained her vision, she cried out that Corey was turning a spit with a man on it at the fireplace. Another of the afflicted, Thomas Putnam's maid Mercy Lewis, seized a stick and tried to strike the apparition but screamed "with a grievous pain in her arm." The girls "grew so bad with pains" that the Putnams ordered Corey to leave, her attempt to dispel the growing suspicions about her a failure. Indeed, that night Mercy Lewis was:

. . . drawn toward the fire by unseen hands as she sat in a chair and two men hold of it. Yet she and chair moved toward the fire though they labored to the contrary. Her feet going foremost and I seeing it stepped to her feet and lifted with my strength together with the other two and all little enough to prevent her from going to the fire with her feet foremost and this distress held until about eleven of the clock in the night.[46]

As with all else that happened that day, witnesses blamed the life-threatening episode on Martha Corey. When Corey's specter began to torment Ann Putnam's mother, Ann, Edward Putnam decided to take legal action. Along with village farmer Henry Kenney, he filed a complaint on Saturday March 19 with Hathorne and Corwin. They ordered the constables to have the woman at Ingersoll's the following Monday for an examination.[47]

The same day that the magistrates issued their warrant, former village pastor Deodat Lawson arrived in Salem Village. Twelve years later, he explained what drew him back:

In pity therefore to my Christian friends, and former acquaintance there, I was much concerned about them, frequently consulted with them, and fervently (by Divine assistance) prayed for them. But especially my concern was augmented, when it was reported, at an examination of a person suspected for witchcraft, that my wife and daughter, who died three years before, were sent out of the world under the malicious operations of the infernal powers; as is more fully represented in the following remarks. I did then desire, and was also desired by some concerned in the court, to be there present, that I might hear what was alleged in that respect.[48]

Shortly after he arranged lodging at Ingersoll's, Lawson encountered one of the afflicted, Mary Walcott. She came in complaining of a pain in her arm. When Lawson held a candle near her wrist, he "saw apparently the marks of teeth both upper and lower set, on each side of her wrist." Unsure of the significance of what he had just seen, or who or what had caused it, Lawson went on to the parsonage to visit with Samuel Parris. There he saw how serious the fits of the afflicted had become:

Abigail Williams, (about 12 years of age,) had a grievous fit. She was at first hurried with violence to and fro in the room, (though Mrs. Ingersoll endeavored to hold her,) sometimes making as if she would fly, stretching up her arms as high as she could, and crying "whish, whish, whish!" several times. Presently after she said there was Goodwife N. and said, "Do you not see her? Why there she stands!" And the said Goodwife N. offered her the Book, but she was resolved she would not take it, saying often, "I won't, I won't, I won't, take it, I do not know what book it is. I am sure it is none of God's Book, it is the Devil's Book, for ought I know." After that, she ran to the fire, and began to throw fire brands, about the house; and run against the back, as if she would run up chimney, and, as they said, she had attempted to go into the fire in other fits.[49]

Lawson did not record his reaction to Abigail's disturbing action. Nor is it evident with what frame of mind he took to the pulpit the next day, in response to Parris's invitation, to preach to his former congregation. He, as well as those in attendance, must have been shocked, however, at what happened that March 20. With Martha Corey in attendance, the afflicted disrupted virtually the entire worship service. After they interrupted his opening prayer with "severe sore fits," the afflicted remained calm during the singing of a psalm. Then Abigail Williams blurted out,

"Now stand up, and name your text." When Lawson complied, she was impatient, "It is a long text." Once he began his sermon, Bethshaa Pope, a woman recently afflicted, spoke out, "Now there is enough of that." As the beleaguered clergyman tried to continue, there were more outbursts. Abigail Williams cried, "Look where Goodwife C. sits on the beam suckling her yellow bird betwixt her fingers!" Lawson later learned that young Ann Putnam whispered to a friend that she saw the yellow bird perched "on my hat as it hung on the pin in the pulpit." The afflicted persisted in the afternoon service. When Lawson referred to his sermon doctrine, Abigail Williams said aloud, "I know no doctrine you had, if you did name one, I have forgot it."[50]

Word that the afflicted had disrupted the sacred decorum of worship rapidly reached those in the village who were not in the meetinghouse that Sunday. It caused them to cease virtually all other activity the following morning as most residents of Salem Village arrived at Ingersoll's to witness Martha Corey's examination. At noon, the magistrates, faced with several hundred interested villagers, decided to move the proceedings up the road into the meetinghouse. Prominent among the spectators was the growing group of afflicted. Additions included Bethshaa Pope, who had interrupted Lawson's sermon the day before, Sarah Bibber, and "an ancient woman, named Goodall."[51] After a "pertinent and pathetic prayer" from Salem minister Nicholas Noyes, John Hathorne once again began a rigorous interrogation.[52] He pressed Corey to explain the questions raised in Edward Putnam and Ezekiel Cheever's deposition of their visit with her nine days earlier. How did she know they had asked Ann Putnam what clothes she would be wearing? How did she know why the two men had come to her house before they arrived? What was she turning on the spit in the fireplace? Did her specter strike Mercy Lewis with an iron rod? Corey responded with denials but also with evasive and contradictory answers. She contended that her husband, Giles, told her about the clothing. When Giles denied he had done so, Martha tried another answer; she understood the afflicted had described the clothing of the other accused so she assumed the Putnam girl would be able to do so as well. When her inquisitors found that response unacceptable, she simply admitted no one had told her. She had guessed that someone would visit her about witchcraft after overhearing conversations among some children who said she afflicted and troubled people. Corey denied turning anything on the spit or harming Mercy Lewis. Indeed, throughout the examination, she refused to admit harming anyone.

Her husband not only failed to confirm her testimony on the Putnam and Cheever visit but also, three days later, offered evidence that lent credence to the charges against her. As William Good had done during his wife Sarah's examination, Giles Corey discussed his doubts and suspicions about his wife. He recalled several curious incidents of the previous week, none of which alone was startling, but, collectively, they caused him to wonder if Martha was dabbling in the occult. Two of the incidents involved farm animals. He had "fetched an ox well out of the woods, about noon, and he laying down in the yard I went to raise him to yoke him but he could not rise but dragged his hinder parts as if he had been hipshot but after did rise." He also had a cat suddenly become ill and thought it would die. Martha even encouraged him to "knock her in the head"; he did not and the animal recovered. The other instances he spoke of involved their daily prayers. On the previous Saturday evening, before retiring, Giles "went to prayer," but "could not utter my desires with any sense, not open my mouth to speak." Sensing his difficulties, Martha moved closer to him, and this enabled Giles to "attend the duty." Finally, he recalled, "My wife hath been want to sit up after I went to bed, and I have perceived her to kneel down to the hearth as if she were at prayer, but heard nothing."[53]

Hathorne asked several questions about Corey's understanding of, as well as her personal involvement in witchcraft. He wanted to know why she tried to prevent her husband from attending the examinations earlier in the month by removing the saddle from his horse. Was it because "she would not have them help to find out witches"? First, she said that she did not know where he was going, but as so often happened during her examination, Martha changed her response to suggest that his attendance would not have been "to any benefit." The afflicted interrupted the exchanges between Hathorne and Corey several times. At one point, they asked "why she did not go to the company of witches which were before the meetinghouse mustering? Did she not hear the drum beat?"[54] In response to their outburst, Hathorne asked, "Do not you believe that there are witches in the country?" Corey replied that she did not know of any.

On a couple of occasions, the afflicted testified that they had seen Corey's specter. Ann Putnam, Jr., said that she had seen her "shape" in the Putnam's house praying to the Devil. Several of the afflicted fell into a "fit" during the examination and claimed they saw "her likeness coming to them, and bringing a book to them."[55] Hathorne again followed their prompting and demanded to know how the Devil could appear to the afflicted in her "shape." Corey could only respond, "How can I know how?" "What book," Hathorne continued, "is that you would have these children write in?" Corey maintained that she "showed them none, nor have none nor brought none." The afflicted made several other charges. They contended that Corey "had covenanted with the Devil for ten years, six of them were gone, and four more to come."[56] Twice, they said, a man was whispering to Corey, and twice they saw a yellow bird with her. Hathorne pursued all of their charges despite Corey's repeated denials. This exchange clearly reveals his dogged persistence:

Do you believe these children are bewitched?

They may for ought I know. I have had no hand in it.

You say you are no witch, maybe you mean you never covenanted with the Devil. Did you never deal with any familiar?

No, never.

What bird was that the children spoke of?

The witnesses, spoke.

What bird was it?

I know no bird.

It may be you have engaged you will not confess, but God knows.

A dramatic departure from the earlier examinations was the apparent power of the accused to harm the afflicted by simply moving her body. Deodat Lawson, who took careful notes of the proceedings, explained:

It was observed several times, that if she did but bite her under lip in time of examination the persons afflicted were bitten on their arms and wrists and produced the marks before the magistrates, ministers and others. And being watched for that, if she did but pinch her fingers or grasp one hand hard in another, they were pinched and produced the marks before the magistrates, and spectators. After that, it was observed, that if she did but lean her breast against the seat, in the meetinghouse, (being the bar at which she stood,) they were afflicted. . . . after these postures were watched, if said C. did but stir her feet, they were afflicted in their feet, and stamped fearfully.[57]

The spectacle was convincing. The Reverend Nicholas Noyes was so sure of Corey's guilt that he interjected his opinion. "I believe it is apparent," he said, "she practiceth witchcraft in the congregation." Indeed, the woman was so effective that she had "no need of images" to work her craft.

One of the afflicted, Bethshaa Pope, struck back at Martha Corey in an act with comic overtones amid a deadly serious exchange. Pope "vehemently accused" Corey as the cause of a "grievous torment in her bowels." It felt, she cried, "as if they were torn out." To stop her tormentor, Pope "threw her muff at her" but missed her target. She then removed her shoe, and her aim was true the second time for she struck Corey "on the head with it."[58]

Throughout her examination, Martha Corey alternately posed as an innocent victim and derided the "blind" magistrates and ministers and "distracted" children. In response to several questions, Corey proclaimed she was guiltless; not only now, but throughout her life, "I never had to do with witchcraft since I was born." Early on, she had attempted to demonstrate that she was not only an innocent woman but also a pious one. "Pray give me leave to go to prayer," she asked Hathorne as he began the questioning, a request that caused much wonder among the spectators, according to Deodat Lawson. Hathorne, nonetheless, would not permit it, pointing out that he "came not there to hear her pray, but to examine her, in what was alleged against her."[59] Corey also reminded the magistrates, in a strikingly accurate characterization of the proceedings, of the unfairness of her situation. "If you will all go hang me," she asked, "how can I help it?"

Corey destroyed what little chance she had of gaining the sympathy of the authorities and spectators with her repeated outbursts of laughter at Hathorne's questions and the actions of the afflicted. The outbursts angered the stern Hathorne: "Is it a laughing matter to see these afflicted persons?" She further displayed her disdain in a boast that she could open the "blinded" eyes of the "magistrates and ministers" to the truth of the witchcraft accusations. Corey was most critical of the afflicted. She derided their charges and told Hathorne and Corwin that they should not pay attention to "poor, distracted children."[60] The magistrates, as well as the Reverend Noyes, tired of her scorn and explained, "It was the judgment of all that were present, they were bewitched, and only she, the accused person said, they were distracted." After the exhausting exchange, Hathorne and Corwin ordered Martha Corey committed to the jail in Salem. "After she was in custody," according to Lawson, "she did not appear to them [the afflicted] and afflict them as before."[61]

Two days after Corey's examination, the Reverend Lawson went to see Thomas Putnam's wife, Ann. For almost a week, she had suffered torments from apparitions. Five days earlier, Ann had spent most of the day caring for her afflicted daughter Ann and maid Mercy Lewis. In the afternoon, she lay down for a brief rest and "was almost pressed and choked to death" by Martha Corey's shape. The apparition brought "a little red book" and "a black pen" and urged her to join with the forces of evil by signing the book. Corey's shape returned the next day, accompanied by Rebecca Nurse's, and the two tortured Ann. She "had a great deal of respite" on March 20 and 21. The following day, however, Nurse's shape appeared once more:

The apparition of Rebecca Nurse did again set upon in a most dreadful manner very early in the morning as soon as it was well light. And now she appeared to me only in her shift . . . [and night cap] and brought a little red book in her hand urging me vehemently to write in her book and because I would not yield to her hellish temptations she threatened to tear my soul out of my body blasphemously denying the blessed God and the power of the Lord Jesus Christ to save my soul and denying several places of scripture which I told her of to repel her hellish temptations. And for near two hours together at this time the apparitions of Rebecca Nurse did tempt and torture me before she left me as if indeed she would have killed me and also the greatest part of this day with but very little respite.[62]

Aware of Ann's afflictions, Lawson intervened. When he arrived, she was lying down, recovering from "a sore fit a little before." Ann asked Lawson to pray for her, but when he acquiesced, she suffered a silent fit. Her husband tried to take her from the bed and help her kneel, but "she could not be bended." Suddenly, Ann began to flail about the room and to argue with Rebecca Nurse's shape:

Goodwife N. be gone! be gone! be gone! Are you not ashamed, a woman of your profession, to afflict a poor creature so? What hurt did I ever do you in my life! You have but two years to live, and then the Devil will torment your soul, for this your name is blotted out of God's Book, and it shall never be put in God's Book again. Be gone for shame, are you not afraid of that which is coming upon you? I know, I know, what will make you afraid; the wrath of an angry God, I am sure that will make you afraid, Be gone, do not torment me, I know what you would have (we judged she meant, her soul) but it is out of your reach; it is clothed with the white robes of Christ's righteousness.

Ann then argued with Nurse's shape "about a particular test of scripture." Ann told the shape that it could not remain if the "third chapter of Revelations" were recited. Lawson took the cue and began to read it "and before I had near read through the first verse, she opened her eyes and was well."[63]

Because of Ann's confrontation with Rebecca Nurse's shape, Edward and Jonathan Putnam filed a complaint that day with Hathorne and Corwin. The magistrates ordered Nurse's arrest and scheduled yet another examination for the following morning. The wife of a prosperous village farmer and a member of the Salem church, Rebecca drew even greater interest than Martha Corey because many had seen in the aged Rebecca a model of Christian piety.[64] It seemed unbelievable to most, not the least of all Rebecca herself, that she could be accused. Her reaction was recorded in a deposition filed by Israel and Elizabeth Porter, Daniel Andrew, and Peter Cloyce. After Ann Putnam began to cry out against her, the foursome decided to visit Rebecca. They found her recovering from a week-long illness, yet she blessed God for "His presence in this sickness." She spoke of her concern for the spreading afflictions especially in Reverend Parris's family and how she grieved for and pitied them. Rebecca worried, though, about individuals who had been accused that she considered as innocent as herself. Finally, her visitors told Rebecca that she had been identified as a witch. After sitting quietly for a moment, the old woman wondered aloud, "What sin hath God found out in me unrepented of that he should lay such an affliction upon me in my old age."[65]

Because of Rebecca Nurse's reputation, John Hathorne took a dramatically different approach during her examination.[66] Rather than assuming her guilt, as he had with the four other women, the magistrate offered the hope that she would be exonerated. When Rebecca proclaimed her innocence, he responded, "Here is never a one in the assembly but desires it." Later, he told her, "I pray God clear you if you be innocent." As never before, Hathorne had doubts about specter evidence, especially when Mary Walcott admitted that although she had seen Nurse's shape, she could recall no harm it had done. He also moved cautiously when trying to determine how far Nurse may have compromised with evil: "Possibly you may apprehend you are no witch, but have you not been led aside by temptations that way?" "Tell us have not you had visible appearances more than what is common in nature?" Nurse denied both suggestions of limited complicity with evil. Hathorne then probed for her understanding of what the afflicted were experiencing:

Do you think these suffer voluntary or involuntary?

I cannot tell.

That is strange; every one can judge.

I must be silent.

They accuse you of hurting them, and if you think it is not unwillingly but by design, you must look upon them as murderers.

I cannot tell what to think of it.

Eventually, Rebecca acknowledged that she believed the afflicted were indeed "bewitched."

Frequent interruptions made Hathorne's tentative interrogation even more difficult. Shortly after Hathorne began, Henry Kenney rose and testified "that since this Nurse came into the house he was seized twice with an amazed condition." Moments later, before Nurse could answer one of Hathorne's questions, Ann Putnam, Sr., broke in: "Did you not bring the Black Man with you, did you not bid me tempt God and die? How oft have you eat and drunk your own" damnation? Before long, several of the afflicted, notably Elizabeth Hubbard, Mary Walcott, and Bethshaa Pope, either yelled accusations at Nurse or fell to the floor in fits. Whenever Nurse moved her hands, changed the position of her head, or bent her back, the afflicted complained of being bitten, pinched, and bruised. When the hard-of-hearing Nurse had trouble with a question, some of the afflicted said it was because the "black man" was whispering to her. Others claimed that they saw her riding past the meetinghouse "behind the Black Man." Of all the afflicted, Ann Putnam, Sr., suffered the most. As the examination drew to a conclusion, she lost all strength and "could hardly move hand, or foot." Her condition so concerned Hathorne that he permitted her husband to carry her from the meeting-house.[67]

The examination developed into a truly frightening experience. Samuel Parris, appointed by the magistrates to serve as clerk, explained at the end of the transcript that he had difficulty recording the questions and answers "by reason of great noises by the afflicted and many speakers." Deodat Lawson, who had to leave before the examination ended to finish preparations for the afternoon sermon, noted that as he walked from the meetinghouse he heard a "hideous screech and noise" that "did amaze" him. He later learned from those who had remained behind that all within were "struck with consternation" at what they had witnessed. Most important for Rebecca Nurse, the actions of the afflicted convinced Hathorne and Corwin to place her in the Salem jail with Martha Corey.

In addition to Rebecca Nurse, the magistrates also examined Sarah Good's daughter, Dorcas. Mary Walcott and Ann Putnam, Jr., had complained that the child's shape had bitten, pinched, and choked them. During her brief examination, whenever Dorcas glanced at the afflicted, they said she bit them. Several even showed the magistrates "the marks of a small set of teeth" on their arms. With little deliberation, Hathorne and Corwin dispatched her to join her mother in the Salem jail. Two days later, the magistrates, along with Salem minister John Higginson, visited the child, and she told them that she "had a little snake that used to suck on the lowest joint of it[s] forefinger." Dorcas pointed to a spot about the size of a "flea-bite" as the place she had given nourishment to the familiar given to her, she said, by her mother.[68]

The accusations, arrests, and examinations of Martha Corey and Rebecca Nurse raised questions about two vital issues. Both Corey and Nurse had contended that specter evidence was not proof that they had entered into covenants with Satan. "I cannot help it," Rebecca told John Hathorne, "the Devil may appear in my shape." More troubling to the villagers than the reliability of specter evidence was the prospect that members of Puritan congregations could be witches. Were not those who professed Christ and who had made a covenant with God above suspicion of practicing witchcraft? That was essentially what Martha Corey had told Ezekiel Cheever and Edward Putnam when they had come calling on March 12. "We told her," the two men explained in their testimony, "it was not her making an outward profession that would clear her from being a witch for it had often been so in the world that witches had crept into churches."[69] John Hathorne clearly shared their concern. "What a sad thing it is," he said during Rebecca Nurse's examination, "that a church member here and now another of Salem, should be thus accused and charged."[70] Apparently, most villagers likewise worried about the likelihood of church members falling prey to the blandishments of the Devil. Amid the chaos of Rebecca Nurse's examination, spectators simply did not know who around them could be trusted; "they were afraid, that those that sat next to them, were under the influence of witchcraft."[71]

After Rebecca Nurse and Dorcas Good were taken to jail, the villagers remained in the meetinghouse to listen to the Thursday lecture day sermon from their former pastor, Deodat Lawson, hoping for an explanation of their crisis.[72] In "Christ's Fidelity the Only Shield Against Satan's Malignity," Lawson reminded his listeners to understand this hellish episode as part of the constant struggle between good and evil, that Satan had set "himself against the infinite and eternal God." That "Grand Enemy of all mankind" was always seeking "to catch devour and destroy souls." In his contracts with those who fall, "after the time of his service to them, he will have their souls, viz intending to torment them forever." To that end, Satan employs various tactics. He seeks to confuse people's understanding by surrounding them in "mists of darkness." He also creates "frightful representations" in individuals' imaginations, and he resorts to "violent tortures of the body." Satan might actually enter and possess the soul of humans, but more often convinces them to do harm.

Because of the extraordinary powers that Satan wields, we should have compassion for his victims, "those poor, afflicted persons that are by divine permission under the direful influence of Satan's malice."[73]

During the course of his sermon, however, Lawson offered strangely equivocal answers to the central questions of concern. In one section, he suggested that specter evidence could legitimately be used, because Satan, through witches, convinces individuals "to subscribe to a book," placing them in subjection to him. Once he has "them in this subjection, by their consent, he will use their bodies and minds, shapes and representations, to affright and afflict others." Significantly, he is particularly interested in prevailing upon "those that make a visible profession" to join him, so that he may "more readily pervert others to consenting unto his subjection." Unfortunately for the congregation, Lawson contradicted these statements in other passages. Satan, he told them, "if it were possible," would deceive "the very Elect," but cannot. Indeed, when dealing with specter evidence against church members, he advised great caution, for Satan was clever:

And (which is yet more astonishing) he who is the accuser of the brethren, endeavors to introduce as criminal, some of the visible subjects of Christ's Kingdom, by whose sober and godly conversation in times past, we could draw no other conclusions than that they were real members of His Mystical Body, representing them, as the instruments of his malice, against their friends and neighbors.[74]

Out of these confusing statements, Lawson drew some lessons and offered advice to the villagers. They must understand that they had brought this crisis upon themselves through their constant quarrels and divisions. "In righteous judgment," God had "sent this fire of His Holy displeasure, to put out some fires of contention, that have been amongst you." Consequently, they must look upon the afflictions as a sign to reform their lives. Certainly mindful of Mary Sibley's effort to help the afflicted through occult means, he instructed them not to try to "charm away witchcraft." Instead, he encouraged the villagers to assist with "spiritual sympathy" the efforts of their "reverend and pious pastor." Above all, as he had intimated in the sermon title, Lawson called upon the congregation to resist the power of Satan through their greatest weapon, "what therefore I say unto one, I say unto all, in this important case: pray, pray, pray."[75]

Three days after Lawson's attempt to explain what had befallen the village, Samuel Parris took to the pulpit and delivered a communion day sermon that left little doubt about his views on specter evidence and the possibility of church members being witches. His sermon title was a model of clarity: "Christ Knows How Many Devils There Are in His Churches and Who They Are." Parris felt compelled to speak out because of the "dreadful witchcraft" that had broken out in the village over the past month. But more important, he spoke out because "one member of this church, and another of Salem upon public examination by civil authority vehemently suspected for she-witches and upon it committed." He drew upon the betrayal of Christ by Judas as described in John 6:70, for his sermon topic: "Have not I chosen you twelve, and one of you is a devil." A devil in this context, Parris explained, was not the "prince or head of the evil spirits," but rather "vile and wicked" sinners. The most "notorious" were the hypocrites: "None are worse than those that have been good, and are naught." They are a threat because hypocrites are found amid the "true saints" in the church. He likened such a congregation to a garden that has both weeds and flowers and a field that has tares as well as wheat. More precisely, he compared it to the twelve apostles among whose ranks was a devil. But, as in that case, Christ knows who the "true believers, or hypocrites and dissembling Judases" are in the church. In taking this position, Parris clearly referred to Nurse and Corey: "Let none then build their hopes of salvation merely upon this, that they are church-members this you and I may be, and yet devils for all that."[76]

Not only did Parris contend that it was likely that some members of the Salem Village church could be witches but he also indicated his belief in specter evidence. In doing so, though, he was careful to make it clear that Satan only had the power to use the shape of some church members. He drew a distinction between the "true saints" and the hypocrites. He prayed that:

God would not suffer devils in the guise of saints to associate with us. One sinner destroys much good; how much more one devil. Pray we also that not one true saint may suffer as a devil either in name, or body. The Devil would represent the best saints as devils if he could, but it is not easy to imagine that his power is of such extent, to the hazard of the church.[77]

Once Parris completed the sermon, but before the congregation shared communion, he read a statement about the outbreak of witchcraft in the village and Mary Sibley's role in it. As had Lawson, Parris emphasized that God "for wise and holy ends" had permitted many villagers "to be grievously vexed and tortured in body." He reminded his listeners, certainly with much chagrin, that it had all begun "in my own family." Not only had the afflictions commenced in his household but also it had been "my Indian man," under Mary Sibley's direction, who had employed countercharms. Such an act was no less than "going to the Devil for help against the Devil." Since Parris considered Sibley "instrumental" in the "distress" suffered since by the village, on the surface, the actions he recommended to deal with her seem curious. Parris asked the church members, by a show of hands, to protest what she had done as "contrary to the Gospel." However, since Sibley "did it in ignorance," and because she confessed to much sorrow and grief for her actions and promised "future better advisedness and caution," Parris also asked that members vote to permit her to "continue in our holy fellowship." Taking their pastor's advice, the members unanimously approved both recommendations.[78] In light of the recent rigorous examinations and jailings of Martha Corey and Rebecca Nurse, the treatment of Sibley for her "diabolical" act appears extraordinarily lenient. Two factors explain the difference. Unlike Nurse and Corey, no one had charged that Sibley's shape had harmed anyone. Moreover, she had employed witchcraft in an effort to help individuals, not harm them, as had been alleged against the other two women.

Parris's message had given the villagers much to think about. He had confirmed the frightening sensation that they had experienced at Nurse's examination: they could not be confident about anyone's fidelity to Christ. Indeed, Parris had suggested that the villagers must accept the possibility that several more within their congregation might be witches. "Christ knows how many devils among us," he had emphasized, "whether one or ten or 20."[79] They had also been startled by Sarah Cloyce's protest of Parris's sermon. When he announced his text—"Have not I chosen you twelve, and one of you is a devil"—Cloyce, a sister of Rebecca Nurse, stood and then walked out of the meetinghouse, the door slamming shut behind her.[80] Most memorable, however, was his prophecy of a long struggle with the forces of evil: "The Devil hath been raised amongst us, and his rage is vehement and terrible, and when he shall be silenced, the Lord only knows."[81]

Samuel Parris's strong words represented the culmination of a process that had developed over four weeks' time, one that would lead to the most massive of the American witch hunts. The accused in Salem Village were suspected of more than mere *maleficium*. Beginning with Tituba's examination, scattered evidence had emerged of an organized witch cult. She had said that there were at least nine witches and admitted attending meetings with them. During Martha Corey's examination, the afflicted had claimed that a company of witches was mustering in front of the meetinghouse. Four days after Parris's communion day sermon, the afflicted began to claim even more. During a public fast, Abigail Williams said that "the witches had a sacrament that day at a house in the village, and that they had red bread and red drink." The following day, Mercy Lewis, during a fit, claimed that the witches had tried to force her to participate in their unholy communion, but she had refused. Mercy also had an extraordinary vision, in which she:

... saw a white man and was with him in a glorious place, which had no candles nor sun, yet was full of light and brightness; where was a great multitude in white glittering robes, and they sung the song in the fifth of Revelation the ninth verse, and the 110 Psalm, and the 149 Psalm; and said with her self, "How long shall I stay here? Let me be along with you." She was loath to leave this place, and grieved that she could tarry no longer.[82]

Moreover, this man in white appeared to several of the afflicted and told them when they would have their next fit. The witches were not only mocking the holy Christian sacraments but Satan was filling the afflicted with visions of glory.

The tools for fighting this growing threat to the Puritan's Christian commonwealth likewise had emerged over the month of March. The judicial procedure for the examination of the accused had become predictable. Constables took the accused to the meetinghouse for public questioning. John Hathorne, the chief interrogator, assumed the guilt of those appearing before him, with the exception of Rebecca Nurse, and became adept at catching suspects in contradictions and lies. The afflicted were permitted to be near the accused during the examination, and they increasingly charged that the accused were audacious enough to harm them in the presence of authorities. Villagers, in ever larger numbers, began to recall incidents of evil associated with the accused and were ever more willing to come forward with their stories. Most important, authorities, religious and secular, were willing to accept specter evidence as proof of the accused's complicity with Satan.

Despite these developments, which had such a powerful cumulative effect, there was a brief time in late March when the witchcraft episode might have ended. The accusations against Rebecca Nurse had caused the villagers to pause; even the diligent Hathorne stumbled during the examination. Deodat Lawson had given them mixed signals from the pulpit. Samuel Parris had handled the occult actions of Mary Sibley with a measure of caution and charity. He may have been able to defuse the sense of crisis in the community had he taken a different approach in his March 27 sermon, rejecting the possibility that a "true saint" of God, like Rebecca Nurse, could ever become a tool of Satan. Another possibility would have been to reject, as most clergymen would do later in the year, the validity of specter evidence. Perhaps that is too much to expect from a clergyman who was fighting a battle to defeat his own "devils," those in the village trying to remove him from his position as pastor. He was also a man who had watched his daughter and niece struggle with their afflictions for over two months. The moment when events might have taken a different path passed quickly. The day after Parris gave his tough sermon, several villagers gathered in Ingersoll's ordinary, and there was considerable discussion "concerning the examining of several persons suspected for witches" and speculation about who else might be accused.[83] The witch hunt was on.

NOTES

1. Cotton Mather, *Magnalia Christi Americana*, edited by Kenneth B. Murdock (Cambridge, MA, 1977), 326.

2. A description and illustration of the parsonage is in Richard Trask, "Raising the Devil," *Yankee*, XXXVI (May 1972), 74–77 and 190–201. On the darkness of colonial New England homes, see David D. Hall, "The Mental World of Samuel Sewall," in Hall, John M. Murrin, and Thad W. Tate, eds., *Saints & Revolutionaries, Essays in Early American History* (New York, 1984), 76.

3. Hale quoted by Chadwick Hansen in *Witchcraft at Salem* (New York, 1969), 55.

4. Hale, "A Modest Inquiry into the Nature of Witchcraft," in George Lincoln Burr, ed., *Narratives of the Witchcraft Cases: 1648–1706* (New York, 1975), reprint, 413.

5. Ibid., 413–414.

6. Ibid., 397.

7. Ibid., 408.

8. Paul Boyer and Stephen Nissenbaum, eds., *The Salem Witchcraft Papers* (New York, 1977), II, 397–398.

9. Hale, "A Modest Inquiry," 412.

10. The proximity of the two homes can be seen on the village map in Boyer and Nissenbaum, eds., *Salem-Village Witchcraft: A Documentary Record of Local Conflict in Colonial New England* (Belmont, CA, 1972), 395. This episode is described in Boyer and Nissenbaum, eds., *Witchcraft Papers*, I, 95–97.

11. Hale, "A Modest Inquiry," 414.

12. Hansen, *Witchcraft*, 57 and 90; Marion Starkey, *The Devil in Massachusetts, A Modern Enquiry into the Salem Witch Trials* (New York, 1969), reprint, 36; and Boyer and Nissenbaum, eds., *Salem-Village Witchcraft*, 395.

13. Hale, "A Modest Inquiry," 413; Robert Calef, "More Wonders of the Invisible World," in Burr, ed., *Witchcraft Cases*, 342; and Boyer and Nissenbaum, eds., *Salem-Village Witchcraft*, 278.

14. Hale, "A Modest Inquiry," 413–414.

15. Ibid. The four afflicted were named in the warrants for the arrest of the three women; see Boyer and Nissenbaum, eds. *Witchcraft Papers*, II, 355 and 609, and III, 745.

16. Their proximity to the parsonage is seen on the village map in Boyer and Nissenbaum, eds., *Salem-Village Witchcraft*, 394–395. The men frequently held village positions in the 1680s and 1690s, and their prosperity is reflected on village tax lists; see ibid., 319–372.

17. Boyer and Nissenbaum, eds., *Witchcraft Papers*, II, 355 and 609, and III, 745–746.

18. Ibid., II, 368; Boyer and Nissenbaum, eds., *Salem-Village Witchcraft*, 139–147 and 353–355; and Carol F. Karlsen, *The Devil in the Shape of a Woman, Witchcraft in Colonial New England* (New York, 1987), 110–112.

19. Boyer and Nissenbaum, eds., *Witchcraft Papers*, II, 356–360.

20. Ibid., 363.

21. Ibid., 357 and 372.

22. Ibid., 368.

23. Ibid., 369.

24. Ibid., 375.

25. Ibid., 357.

26. Her husband was in the upper one-fourth of taxpayers in 1689; see Boyer and Nissenbaum, eds., *Salem-Village Witchcraft*, 353–355.

27. Boyer and Nissenbaum, eds., *Salem Possessed: The Social Origins of Witchcraft* (Cambridge, MA, 1974), 193–194; and *Witchcraft Papers*, II, 611.

28. Ibid., 610 and 609.

29. Ibid., 610–611.

30. The next three paragraphs were drawn from Ibid., III, 746–753.

31. Ibid., 753–755.

32. Calef, "More Wonders," 343.

33. Hansen, *Witchcraft,* 64.

34. Boyer and Nissenbaum, eds., *Witchcraft Papers*, III, 746–747.

35. See chapter 1, 11–12.

36. Calef, "More Wonders," 343.

37. Burr, ed., *Witchcraft Cases*, 400.

38. Hale, "A Modest Inquiry," 414; and Calef, "More Wonders," 342.

39. Deodat Lawson, "A Brief and True Narrative of Witchcraft at Salem Village," in Burr, ed., *Witchcraft Cases*, 160.

40. Boyer and Nissenbaum, eds., *Witchcraft Papers*, II, 370, 373, and 377.

41. Ibid., 371–372.

42. Ibid., I, 260.

43. Boyer and Nissenbaum, *Salem Possessed*, 146, and *Salem-Village Witchcraft*, 277.

44. The visit of the two men is described in their deposition, Boyer and Nissenbaum, eds., *Witchcraft Papers*, I, 260–262.

45. Ibid., 258.

46. Ibid., 264–265.

47. Ibid., 247.

48. Burr, ed., *Witchcraft Cases*, 148.

49. Lawson, "Brief Narrative," 153–154. The "Goodw. N." mentioned in Lawson's account of Abigail Williams's accusation was Rebecca Nurse.

50. Ibid., 154.

51. Ibid., 155. The "ancient woman, named Goodall," was most likely Eliza Goodell, the eldest female Goodell in the village; see Boyer and Nissenbaum, eds., *Salem-Village Witchcraft*, 384.

52. Martha Corey's examination that follows, except where noted, is drawn from Boyer and Nissenbaum, eds., *Witchcraft Papers*, I, 248–254.

53. Ibid., 259–260.

54. Lawson, "Brief Narrative," 156.

55. Ibid., 156 and 155.

56. Ibid., 156.

57. Ibid.

58. Ibid.

59. Ibid., 155.

60. Ibid., 156.

61. Ibid., 156–157.

62. Boyer and Nissenbaum, eds., *Witchcraft Papers*, II, 604.

63. Lawson, "Brief Narrative," 157–158.

64. Boyer and Nissenbaum, *Salem Possessed*, 199–200.

65. Boyer and Nissenbaum, eds., *Witchcraft Papers*, II, 593–594.

66. Nurse's examination is in ibid., 584–587.

67. The additional information for this paragraph is drawn from ibid., 604–605; and Lawson, "Brief Narrative," 158–159.

68. Boyer and Nissenbaum, eds., *Witchcraft Papers*, II, 351–353; and Lawson, "Brief Narrative," 159–160.

69. Boyer and Nissenbaum, eds., *Witchcraft Papers*, I, 261.

70. Ibid., II, 586.

71. Lawson, "Brief Narrative," 159.

72. Lawson, *Christ's Fidelity the Only Shield Against Satan's Malignity* (Boston, 1693).

73. Ibid., 11, 14, 15, 16, 24, and 69.

74. Ibid., 25, 28, and Introduction.

75. Ibid., 62, 49, 65, Introduction, and 73.

76. Parris, Sermon Book, March 27, 1692, 147–150. Deodat Lawson inaccurately dated the sermon as April 3, 1692, "Brief Narrative," 161.

77. Parris, Sermon Book, March 27, 1692, 151.

78. Boyer and Nissenbaum, eds., *Salem-Village Witchcraft*, 278–279.

79. Parris, Sermon Book, March 27, 1692, 149.

80. Lawson said that Cloyce slammed the door in anger; see "Brief Narrative," 161. Robert Calef, however, claimed that the wind blew it shut; see "More Wonders," 346. Given the circumstances, Lawson's version is probably the most accurate.

81. Boyer and Nissenbaum, eds., *Salem-Village Witchcraft*, 278.

82. Lawson, "Brief Narrative," 160–161.

83. Boyer and Nissenbaum, eds., *Witchcraft Papers*, II, 670.

Four

The Crisis Grows

In the few weeks between Samuel Parris's March 27 witchcraft sermon and the first trial on June 2, the impact of his words was clear. By arguing that hypocrites were to be found in Christ's Church, he had made almost everyone vulnerable to accusations of witchcraft. Otherwise respected and trusted members of the community appeared to the afflicted in their fits. Many in Salem Village, after overcoming initial doubts, became convinced that Satan's minions had infiltrated their neighborhoods, and as warriors for Christ, they stood ready to offer evidence of the malevolent activities in their besieged community.

Sarah Cloyce's dramatic departure during Parris's sermon had an almost immediate impact on the afflicted. Within days, they began to see her specter during their fits. They claimed that she had stormed out of the meetinghouse to avoid the Christian communion. Instead, they saw her take red bread and drink with other witches at a house in the village: "is this a time to receive it in the meeting-house, and, is this a time to receive it? I wonder at you?"[1] Several, including Abigail Williams, John Indian, Mary Walcott, Ann Putnam, and Mercy Lewis, claimed that her specter had harmed them. Reacting to their cries, Jonathan Walcott and Nathaniel Ingersoll filed complaints against Sarah Cloyce on April 4.[2]

There was nothing in Sarah Cloyce's background to suggest that she might be a witch. One of Rebecca Nurse's sisters, Sarah lived with her husband, Peter, on a farm about two miles from the meetinghouse in Salem Village. Both of them had joined the village congregation; indeed Peter had been the sixth man to sign the new village covenant in 1689.

He had rarely been a party to any of the conflicts involving ministers Bayley, Burroughs, Lawson, or Parris or the separatist struggle with Salem town. While he never held any positions of distinction in the village, Peter had been careful to fulfill his obligations to the community; his name appeared on none of the delinquent tax lists. A couple with a large family (there were at least five children in the household) of modest means (on the 1681 and 1689 tax lists, Peter's assessment was slightly above the median), Peter and Sarah Cloyce led lives that fit the Puritan ideal. A sturdy yeoman with a sense of responsibility to the community, Peter had, along with his wife, avoided conflict, embraced the reformed faith, and reared a substantial Christian family.[3]

As magistrates Jonathan Corwin and John Hathorne considered issuing warrants for Sarah Cloyce's arrest, they encountered charges against Elizabeth Proctor as well. Like Sarah Cloyce, Proctor was a surprising target of accusation. She and her husband, John, had fashioned a prosperous life on the periphery of Salem Village. Originally from Ipswich, John had leased a 700-acre farm just south of the village in 1666. Because his house was on a sparsely populated stretch of the road from Ipswich to Boston, travelers often stopped in search of refreshment. Proctor tired of accommodating them "upon free cost" and secured a license to operate a "house of entertainment to sell beer, cider, liquors." Besides his tavern and farm, Proctor was an absentee landlord over property in Ipswich that he had inherited from his father. Both he and Elizabeth attended the church in Salem, and when the town constructed a new meetinghouse in 1677, they received a prominent place in the "seating" arrangement. The church placed John in the fourth row and Elizabeth beside Rebecca Nurse in the "women's seats." He was more prosperous than Peter Cloyce, and he had served as a village constable. Still, John Proctor was scarcely more involved than Cloyce in the public life of Salem Village. The thrice-married father of sixteen had avoided most village squabbles. Because he lived just beyond its boundary, John Proctor did not even pay taxes to support the village ministry.[4]

Outward appearances, then, afford no good clues to the afflicted's accusations against Elizabeth Proctor. She appeared to be a solid matron of the community. Married to John for eighteen years, she was pregnant with his seventeenth child in April 1692. Apparently, Elizabeth ran the Proctor tavern while her husband tended to his substantial acreage. There is only the slightest evidence of trouble in her operation of the tavern. In a June deposition against her, Elizabeth Booth mentioned "some difference in a reckoning" with Robert Stone and a confrontation with Hugh Jones over "a pot of cider . . . which he had not paid her for."[5]

Further, there was no hint of suspicion of her practicing witchcraft, although she did sit each week with the recently accused Rebecca Nurse in the Salem meetinghouse. Residents of Lynn, many years earlier, had suspected Elizabeth's grandmother, Ann Burt, of witchcraft.[6] Yet if anyone linked Ann Burt's reputation with Elizabeth in the spring of 1692, it does not appear in the surviving documents.

When they first heard of her accusation, several villagers clearly had difficulty believing that Elizabeth Proctor could be a witch. The day after Parris's witchcraft sermon, villagers gathered in Ingersoll's tavern, and the conversation inevitably turned to the growing witchcraft crisis. When William Rayment said, "I heard that Goody Proctor was to be examined tomorrow," Hanna Ingersoll refused to believe the rumor "for she heard nothing of it." Picking up on the conversation, some afflicted in the tavern "cried out there Goody Proctor there Goody Proctor and old witch I'll have her hang." Again, Ingersoll challenged the charge. When she "sharply reproved" the girls, they seemed "to make a jest of it."[7] Proctor's standing in the community gave the afflicted pause in their accusations. When immediately and directly challenged, they tried to explain their statements away as a jest, or as one allegedly put it: "She did it for sport; they must have some sport."[8]

The following day, John Houghton and Samuel Barton witnessed similar uncertainty when they visited the home of Thomas Putnam. Putnam's wife, Ann, daughter, Ann, and their nineteen-year-old servant Mercy Lewis had all suffered fits. Barton and Houghton may have dropped by out of curiosity although they said that they were there "helping to tend the afflicted folks." Thomas and his wife were discussing the names the afflicted had mentioned, and they told Mercy Lewis "she cried out of Goody Proctor." Even with this prompting, Lewis was unsure: "She did not cry out of Goody Proctor nor nobody she said she did say there she is but did not tell them who." When the Putnams persisted that she had named Proctor in one of her fits, Lewis replied that "if she did it was when she was out in her head."[9] The obvious caution among the afflicted was also evident in at least one who testified in the Proctor case later in the summer. Stephen Bittford, in late June, said:

. . . about the beginning of April 1692 about midnight as I was a bed at the house of James Darling of Salem I being perfectly awake I saw standing in the chamber Rebecca Nurse and Elizabeth Proctor the wife of John Proctor . . . and I was in very great pain in my neck and could not stir my head nor speak a word . . . and for 2 or 3 days after I could not stir my neck but as I moved my whole body.

Though Bittford was convinced that he had been the victim of *maleficium* and that he knew both Elizabeth Proctor and Rebecca Nurse well, he admitted, "I cannot say that it was they that hurt me."[10]

As when John Hathorne dealt with Rebecca Nurse in her examination, there was an unmistakable hesitation in the words of those who accused Sarah Cloyce and Elizabeth Proctor. Yet they continued to suffer afflictions even though they were unsure, and they certainly remembered Samuel Parris's emphatic message of the previous week, "Christ knows how many Devils among us whither one or ten or 20."[11] Convinced that the suffering in their midst was genuine, magistrates Corwin and Hathorne issued warrants for the arrest of both women on April 8 and scheduled their examination for April 11.[12] Because the list of the accused had continued to grow, and because it included ever more people with sober reputations, Deputy Governor Thomas Danforth and four other magistrates—James Russell, Isaac Addington, Samuel Appleton, and Samuel Sewall—journeyed to Salem for the proceedings. Notable among the group was Sewall. A Harvard graduate, successful Boston merchant, and prominent municipal, county, and provincial officeholder, Sewall brought a singular curiosity to the examinations. In his diary, he displayed a fascination with coincidences and portents—eclipses, lightning, thunder, earthquakes, comets, and rainbows that revealed to him the workings of God.[13] Drawn by a sense of responsibility and concern to be sure, Sewall, nonetheless, must have been eager to observe another dimension of the "invisible world."

Those who filed into the meetinghouse that April morning assuredly shared Sewall's sense of anticipation. The witchcraft crisis was assuming ever greater significance. No longer an exclusively local concern, the increased interest had forced authorities to move the examinations from Salem Village to the larger accommodations of the Salem meetinghouse. As they searched for places to sit, the onlookers wondered if they would witness the terror and confusion that had developed during Rebecca Nurse's examination scarcely three weeks earlier. Upon settling in, they noted the larger, more august panel of interrogators primarily from the provincial capital and the five afflicted—John Indian, Mary Walcott, Abigail Williams, Mercy Lewis, and Ann Putnam—assembled in front of them. The Reverend Mr. Parris was there serving as a clerk of the proceedings. Most attention, however, must have been focused upon the accused, Sarah Cloyce and Elizabeth Proctor. Since Tituba had insisted, over a month before, that there were still seven unnamed witches in their midst, Martha Corey, Dorcas Good, and Rebecca Nurse had been accused and examined. In addition, John Lee, about whom almost nothing is known, and Rachel Clinton of Ipswich had faced charges.[14] Would the magistrates discover the remaining two agents of the Devil masquerading as church members?

After a prayer by the Reverend Nicholas Noyes, Deputy Governor Danforth took control of the examination.[15] Unlike Hathorne, who had begun his examinations by directly confronting the accused, Danforth directed his initial questions at the afflicted, an approach that enhanced the former's role in the deliberations, particularly Abigail Williams. John Indian told him that both women had hurt him, especially Sarah Cloyce, who had choked, bit, and pinched him several times. With Abigail Williams and Mary Walcott, he also supplied testimony that the accused were guilty not only of *maleficium* but also of contributing to the growing witch conspiracy. The accused had attempted to coerce them into signing the Devil's book. Also, the afflicted had seen them at large gatherings of witches. In an intriguing inversion of the male-dominated Christian communion service, Goody Cloyce and Goody Good, according to Abigail Williams, had served as deacons when forty witches had met at the Reverend Mr. Parris's house to take the Devil's sacrament. She had also seen Good, Cloyce, Nurse, and Corey at a witch gathering at Deacon Ingersoll's. The afflicted reported that while unable to recruit many, Elizabeth Proctor had successfully brought Mary Warren into the conspiracy. Abigail Williams charged that Proctor "saith she hath made her maid [Warren] set her hand to" the Devil's book.

The women reacted differently to the accusations. Sarah Cloyce initially challenged the charges made against her. When John Indian said that she had choked him, she demanded, "When did I hurt thee?" "A great many times," John responded. "Oh!" she snapped back, "You are a grievous liar." As the afflicted continued to testify against her evil acts, however, she dropped her defiant demeanor. As Abigail Williams detailed her attendance at witch meetings, Cloyce "asked for water, and sat down as one seized with a dying fainting fit." That simple act triggered an immediate reaction among the afflicted who "fell into fits," and they cried, "Oh! her spirit is gone to prison to her sister Nurse." Elizabeth Proctor assumed a stance of innocence in the same manner as Rebecca Nurse. When Danforth asked what she thought of the sufferings of the afflicted, she answered, "I take God in heaven to be my witness, that I know nothing of it, no more than the child unborn." She also tried to reason with her accusers. When Abigail Williams contended that she had persuaded Mary Warren to sign the Devil's book, Elizabeth looked to her and said, "Dear child, it is not so. There is another judgment, dear child." Her approach, like Cloyce's, did no good. As soon as she had spoken to Abigail Williams, the girl and Ann Putnam fell into fits.

The only time that the afflicted seemed unsure was when Danforth warned them of the penalty should they lie. "You must speak the truth," he said, "as you will answer it before God another day." With that injunction, he asked Mary Walcott if Elizabeth Proctor had truly harmed her. She admitted, "I never saw her so as to be hurt by her." Some of the others were unable to answer questions, but only briefly. During Elizabeth Proctor's examination, two of them, Ann Putnam and Abigail Williams, boldly approached her and attempted to strike her:

But when Abigail's hand came near, it opened, whereas it was made up into a fist before, and came down exceeding lightly, as it drew near to said Proctor, and at length with open and extended fingers, touched Proctor's hood very lightly. Immediately Abigail cried out, her fingers, her fingers, burned and Ann Putnam took on most grievously, of her head, and sunk down.

Apparently, Danforth also employed the test of the Lord's Prayer during the examination.[16] Tradition dictated that a witch would err when asked to repeat the prayer, because she had become so accustomed to saying it backward at the gatherings of witches.[17] Given Sarah Cloyce's fainting spell, it is likely that Danforth directed Elizabeth Proctor to attempt the prayer. Instead of the words "deliver us from evil," the accused said "deliver us from all evil." The magistrates felt that this revealed that "she prayed against what she was now justly under." Asked to try the prayer again, the accused said "hollowed be thy name," rather than "hallowed be thy name." The magistrates considered this second error "a depraving the words, as signifying to make void, and so a curse rather than a prayer." Consequently, they concluded that the test verified that the accused was indeed a witch.[18]

During one of their fits, the afflicted suddenly charged that John Proctor "was a wizard."[19] Proctor had been an early and consistent critic of the afflicted. The day after Rebecca Nurse's examination, he encountered Samuel Sibley and asked "how the folks did at the village." Sibley understood that they had had a very bad night, but he did not know if they were better. Proctor then told Sibley that he "was going to fetch home his jade . . . and had rather given 40d than let her come up." When Sibley asked why he talked that way about his servant, Mary Warren, Proctor said:

If they were let alone so we should all be devils and witches quickly. They should rather be had to the whipping post but he would fetch his jade home and thrash the Devil out of her. . . . And also added that when she was first taken with fits he kept her close to the wheel and threatened to thrash her, and then she had no more fits till the next day he was gone forth, and then she must have her fits again.[20]

Proctor maintained his low opinion of the afflicted through the day of his wife's examination. Several overheard him say that "if Mr. Parris would let him have his Indian he the said Proctor would soon drive the Devil out of him."[21]

Proctor's stern opposition did not prevent the afflicted from turning on him. When Ann Putnam and Abigail Williams claimed that he was a wizard, most of the remaining afflicted "had grievous fits." When Thomas Danforth asked Proctor to explain the scene in front of him, the formerly tough-talking farmer offered a lame response: "I know not, I am innocent." His claim of innocence, as in many previous examinations, triggered a reaction among the afflicted. Samuel Parris described the scene, which obviously convinced Danforth, who interjected a comment:

Abigail Williams cried out, there is Goodman Proctor going to Mrs. Pope, and immediately, said Pope fell into a fit. You see the Devil will deceive you; the children could see what you was going to do before the woman was hurt. I would advise you to repentance, for the Devil is bringing you out. Abigail Williams cried out again, there is Goodman Proctor going to hurt Goody Bibber; and immediately Goody Bibber fell into a fit. There was the like of Mary Walcott, and divers others.[22]

The "hideous clamors and screechings" prompted one man who had not participated in any of the previous examinations to offer testimony.[23] Benjamin Gould told the magistrates that four nights before "he had seen Goodman Corey and his wife, Proctor and his wife, Goody Cloyce, Goody Nurse, and Goody Griggs in his chamber."[24]

The testimony offered, the sufferings of the afflicted, and the responses of the accused to their questions convinced the magistrates that there was sufficient evidence to hold the Proctors and Sarah Cloyce for trial. Accordingly, they ordered the three, with Martha Corey, Rebecca Nurse, and Dorcas Good, to be taken to Boston to join Sarah Good, Sarah Osborne, and Tituba in prison.[25] The experiences of that day profoundly affected the magistrates, particularly Samuel Sewall. In his diary, he noted the large crowd at the examinations and how awful it was "to see how the afflicted persons were agitated." Convinced that their fits were genuine, he added in the margin of his diary, "Vae, Vae, Vae, Witch-craft."[26]

Provincial officials, as well as local ones, were now convinced of the severity of the crisis, thus eliminating a potential check to the spread of accusations. Over the next seven weeks, with only brief pauses, the number of people accused multiplied rapidly: four on April 18, nine on April 21, five on April 30, eight on May 14, and eleven on May 28. Altogether, seventy people stood accused by June 2.[27] Besides increasing dramatically in numbers, the accusations spread geographically. The following list shows the number of people accused in the various towns in eastern Massachusetts:

Salem Village	25
Salem Town	10
Topsfield	7
Reading	4
Beverly	3
Billerica	3
Lynn	3
Charleston	2
Malden	2
Woburn	2
Amesbury	1
Andover	1
Boston	1
Ipswich	1
Marblehead	1
Rumney Marsh	1
Salisbury	1
Wells, Maine	1
Unknown	1
TOTAL	70[28]

Included among those from Salem Village were six men, most of whom were related to women accused of witchcraft. Giles Corey seemed the most likely suspect because of his unsavory reputation. Generally regarded as a "scandalous person," the seventy-two-year-old Corey had a substantial criminal record ranging from petty to serious breaches of the law. Twice, in 1649 and 1670, the Essex County Court found Corey guilty of theft. He took only "small things," food, tobacco, and knives, but the convictions earned for him an enduring reputation.[29] In 1678, for example, when Corey's neighbor Robert Moulton discovered the disappearance of wood, hay, tools, and twelve bushels of apples, he assumed that Corey had taken them.[30] That same year, another neighbor, John Proctor, made light of Corey's repute as a common thief. Meeting him on the road to Salem with a cartload of wood, Proctor said, "How now Giles what wilt thou never leave thy old trade? Thou has got some of my wood here upon thy cart."[31] Proctor clearly believed that Corey was also capable of committing arson. When his house caught fire and there were signs of arson, Proctor assumed that Corey had done it. In this case, however, Corey provided evidence that he was home the night of the fire.[32]

Cursed with a quick temper, Corey was easily provoked. The Essex County Court records reveal him arguing with or threatening neighbors over fences, sawmills, horses' fetters, and his reputation.[33] Robert Moulton, a frequent antagonist, characterized Corey as "a very quarrelsome and contentious bad neighbor."[34] His first wife, Mary, did little to improve the family's image. Her boorish behavior in the summer of 1678 led to an embarrassing trial. The judges found her guilty of cursing, excessive drinking, and abusive speech. One witness claimed that he saw her "drunk upon the highway, and that she tumbled off her horse several times, and was not able to go or stand." The court also charged Mary, though it did not convict her, of beating a servant.[35] Occasionally, Corey's temper led to extraordinarily violent confrontations. In 1651, John Kitchin sought out Corey to settle an old score. After he pinched, choked, and kicked Corey, Kitchin threw "stinking water" on him and "thrust him out of doors." Not satisfied, Kitchin chased Corey, who tried to elude him by jumping over a rail fence. Kitchin caught him and "threw him off the rails and beat him until he was all bloody."[36] Twenty-four years later, Corey beat his servant, Jacob Goodale, so badly that the man died from the wounds several days later. Using a large stick, Corey furiously assaulted Goodale. Before a neighbor could stop him, Corey had struck Goodale almost one hundred times and then audaciously told the injured man's brother that Jacob had fallen and broken his arm. For several days, Goodale lingered in a daze. Witnesses noted that he was pale and had great difficulty walking. Goodale would not relate what had happened to him and apparently Elisha Keebe, who had stopped the beating, disclosed little, if anything. Nonetheless, when Goodale died, an inquest was held and, besides his broken arm, the jurors found enormous bruises on his arms, back, and buttocks. Because of a lack of sufficient evidence to link Corey directly to Goodale's death, the court could only fine him for abuse.[37]

Beyond his power to intimidate physically, some villagers believed that Corey possessed occult powers. During an argument with Robert Moulton, Corey allegedly told him that his "saw mill should saw no more." Shortly afterward, Moulton contended, "The mill would not work."[38]

Surprisingly, this angry, violent, much maligned man sought membership in the Salem church in 1691. Although his wife was a member of the Salem Village church, Corey clearly felt that he had little chance of gaining entry into a congregation of people with whom he had frequent heated confrontations. The Salem church record notes an apparently remarkable change in Corey from his tempestuous past:

Giles Corey a man of 80 years of age [actually he was closer to 70] having been a scandalous person in his former time, and God having in his later time awakened him unto repentance he stood propounded a month, and making a confession of such evils as had been observed in him before. He was received into the Church with consent of the brethren.[39]

Corey's failure to defend his wife during her examination and his responses during the magistrates' interrogation of him reveal a change in the once defiant Salem farmer. Giles's examination on April 19 proceeded in a now familiar pattern. Several of the afflicted accused Corey of harming them, and whenever he moved his head, they suffered from fits. Like most of the accused, he denied harming anyone or signing a pact with Satan. There were, however, some particularly revealing moments during his examination. Three witnesses testified that only hours earlier, this once menacing man admitted that he was afraid of what was happening. Although Corey adamantly denied disclosing his fears, he did admit that he had contemplated suicide.[40] A chastened Giles Corey lingered in a Salem jail for almost a month where his specter repeatedly appeared to Mary Warren. On May 13, magistrates ordered his removal to a Boston jail with ten others to await trial.

Besides Corey, there were twenty-six people languishing in Boston jails when the colony's new royal governor, Sir William Phips, arrived from England on May 14. Phips had experienced an amazing rags-to-riches life. The son of a frontier Maine gunsmith, Phips was born in 1651. After migrating to Boston and completing an apprenticeship as a ship's carpenter, he became a ship captain and shipbuilder. He used the profits of that trade and the proceeds of a shrewd marriage to a wealthy

Boston widow to finance a six-year effort to find sunken Spanish treasure. He even obtained the support of Charles II who provided the H.M.S. *Algier Rose* in 1683. After many vain efforts, his crew brought up over thirty tons of silver and gold from a wreck off the coast of Haiti in 1687. Phips not only received a knighthood from James II for his efforts but also an £11,000 share of the booty. Because of his experiences at sea and connections at court, Phips obtained command of an expedition in 1690 that captured Port Royal in Nova Scotia for the English. That success led to his selection as commander of an amphibious assault on the French stronghold of Quebec. The attack ended in disaster. Unable to take the fortified city, Phips lost over 200 men out of a force of about 2,000. Moreover, the operation cost Massachusetts over £50,000, forcing the province to raise taxes. Undaunted, Phips journeyed to London in 1691 in search of royal approval for another assault. There he lent support to the efforts of his Boston minister, Increase Mather, who was negotiating with King William for a new charter for the Bay colony. Successful, Mather also won the privilege to nominate the first royal governor, and the king agreed with his selection of Phips for the position.[41]

Boston greeted their new governor with as much pageantry as a Sabbath's eve would permit. Samuel Sewall was among many who gathered at the docks and described the reception:

Sir William arrives in the *Nonesuch* frigate. Candles are lighted before he gets into Townhouse. Eight companies wait on him to his house, and then on Mr. [Increase] Mather to his. Made no volleys because it was Saturday night.[42]

Phips had little time for ceremony, however, as he faced several formidable problems. He had to establish a government under the auspices of the new charter, and continuing Indian conflict along the frontier, Phips concluded, required his direct command. Yet most pressing was that he "found this province miserably harassed with a most horrible witchcraft or possession of devils."[43] Daily, friends and relatives of the afflicted called upon Phips to do something. They related stories of all that had happened to loved ones over the previous two months. "Scores of poor people," he learned, "were taken with preternatural torments some scalded with brimstone some had pins stuck in their flesh others hurried into the fire and water and some dragged out of their houses and carried over the tops of trees and hills for many miles together."[44] Most incessant were the pleas that he do something to stop the jailed suspects from continuing to harm the afflicted.

A man of action, Phips responded decisively to the appeals. First, he ordered that jailers place irons on several of the accused.[45] Phips worked under the commonly held assumption that if a witch was manacled, she could do no harm. Second, he issued a commission for the creation of a court of Oyer and Terminer "for discovering what witchcraft might be at the bottom or whether it were not a possession."[46] Clearly, Phips exceeded his authority in naming the special tribunal. The charter that he and Increase Mather had brought to Massachusetts Bay gave the provincial legislature the power to create such a special court, and he would not convene a session until June. But Phips should not have proceeded for another compelling reason. Under the first charter government, "if any man or woman be a witch, that is, hath or consulteth with a familiar spirit, they shall be put to death."[47] Still, until the new legislature met, no laws of the old regime were assured of confirmation. Although no one doubted that legislators would confirm the law against witchcraft (they did so in early June), Phips, nonetheless, proceeded without a statute against that crime.[48]

Through the Governor's Council, Phips issued the order on May 27:

Upon consideration that there are many criminal offenders now in custody, some whereof have lain long, and many inconveniences attending the thronging of the jails at this hot season of the year, there being no judicatories or courts of justice yet established: Ordered, that a Special Commission of Oyer and Terminer be made out to William Stoughton, John Richards, Nathaniel Saltonstall, Wait Winthrop, Bartholomew Gedney, Samuel Sewall, John Hathorne, Jonathan Corwin and Peter Sergeant, Esquires, assigning them to be justices, or any five of them.[49]

Phips had selected a truly august body to try the cases. William Stoughton, who served as the presiding judge during the trials, had a distinguished career as both a minister and a magistrate. A graduate of Harvard and Oxford, Stoughton had served briefly as a curate in Sussex and had preached several years in Dorchester, Massachusetts. In addition to a decade and a half of service on the General Court, a variety of provincial appointments, and service on Governor Edmund Andros's Council, Stoughton had been a judge on several different courts in the colony.[50] John Richards, a wealthy Boston merchant, had served as a captain in the militia, a town selectman, and treasurer of Harvard College.[51] Nathaniel Saltonstall, a large property owner from Haverhill, was an experienced Essex County judge and member of the provincial Court of Assistants.[52] Wait Winthrop of Boston, the grandson of the colony's first governor, a major general in the militia, and a member of the Governor's Council, had a keen interest in science.[53] Bartholomew Gedney, a respected Salem physician and selectman, had also represented his community in the 1670s and 1680s in the provincial government.[54] Like John Richards, Peter Sergeant was a prominent Boston merchant who, with Stoughton, Winthrop, Richards, and Gedney had been active in the opposition to deposed governor Edmund Andros.[55] With Samuel Sewall, John Hathorne, and Jonathan Corwin, these men were charged with winning the colony's confrontation with the forces of Satan.

By any measure it was an impressive group. "No more experienced or distinguished a court," Chadwick Hansen has claimed, "could have been assembled anywhere in English America."[56] Most of them had some experience with witchcraft cases. Not only had Hathorne and Corwin conducted most of the preliminary examinations but Gedney, Sewall, Winthrop, Sargeant, and Stoughton all had attended at least one. Richards, with Gedney and Stoughton, had been on the Court of Assistants that had tried Newbury's Elizabeth Morse for witchcraft in 1680.[57]

Given these intimate connections with witchcraft cases, one scholar has concluded that the Court of Oyer and Terminer brought a "predisposition toward conviction" to the trials of the accused.[58] Yet at least one judge, Nathaniel Saltonstall, reluctantly participated. He excused himself from a session of the Essex County Court in March scheduled to examine accused witch Rachel Clinton. He also refused to sign the witchcraft charges against three Haverhill women. Most important, Saltonstall withdrew from the Court of Oyer and Terminer shortly after the first trial.[59] John Richards also had some concerns about the task ahead of him. He asked his long-time friend Cotton Mather to advise him on how to proceed against the accused and to accompany him to Salem for the trials. Desperately ill, Mather could not attend any of the proceedings in Salem until August, but he did offer a lengthy letter of advice to Richards and his colleagues on the special court.

Mather believed that the troubles in Salem Village were due to a "horrible witchcraft." Yet throughout his letter, he pleaded for caution and discretion. In particular, Mather urged the judges to use "specter" evidence with care. Questions about this type of evidence had emerged in the Sarah Osborne examination and became especially important in the questioning of Rebecca Nurse. Deodat Lawson had revealed his uncertainty about it in his March sermon to the villagers. Samuel Parris had attempted to remove the ambiguities by asserting that the Devil could use an individual's shape to perform evil acts only with their permission. Mather remained unpersuaded. "It is very certain," he told Richards, "that the devils have sometimes represented the shapes of persons not only innocent, but also very virtuous."[60] The clergyman raised the frightening possibility of ever escalating accusations "if mankind . . . once consented unto the credit of diabolical representations, the door is opened."[61] Mather, nonetheless, believed that specter evidence had some value. Though not sufficient in itself to convict, he argued that it offered an important "presumption" of guilt. There were other types of evidence that judges needed to obtain valid convictions. A "credible confession" was the best proof. He trusted in the "sagacity" of Richards and the other judges to discriminate between the "credible" confessions and those that result from a "delirious brain, or a discontented heart."[62] The difficulty lay in how to obtain such valid confessions. Mather rejected the use of torture and instead recommended a rigorous use of "cross and swift questions."[63] Should that fail, the judges could, as magistrates had done during the April 11 examinations of Sarah Cloyce and Elizabeth Proctor, order the accused to recite the Lord's Prayer.

If the accused passed that test, Mather advised that the judges might goad them into an admission of their occult powers:

For if there have been those words uttered by the witches, either by way of threatening, or of asking, or of bragging, which rationally demonstrate such a knowledge of the woeful circumstances attending the afflicted people, as could not be had without some diabolical communion, the proof of such words is enough to fix the guilt.[64]

Further, Mather thought physical evidence like the discovery of puppets possessed by the accused or of witch marks on their bodies were appropriate to use in the trials.[65]

Besides Richards's request of help from Cotton Mather, the judges, in the brief time between their appointment and the first trial, read the records from the preliminary examinations and "consulted the precedents of former times and precepts laid down by learned writers about witchcraft."[66] Notably, they examined Richard Bernard's *Guide to Jury-Men . . . in Cases of Witchcraft*; a chapter on conjuration in Joseph Keeble's *An Assistance to Justices of the Peace*; Matthew Hale's *A Tryal of Witches at the Assizes Held at Bury St. Edmonds*; Joseph Glanvill's *Collection of Sundry Tryals in England and Ireland*; Richard Baxter's *Certainty of the World of Spirits*; and Cotton Mather's *Memorable Providences Relating to Witchcrafts*.[67] They also worked with Thomas Newton, Phips's appointee to serve as king's attorney, the special prosecutor for the witch trials.[68]

Newton went to Salem with several members of the Governor's Council on May 31 to observe seven examinations. He came away from the experience, as had so many officials before him, a believer. "I have beheld," he wrote, "most strange things scarce credible but to the spectators."[69] Initially, Newton had intended to try several of the accused during the first week of June. Because of what he saw in Salem, however, he concluded that he had been too optimistic about his timetable. He now thought "the trials will be tedious" because "the afflicted persons cannot readily give their testimonies, being struck dumb and senseless for a season at the name of the accused."[70]

Unfortunately, there are only slight clues on the judges' deliberations on how to proceed. Thomas Newton did recommend that they use a couple of the accused who had already confessed to testify against other suspects. On May 31, he asked that "Tituba the Indian and Mrs. Thatcher's maid may be transferred as evidences." Significantly, he indicated that the two should not be brought with the other prisoners back to Salem but "rather by themselves."[71] Newton was acting on the opinion of witchcraft experts like William Perkins. In *A Discourse of the Damned Art of Witchcraft*, published in 1608, Perkins wrote that if another witch "either voluntarily, or at his or her examination" testified that an accused was also a witch, that would serve as a necessary presumption (though not conclusive proof) of guilt.[72] From their subsequent actions, it is clear that the judges also decided, as Cotton Mather had advised, to accept physical evidence such as puppets and witch's teats in the trials. Most important, they deemed admissible the testimony of villagers, notably the afflicted girls who claimed they had seen the specters of individuals doing harm. In this crucial decision, they were simply following traditional English legal procedure; specter evidence had been used there as early as 1593.[73] Yet contrary to Mather's cautions, they concluded that specter evidence was the key to convictions. Moreover, they were willing to accept a single witness's testimony as sufficient rather than the traditional practice of requiring two.[74]

Having resolved how to proceed, the judges and prosecutor Newton were clearly eager to select the suspect most likely to fit their model procedures. Given the crisis atmosphere sweeping through the province, the court had to demonstrate that it was taking effective action. On May 31, Newton had ordered the return to Salem of Sarah Good, Rebecca Nurse, John Willard, John and Elizabeth Proctor, Susannah Martin, Bridget Bishop, and Alice Parker. From that group, Bishop was the ideal suspect, as the first trial on June 2 revealed.

Bridget Bishop had a well-established reputation as a witch. Before her preliminary examination in April, she had even admitted to a bystander that she "had been accounted a witch these ten years."[75] Thomas Newton carefully cultivated this perception in making his case against Bishop. He began by drawing upon the records of her 1680 appearance before the Court of Assistants on witchcraft charges. He also introduced statements made during her April 19 examination concerning her reputation in the village. Then the afflicted had accused her of using witchcraft in the past to commit murder. Notably, they charged that Bishop had bewitched her "first husband to death."[76]

Aside from the charges of the afflicted, Newton introduced the testimony of several villagers who claimed that they had suffered from Bishop's evil in the past. On May 30, William Stacy came forward with a vivid record of her occult powers. He recalled that over a decade earlier, Bishop had said to him that "folks counted her a witch." Stacy agreed. He became acquainted with her "about fourteen years ago" when he "was visited with the smallpox." The town selectmen had ordered him to remain at home for three weeks and "not frequent any company till he be wholly clear of that infection."[77] Yet Bishop visited Stacy and "professed a great love for" him, "more than ordinary at which this deponent admired."[78] It is not clear whether Stacy's admiration resulted from Bishop's love for him or from her courage (perhaps a consequence of her occult powers) to violate the town's orders and visit him.

Whatever the case, Stacy reported that at about that time, Bishop began to play her "pranks." Over the years, Bishop had made money vanish from his pocket, caused potholes to appear in the road, destroyed his cart, and prevented him from lifting a bag of corn. More serious than these antics, Stacy blamed Bishop for an injury that he had suffered. One night, as he approached his barn, Stacy "was suddenly taken or hoisted from the ground and threw against a stone wall after that taken up again a throwed down a bank at the end of his house." He closed his testimony with an attempt to confirm Bishop's reputation as a murdering witch. He believed that she had killed his daughter in 1690. The girl had been "a likely thriving child," but "suddenly screamed out and so continued in an unusual manner for about a fortnight and so died in that lamentable manner."[79]

Samuel and Sarah Shattuck testified on the day of Bishop's trial of the harm she done to their family. Shattuck, a Quaker, had occasionally dyed clothing for Bishop. They recalled that their problems with her began in 1680, the year she first faced witchcraft charges. Bridget dropped by their house often for "very slighty errands" and always "in a smooth flattering manner." Not coincidentally, they believed, their eldest son "was taken in a very drooping condition." The more Bishop visited, the worse he became. Repeatedly, he fell upon the stone steps at their front door "hitting his face in a very miserable manner." Perhaps suffering from epilepsy, the boy never improved. Shattuck described his fits as "his mouth and eyes drawn aside and gasped in such a manner as if he was upon the point of death." For several months, the child's life was little more than alternating bouts of weeping, moaning, and sleeping. "Ever since," Shattuck told the court, "he has been stupefied and void of reason his fits still following of him."

After observing their suffering child for over a year, the Shattucks decided that "some enchantment" had caused the illness. A curious visit with a stranger confirmed their conclusion.

[He] pitied this child and said among other words we are all born some to one this and some to another. I asked him and what do you say this child is born to? He replied he is born to be bewitched and is bewitched. I told him he did not know. He said he did know and said to me you have a neighbor that lives not far off that is a witch. I told him we had no neighbor but what was honest folk. He replied you have a neighbor that is a witch and she has had a falling out with your wife and said in her heart your wife is a proud woman and she would bring down her pride in this child.

At that point, Shattuck recalled a disagreement his wife had had with Bridget (then Bridget Oliver).

Shattuck and the stranger then concocted an occult ruse to determine if Bridget really was a witch. Shattuck's son would take the stranger to Bridget's tavern ostensibly to buy a pot of cider. While there, the man would "fetch blood of her" for some unexplained occult test. The subterfuge failed, Shattuck admitted, because he had not accounted for Bridget's fierce temper. She chased the man away with a spade, and when she spied the boy, Bridget "scratched his face & made it bleed: saying to him thou rogue what dost thou bring this fellow here to plague me." From that episode, the boy's fits became ever more "grievous." The Shattucks concluded their testimony by pointing out that they had consulted physicians about their son's condition, and the physicians had conceded "that he is under an evil hand of witchcraft."[80]

Another couple, John and Rebecca Bly, offered evidence of Bishop's evil powers. John had purchased a sow from Bridget's husband, Edward, and had agreed to pay Jeremiah Neale of Salem to whom Edward was in debt. When Bridget discovered that she "could not have the money," she flew into a rage. Shortly afterward, the sow "was taken with strange fits jumping up and knocking her head against the fence." The Blys believed that Bishop had bewitched the pig into acting as if it were "stark mad" out of spite.[81]

Besides documenting Bishop's reputation as a witch, Thomas Newton submitted physical evidence. A surgeon and eight women examined Bridget on the morning of her trial and reported "a preternatural excrescence of flesh between the pudendum and anus much like to teats and not usual in women." Although a second examination in the afternoon revealed her "clear and free . . . from any preternatural excrescence," the damage had been done; the judges had heard evidence of a witch's teat.[82] Still, the most damaging physical evidence in her case came from John Bly and his son, William, who offered proof of her use of image magic to harm individuals. They testified that Bishop had hired them to remove a cellar wall in a house that she had once lived in. "In holes of the said old wall," they found several puppets "made up of rags and hogs bristles with headless pins in them with the points out ward."[83]

As damning as this physical evidence of Bishop's occult activities seemed, the decisive factor in her case, as it would be in all those convicted, was specter evidence. The afflicted continued to claim that her shape harmed them. Deliverance Hobbs, Mary Warren, Susannah Sheldon, and Elizabeth Hubbard all said that Bishop's shape appeared to them right up to the day of the trial.[84] Beyond the afflicted, five people offered detailed evidence that Bridget Bishop's shape had been active in Salem as far back as the 1670s. Between May 30 and June 2, John Cook, William Stacy, Samuel Gray, Richard Coman, and John Louder testified about the mischief and harm her specter had caused.

In his testimony, John Cook portrayed Bishop's specter as a mere prankster. Cook recalled that about six years earlier, he had awakened one morning at sunrise and had seen Bishop's specter near his bed. She grinned at him, whacked him on the head, and vanished "under the end window at a little crevice about so big as I could thrust my hand into." Later in the day, as Cook sat with company, Bishop's specter reappeared. She knocked an apple from his hand into his mother's lap several feet away.[85] Her specter also bothered William Stacy. He explained that one night in the 1680s near midnight, he saw Bishop "or her shape" near his bed wearing a black hat and red coat.

Although Bishop's specter made a solitary pass through Stacy's bed chamber, it repeatedly harassed Richard Coman. One night in 1684, Coman retired with his wife after locking the door to their house. He was awakened by the specters of Bishop and two other women he did not know. He recognized Bishop because of her familiar attire, particularly her "red paragon bodice." Pulling aside the curtain at the end of the bed, Bishop's specter came onto the bed and sat on his chest. The weight was so oppressive, Coman claimed, that he "could not speak nor stir," not even to awake his wife who amazingly slept through it all. When the same thing happened the following night, Coman convinced his "kinsman William Coman" to join him in a confrontation with the specters. Armed with a sword, the two men discussed the nocturnal visitors well into the night. When the three specters finally appeared, William Coman proved to be no help at all; he "was immediately struck speechless," and Richard had to struggle to keep Bishop and her allies from taking his sword. Coman's resistance worked, however, because the specters never again bothered his household.[86]

Samuel Gray's account shared none of the comic overtones of the previous testimony. About fourteen years earlier, Gray explained to the court, he was asleep with his child nearby in a cradle. He awakened to see a woman's specter in the room, although he had locked his doors, as Richard Coman had done. The specter had something in her hands when she approached the sleeping child. The infant then "gave a great screech" and could not be quieted. Though "a very likely thriving child" before this incident, over the next several months it pined away and died. Within a week of the child's death, Gray saw "the same woman in the same garb" that had been in his bed chamber, but he did not know her name. Despite not knowing then, Gray was willing now to identify her as the accused—"Bridget Bishop alias Oliver of Salem."[87]

Thirty-two-year-old John Louder of Salem gave testimony not only of Bishop's specter but also of her frightening familiar spirit. As had happened with some of the other witnesses, Louder had had an argument with Bishop before her specter appeared to him. At roughly the same time as Coman had claimed to have seen Bishop's specter, "about seven or eight years since," Louder said that Bishop's specter had also invaded his house. Similarly, she choked him, and he was likewise powerless to push her away. When he later confronted Bishop about the incident, she denied it and "threatened me."

Not long after her threat, Louder fell ill on a Sunday and stayed home from worship. That afternoon, Bishop's familiar got into his locked house and invited him to join the forces of Satan. Initially, the familiar came as a black pig that Louder chased about the room and unsuccessfully tried to kick before it vanished. When it returned, it "looked like a monkey only the feet were like a cock's feet with claws and the face somewhat more like a man's than a monkey." Louder claimed that the odd-looking familiar spoke. "I am a messenger sent to you," it said, "for

I understand you are troubled in mind, and if you will be ruled by me you shall want for nothing in this world." Being a good Christian, Louder chased the familiar away and realized that it belonged to Bridget Bishop for, as he went out the door, he saw her walking toward her house. Just as he saw her, Louder "had no power to set one foot forward" and retreated to his house. There he encountered the familiar yet again flying at him. When Louder cried out, "The whole armor of God be between me and you," it disappeared for good.[88]

The strong-willed, outspoken, occasionally violent Bridget Bishop, despite the body search, the physical evidence, and the specter evidence, remained adamant in her protestations of innocence.[89] She had taken the same position during her April 19 examination. "I am as innocent as the child unborn," she had told the magistrates. At one point, her dogged persistence led Bishop into a lie. Stephen Sewall, who served as clerk for the Court of Oyer and Terminer, noted that she claimed not to know John Louder. Clearly, Bishop lied since, as Sewall pointed out, their property joined, and "they often had difference for some years together."[90]

Prosecutor Newton introduced one last piece of evidence against Bishop. One day, while under guard, Bishop walked by the Salem meetinghouse. When she shifted her glance toward the building, something curious happened. In his account of the trial, Cotton Mather explained:

Immediately a demon invisibly entering the meetinghouse, tore down a part of it; so that though there were no person to be seen there, yet the people at the noise running in, found a board, which was strongly fastened with several nails, transported unto another quarter of the house.[91]

Once Newton had completed his case, Judge Stoughton gave his instructions to the jury. He explained that Bridget Bishop had been charged with five counts of witchcraft. Specifically, she stood indicted with using witchcraft against Abigail Williams, Ann Putnam, Jr., Mercy Lewis, Mary Walcott, and Elizabeth Hubbard: "Their bodies were hurt, afflicted, pined, consumed, wasted and tormented." Yet Stoughton told the jury that a guilty verdict did not require that the five actually suffered the harm specified:

They were not to mind whether the bodies of the said afflicted were really pined and consumed, as was expressed in the indictment; but whether the said afflicted did not suffer from the accused such afflictions as naturally *tended* to their being pined and consumed, wasted, etc. This . . . is a pining and consuming in the sense of the law.[92]

The jury found Bishop guilty of the charges, but the Court of Oyer and Terminer could not impose a sentence because the General Court had not yet met to confirm the statute against witchcraft. At their June 8 session, the legislators ordered that laws "made by the late governor and company of Massachusetts Bay" would "remain and continue in full force."[93] Judge Stoughton quickly issued a death warrant for Bridget Bishop, ordering Essex County Sheriff George Corwin to "cause her to be hanged by the neck until she be dead" on June 10.[94]

As examination procedures had become structured and predictable by late March, Bridget Bishop's trial formalized the Court of Oyer and Terminer's approach to trying the accused. The testimony and reactions of the afflicted, villagers' recollections of the accused's specter doing harm, and body searches all became standard components of the proceedings. It appeared that the special court would now move swiftly to try the nearly six dozen remaining accused witches. Yet the judges would not convene the court for another three weeks. The absence of records of their deliberations makes it difficult to be completely confident in the reasons for not moving with dispatch. Still, there are some clues. A division apparently developed among the judges on the propriety of their procedures. Most likely after the execution of Bridget Bishop, Nathaniel Saltonstall resigned from the tribunal, according to one source, "very much dissatisfied with the proceedings of it."[95] The best evidence of conflict among the judges is their request that the province's leading clergymen offer advice on the soundness of their approach. The resolution of the witchcraft crisis had reached another crucial moment. The learned judges had some reservations about continuing the trials, and their sense of uncertainty had an impact on the general population. Between June 6 and July 2, no one filed formal charges of witchcraft.[96] All seemed to be waiting for the advice that their spiritual leaders would offer on what to do next.

NOTES

1. Deodat Lawson, "A Brief and True Narrative of Witchcraft at Salem Village," in George Lincoln Burr, ed., *Narratives of the Witchcraft Cases, 1648–1706* (New York, 1975), reprint, 161.

2. Paul Boyer and Stephen Nissenbaum, eds., *The Salem Witchcraft Papers* (New York, 1977), II, 657–658.

3. Material on the lives of Peter and Sarah Cloyce is in Sidney Perley, *The History of Salem, Massachusetts* (Salem, 1924–1928), II, 405, and III, 5 and 110; and Paul Boyer and Stephen Nissenbaum, eds., *Salem-Village Witchcraft, A Documentary Record of Local Conflict in Colonial New England* (Belmont, CA, 1972), 250, 251, 269, 270, 321, 322, 326, 329, 350, 353, 355, 385, 395, and 396.

4. The details of the Proctors's lives are in *Town Records of Salem, Massachusetts* (Salem, 1913–1934), II, 199; Perley, *Salem*, II, 22–25, 402, and 433; Charles W. Upham, *Salem Witchcraft* (Boston, 1867), I, 179; and Boyer and Nissenbaum, *Salem Possessed, The Social Origins of Witchcraft* (Cambridge, MA, 1974), 200–202.

5. Boyer and Nissenbaum, eds., *Witchcraft Papers*, II, 672–673.

6. Carol F. Karlsen, *The Devil in the Shape of a Woman, Witchcraft in Colonial New England* (New York, 1987), 278 n.120.

7. Boyer and Nissenbaum, eds., *Witchcraft Papers*, II, 665 and 670.

8. Ibid., 665.

9. Ibid., 674–675.

10. Ibid., 669.

11. Parris, Sermon Book, March 27, 1692, 149.

12. Boyer and Nissenbaum, eds., *Witchcraft Papers*, II, 658.

13. David D. Hall, "The Mental World of Samuel Sewall," *Worlds of Wonder, Days of Judgment* (New York, 1989), 212–238.

14. The only documentation on the Lee case is a brief deposition of Elizabeth Fuller's. She testified that Lee once told her that "he had laid one of Mr. Clarke's hogs fast asleep and this was when Mr. Clarke lived here." This may have been the only evidence presented against Lee, forcing the magistrates to dismiss the case; see Boyer and Nissenbaum, eds., *Witchcraft Papers*, II, 535. Essex County Court justices had summoned Rachel Clinton to appear before their March 30 session in Ipswich. The record of her examination no longer exists, but there are five depositions that were filed against her. Neighbors charged that Rachel had familiar spirits, had caused the deaths of farm animals and the illness of a little girl, and had even caused beer to disappear from a barrel; see ibid., I, 215–219.

15. Mark Van Doren, ed., *Samuel Sewall's Diary*, (New York, 1963), 107. The examination is in Boyer and Nissenbaum, eds., *Witchcraft Papers*, II, 658–661.

16. Robert Calef, "More Wonders of the Invisible World," in Burr, ed., *Narratives*, 347.

17. Chadwick Hansen, *Witchcraft at Salem* (New York, 1969), 78.

18. Calef, "More Wonders," 347.

19. Boyer and Nissenbaum, eds., *Witchcraft Papers*, II, 660.

20. Ibid., 683–684.

21. Ibid., 678 and 683.

22. Ibid., 660.

23. Calef, "More Wonders," 346.

24. Boyer and Nissenbaum, eds., *Witchcraft Papers*, II, 660.

25. Ibid., 662.

26. "Woe, Woe, Woe, Witchcraft," in Harvey Wish, ed., *The Diary of Samuel Sewall* (New York, 1967), 71.

27. Boyer and Nissenbaum, eds., *Salem-Village Witchcraft*, 376–378.

28. Ibid.

29. *Records and Files of the Quarterly Courts of Essex County, Massachusetts* (Salem, 1911–1921), I, 172, and IV, 275.

30. Ibid., VII, 91.

31. Ibid., 89.

32. Ibid., 77, 78, and 89–91.

33. Ibid., 89, 91, 147, and 148.

34. Ibid., 91.

35. Ibid., 147–148. After Mary's death in 1684, Giles married Martha Rich; see Karlsen, *Devil*, 107.

36. *Essex County Records*, I, 208–209.

37. Perley, *Salem*, III, 106–107; and Boyer and Nissenbaum, eds., *Witchcraft Papers*, I, 246.

38. *Essex County Records*, VII, 91.

39. Richard D. Pierce, ed., *The Records of the First Church in Salem, Massachusetts, 1629–1736* (Salem, 1974), 170–171.

40. Samuel G. Drake, ed., *The Witchcraft Delusion in New England* (Roxbury, MA, 1866), III, 169–173.

41. The material for Phips's life is in Kenneth Silverman, *The Life and Times of Cotton Mather* (New York, 1984), 75, 79–81, and 164–165; Dumas Malone, ed., *Dictionary of American Biography* (New York, 1934), XIV, 551; and James Savage, *A Genealogical Dictionary of the First Settlers of New England* (Baltimore, 1986), reprint, III, 36.

42. Van Doren, ed., *Diary of Sewall*, 107.

43. Boyer and Nissenbaum, eds., *Witchcraft Papers*, III, 861.

44. Ibid.

45. Calef, "More Wonders," 349. The Boston jailer put shackles on at least ten prisoners on May 23; see Boyer and Nissenbaum, eds., *Witchcraft Papers*, III, 953.

46. Boyer and Nissenbaum, eds., *Witchcraft Papers*, III, 861.

47. Burr, ed., *Narratives*, 381 n. 3.

48. For the General Court's action, see *Acts & Resolves, Public and Private, of the Province of the Massachusetts Bay, 1692–1780* (1869), I, 27.

49. Hansen, *Witchcraft*, 161.

50. Malone, ed., *Dictionary*, XVIII, 113.

51. Silverman, *Mather*, 101.

52. Robert E. Moody, ed., *The Saltonstall Papers, 1607–1815* (Boston, 1972), I, 48–51.

53. Richard Weisman, *Witchcraft, Magic, and Religion in 17th Century Massachusetts* (Amherst, MA, 1984), 148; Silverman, *Mather*, 68, 102, and 246; and G. B. Warden, *Boston, 1689–1776* (Boston, 1970), 9.

54. Christine Alice Young, *From 'Good Order' to Glorious Revolution: Salem, Massachusetts, 1628–1689* (Ann Arbor, MI, 1980), 119 and 214 n. 44; and Weisman, *Witchcraft*, 148.

55. Savage, ed., *Dictionary*, IV, 18.

56. Hansen, *Witchcraft*, 122.

57. Weisman, *Witchcraft*, 149.

58. Ibid.

59. Moody, ed., *Saltonstall Papers*, I, 207–208; and David Thomas Konig, *Law and Society in Puritan Massachusetts, Essex County, 1629–1692* (Chapel Hill, NC, 1979), 177.

60. Kenneth Silverman, ed., *Selected Letters of Cotton Mather* (Baton Rouge, LA, 1971), 36.

61. Ibid.

62. Ibid., 36–38.

63. Ibid., 38.

64. Ibid., 38–39.

65. Ibid., 39.

66. John Hale, "A Modest Inquiry into the Nature of Witchcraft," in Burr, ed., *Narratives*, 415.

67. Ibid., 416.

68. Born in England, the thirty-two-year-old Newton had limited legal training; most likely he read law in an attorney's office. In 1688, Newton had taken an oath to practice law in front of Judge Samuel Sewall. Following Edmund Andros's overthrow, Newton had fled to New York where he had served as prosecutor for the crown in the Jacob Leisler trial. See David H. Flaherty, "Criminal Practice in Provincial Massachusetts," in Daniel R. Coquillette, ed., *Law in Colonial Massachusetts, 1630–1800* (Boston, 1984), 194; and John M. Murrin, "The Legal Transformation: The Bench and Bar of Eighteenth-Century Massachusetts," in Stanley N. Katz and John M. Murrin, eds., *Colonial America, Essays in Politics and Social Development* (New York, 1983), 545.

69. Boyer and Nissenbaum, eds., *Witchcraft Papers*, III, 867.

70. Ibid.

71. Ibid.

72. Perkins, *A Discourse of the Damned Art of Witchcraft* (Cambridge, England, 1608), 201–202.

73. Konig, *Law and Society*, 172.

74. Ibid., 171.

75. Boyer and Nissenbaum, eds., *Witchcraft Papers*, I, 83.

76. Ibid.

77. *Salem Town Records*, II, 273.

78. Boyer and Nissenbaum, eds., *Witchcraft Papers*, I, 92.

79. Ibid., 92–94.

80. Ibid., 97–99.

81. Ibid., 103.

82. Ibid., 106–108.

83. Ibid., 101.

84. Ibid., 91, 92, and 103–106.

85. Boyer and Nissenbaum, eds., *Witchcraft Papers*, I, 104.

86. Ibid., 101–102.

87. Ibid., 94–95.

88. Ibid., 99–100.

89. Calef, "More Wonders," 356.

90. Boyer and Nissenbaum, eds., *Witchcraft Papers*, I, 101.

91. Cotton Mather, "The Wonders of the Invisible World," in Burr, ed., *Narratives*, 229.

92. "Letter of Thomas Brattle," In Burr, ed., *Narratives, 187–188.*

93. *Acts and Resolves*, I, 27.

94. Boyer and Nissenbaum, eds., *Witchcraft Papers*, I, 109.

95. "Letter of Brattle," 184.

96. Boyer and Nissenbaum, eds., *Salem-Village Witchcraft*, 376–378.

Five

The Witches of Salem: A Break with the Past

On June 15, over a dozen of the province's leading ministers presented to Governor William Phips a document of curious advice. Drafted by Cotton Mather, "The Return of Several Ministers Consulted" revealed that clergymen as well as judges remained uncertain about the precise way to proceed with the trials.[1] In evaluating the pretrial examinations and the first trial, the ministers offered a strange mixture of criticism and praise, concern and hope. Their quandary reflected the general unease with the growing witch crisis in Massachusetts.

They opened by expressing sympathy for "our poor neighbors that are now suffering by molestations from the invisible world." They then offered thanks for "the sedulous and assiduous endeavors of our honorable rulers to detect the abominable witchcrafts which have been committed." Yet their dissatisfaction with the judicial procedures is clear. They hoped that a means of discovering the source of the "wickednesses may be perfected."

The ministers provided specific examples of the shortcomings of the judges' actions. They rejected the often chaotic procedures used during the examinations as prejudicial against the accused. In particular, they criticized the boisterous actions of the afflicted. "When the first inquiry is made into the circumstances of such as may lie under any just suspicion of witchcrafts," the ministers recommended "that there may be admitted as little as is possible of such noise, company, and openness, as may too hastily expose them that are examined." The clergymen also opposed the use of any test for witchcraft because "the people of God" doubted the "lawfulness" of their use. Specifically, they could not "esteem alterations made in the sufferers by a look or touch of the accused to be an infallible evidence of guilt." In several of the examinations, the magistrates had instructed the accused to touch those experiencing fits. The action almost always ended the suffering. During Elizabeth Cary's examination, for example, Samuel Parris's slave John Indian fell to the floor in a fit, and the magistrates:

ordered her to touch him, in order to his cure, but her head must be turned another way, least instead of curing, she should make him worse, by her looking on him, her hand being guided to take hold of his. But the Indian took hold on her hand, and pulled her down on the floor, in a barbarous manner. Then his hand was taken off, and her hand put on his, and the cure was quickly wrought.[2]

On the issue of tests, the ministers faulted the judges for not carefully researching the authorities on witchcraft trials and suggested that they once again consult the works of William Perkins and Richard Bernard.[3]

The use of specter evidence worried the ministers the most. In their judgment (and here they echoed the positions taken by Sarah Osborne, Rebecca Nurse, and Susannah Martin during their examinations, and Cotton Mather in his letter to John Richards in May), an accused person should not be convicted solely on the basis of such evidence. There is unmistakable clarity in their pronouncement that "inasmuch as it is an undoubted and a notorious thing that a demon may, by God's permission, appear, even to ill purposes, in the shape of an innocent, yea, and a virtuous man."

Essentially the ministers criticized the entire approach of the magistrates and judges, in part because so much of what was being done suggested to them the devious ways of Satan. "A very critical and exquisite caution" was required, they believed, "lest by too much credulity for things received only upon the Devil's authority, there be a door opened for a long train of miserable consequences."

Though written by Cotton Mather, this document revealed a departure in at least one important respect from his advice to John Richards less than three weeks earlier. Then Mather had approved the use of tests like the Lord's Prayer. Now he was willing to compose a document that interpreted such techniques as another one of the "devices" used by Satan to gain "an advantage over us." On the surface, such an about-face is puzzling. Yet Mather's first letter represented his thoughts exclusively, and this second one was the collective wisdom of several men of God.

Among them was Cotton's father, Increase, who clearly opposed the use of tests for witchcraft.[4]

The grand irony of "The Return of Several Ministers Consulted" is its closing paragraph. After repudiating the judges' work and raising serious questions about the evidence introduced, the clergymen seemed on the verge of denouncing the trials. Yet the last paragraph begins with a significant "nevertheless." Despite all they had just said, the ministers concluded, "We cannot but humbly recommend unto the government the speedy and vigorous prosecution of such as have rendered themselves obnoxious, according to the direction given in the laws of God, and the wholesome statutes of the *English* nation, for the detection of witch-crafts."[5]

Doubtless, the ministers did not want to offend the esteemed panel of judges. This obsequious attitude is most apparent in Cotton Mather. His biographer, Kenneth Silverman, has argued that the letter reveals Mather's "feelings of deference, loyalty, and youthful subordination to the judges."[6] These men were not only rich and politically powerful but also "neighbors, old friends, members of his church, persons to whom he owed favors and 'for whom,' he wrote, 'no man living has a greater veneration.'"[7]

In sorting through the contradictory messages in this document, there is a significant clue that helps explain the emphasis upon caution. The clergymen were distressed with the accusations against persons not usually associated with the use of occult powers. They urged "an exceeding tenderness towards those that may be complained of, especially if they have been persons formerly of an unblemished reputation."[8] Their statement betrays a growing conviction among observers that Massachusetts faced an extraordinary situation in the emerging pattern of accusation. Thomas Newton had noted the unaccustomed trend in late May. After attending a day of examinations, Newton concluded, "The afflicted spare no person of what quality soever."[9] Five years later, the Reverend John Hale recalled the general amazement at the "quality of the persons accused."[10]

This is not to say that there were not accusations against individuals who fit the stereotypical view of witches. Several of the accused, like Susannah Martin, Sarah Bibber, Martha Carrier, a slave named Candy, and Dorcas Hoar, surprised few.

Born in England in 1625, Susannah Martin had lived most of her life in Salisbury and Amesbury, Massachusetts. Married to George Martin, her life at first glance seemed hardly exceptional. She had nine children, and her husband busily sought to enhance the growing family's security through numerous land transactions.[11] Below the surface, however, conflict dominated domestic life in the Martin household. One of their sons fought often with his father. A frustrated George Martin took his son to court where the judges found him guilty of the "abusing of his father, and throwing him down, and taking away his clothes."[12] The elder Martin also had violent confrontations with his wife. Susannah appeared in court on charges of assaulting her husband.[13] Susannah's disputes spread beyond her nuclear family as she fought relations in court for three years over the disposition of her father's estate. She was also hauled into court for calling a neighbor a liar and a thief.[14]

Her contentious demeanor clearly contributed to her neighbors' acceptance of charges of witchcraft against her in the 1660s. William Sargeant talked openly about Susannah being a witch and killing an infant that she had given birth to while still single. Thomas Sargeant added to the rumors, saying that her son George "was a bastard and that Richard Martin was Goodwife Martin's imp." Susannah's husband sued the two men for slander. While Martin withdrew his suit against Thomas Sargeant, the Salisbury court found William guilty. As that litigation proceeded, Susannah appeared at the summer session of the Court of Assistants "upon suspicion of witchcraft." The judges apparently found her innocent because there is no record of a conviction.[15]

Although Susannah Martin suffered no legal penalties in 1669, her reputation as a witch had been firmly established. Several people from her neighborhood offered evidence during Martin's 1692 trial of her evil acts, notably her long-held fame as a witch. William Brown of Salisbury explained that in the 1660s his wife, Elizabeth, testified in front of a grand jury about Martin's occult powers. Shortly afterward, Brown contended that Susannah Martin told his wife that "she would make her the miserablest creature for defa[m]ing her name at the court." Since that time, Brown told the court that his wife had suffered "a strange kind of distemper & frenzy incapable of any rational action."[16] John Pressy of Amesbury likewise testified that after he had given evidence against Martin, she prophesied that he and his wife would "never prosper." Specifically, Martin said that they "should never have but two cows."[17]

Robert Downer of Salisbury recalled that the testimony in Martin's previous court appearance on witchcraft charges had convinced him of her guilt. When he told her this, Martin allegedly warned Downer that "some she devil would fetch him away." Downer said that he gave little thought to the threat until the following night:

As he lay in his bed in his own house alone there came at his window the likeness of a cat and by and by come up to his bed took fast hold of his throat and lay hard upon him a considerable while and was like to throttle him. At length he minded what Susannah Martin threatened him with the day before. He strove what he could and said avoid thou she devil in the name of the Father & the Son & the Holy Ghost & then it let him go & slumped down upon the floor and went out at window again.[18]

It is difficult to draw reliable conclusions about the characters of most seventeenth-century people. They seldom appear in documents unless they had been involved in conflict of some sort. In Susannah Martin's case, she appears, from the limited record of her life before 1692, as a tough, vengeful woman who may have used her repute as a witch to intimidate neighbors. The image, in the scattered court documents, of some of the other accused is similar. Yet in their pretrial interrogations, they emerge as sympathetic to the afflicted, or confused by the clamor about them, or frightened by the experience. Susannah Martin's demeanor at her examination, however, did nothing to dispel her neighbors' long-accepted negative perception of her.

Martin displayed contempt for the May 2 proceedings and ridicule for the afflicted. As soon as the constable brought her into the meetinghouse, the afflicted fell to the floor in fits. When one of them, Ann Putnam, threw her glove at Martin, the latter laughed at the gesture. "What do you laugh at it?" John Hathorne asked. "Well I may at such folly," Martin replied. "Is this folly? The hurt of these persons," Hathorne persisted. She was clear in her response: "I never hurt man woman or child." When Hathorne asked Martin to explain the behavior of the afflicted if she had not used witchcraft to harm them, she said simply, "I do not desire to spend my judgment upon it." The magistrate refused to accept her cavalier attitude and demanded that she explain why they suffered if not bewitched. "Why my thoughts are my own, when they are in," Martin replied, "but when they are out they are another's."

Having no success with this stubborn suspect, Hathorne tried another approach—to raise the issue of specter evidence. He charged that Martin's "appearance" harmed the afflicted, a charge that she adamantly denied. Further, she repeated the response used by Martha Corey, Rebecca Nurse, and others that Satan may appear in an innocent's image: "He that appeared in Sam[uel]s shape a glorified saint can appear in anyone's shape." The more Hathorne pressed her, the more cynical Martin became. As the afflicted writhed in agony before them, Hathorne asked, "Have you not compassion for these afflicted?" Martin answered acidly,

"No, I have none." A frustrated Hathorne concluded with the comment that it was clear to him that the entire congregation thought she was a witch. Martin's response revealed her disdain for the way the community had treated her for decades. "Let them think what they will," she said.[19]

Susannah Martin's loathing for the legal proceedings against her continued during her trial. In his account of it, Cotton Mather inserted a special note on her conduct. "This woman was one of the most impudent, scurrilous, wicked creatures in the world," he wrote. Worse, when asked "what she had to say for herself," Martin had the audacity to reply "that she had led a most virtuous and holy life!"[20]

Martha Carrier had a reputation scarcely better than Susannah Martin's. From a prosperous Andover family, Martha married a poor servant named Thomas Carrier after becoming pregnant with his child. Because of their poverty, the couple moved about, ending up in Andover in the late 1680s. Initially, the Andover selectmen intended to "warn" them out of the village but, upon reflection, granted them some land. The difficulties that the Carriers (and their five children) faced in Andover extended beyond their continued economic hardship. In 1690, Martha and some of her children contracted smallpox, and the town officials offered no help. They were concerned only that the family would "spread the distemper with wicked carelessness which we are afraid they have already done."[21]

More important, Martha's reputation as a witch grew during her years in Andover. Suspicions about her occult powers had first emerged during the Carriers' brief stay in the town of Billerica. In 1685, John Roger, a neighbor of the Carriers' had some arguments with Martha, and he recalled her giving "forth several threatening words as she often used to do." Shortly after their heated exchange, Roger found one of his sows next to the Carriers' house "with both ears cut off."[22] The removal of body parts and use of them in occult rituals, according to Chadwick Hansen, "was one of the commonest means of working either white or black magic on a person or an animal."[23] Roger also believed that Carrier, "by means of witchcraft," caused one of his best cows to stop giving milk in the mornings.[24]

Several Andover neighbors testified at her examination and trial that she had not changed her wicked ways after moving to their community. They described her as an "angry" woman who had poisoned the neighborhood with her malice. More important, they believed her guilty of a number of occult acts. Benjamin Abbot testified that in March 1691, just after the town had granted him land next to the Carriers, he had a confrontation with Martha. As the surveyors "laid out" the grant, an angry Carrier told Abbot:

She would stick as close to Benjamin Abbot as the bark stuck to the tree & that I should repent of it before seven years came to an end & that Doctor Prescott could never cure me . . . she would hold my nose so close to the grindstone as ever it was held.[25]

Ever since that threat, Abbot contended, he had suffered a variety of maladies, including a number of sores on his side and in his groin that a physician had lanced. Most of the past year, he had been in "very great misery" even "to death's door." Yet when a constable arrested Carrier, Abbot's health began to improve.[26] Twelve-year-old Phoebe Chandler believed that Carrier had caused her hand and face to swell. Samuel Preston and Carrier's nephew Allen Toothaker were convinced that she had used witchcraft to kill some of their livestock.[27] Her minister, Frances Dane, Sr., acknowledged to authorities "that there was suspicion of Goodwife Carrier among some of us before she was apprehended."[28]

When examined on May 31, Martha Carrier exhibited a defiance that exceeded that of Susannah Martin earlier that month. Showing no fear, Carrier challenged the integrity of the magistrates and the afflicted. When the afflicted said that she "looks upon" a black man, John Hathorne demanded that Carrier identify him. She glared at Hathorne and said, "I saw no black man but your own presence." When Hathorne charged that her gaze caused the afflicted to tumble to the floor, she shot back, "I looked upon none since I came into the room but you." Four of the afflicted claimed that Carrier had murdered thirteen people in Andover, an apparent reference to the smallpox outbreak two years earlier. After listening to their charge, Carrier told the magistrates, "It is a shameful thing that you should mind these folks that are out of their wits." Then the afflicted cried that the ghosts of the murdered had entered the meetinghouse. Hathorne asked, "Do not you see them?" An exasperated Carrier answered, "If I do speak you will not believe me." She then turned to the afflicted and said, "You lie, I am wronged."[29]

During the questioning of Martha Carrier, the afflicted suffered ever worse seizures. The clerk of the proceedings described the scene:

The tortures of the afflicted was so great that there was no enduring of it, so that she was ordered away & to be bound hand & foot with all expedition. The afflicted in the meanwhile almost killed to the great trouble of all spectators magistrates & others.[30]

This happened to be the day that Thomas Newton, Governor Phips's appointee as prosecutor for the trials, and several of the Governor's Council decided to attend some preliminary examinations. No wonder they came away from the experience convinced of the reality of the accusers' pain and the guilt of the accused.

In his account of her examination and trial, Cotton Mather was particularly vicious in his characterization of Martha Carrier. Yet Mather probably spoke for many when he described her as both a "rampant hag" and the "Queen of Hell."[31]

Sarah Bibber also shared the traits early Americans associated with witches. Married and from Wenham, Sarah Bibber had accused eleven people of harming her before she became the target of charges.[32] Neighbors and people who had shared their homes with Bibber and her family testified about her "unruly turbulent spirit." Bibber, they said, quarreled often with her husband. In their fights, Lydia Porter contended, Sarah "would call him very bad names." Worse, Bibber's accusers related stories of her as a horrid gossip. Joseph Fowler knew her to be "very idle in her calling." Bibber, he said, was "very much given to tattling & tale bearing making mischief among her neighbors." Thomas and Mary Jacob agreed. They testified that Sarah often said things about people "that were very false." Lydia Porter saw her as a neighborhood scourge, a woman who was "double tongued." The Jacobs and the Porters also had serious questions about Bibber's credibility as an accuser. They believed that she "could fall into fits as often as she pleased." In particular, she seemed to "have strange fits" whenever "she was crossed."[33]

Unlike Susannah Martin and Martha Carrier, Sarah Bibber stood accused not because of any specific witchcraft accusations but because of her shrewish behavior. That was not true in the case of Candy, a slave belonging to Margaret Hawks of Salem. Although she had not been a witch in her native Barbados, Candy admitted to practicing the art in Massachusetts. When the magistrates wanted to know, during her July 4 examination, how she harmed the afflicted, Candy, like Tituba earlier in the year, quickly obliged them. The magistrates granted her permission to leave the meetinghouse to recover the tools of her witchcraft. Accompanied by a guard, Candy returned with two rags fashioned into puppets. Once the afflicted saw the images, they immediately "fell into violent fits."

Surprisingly, the magistrates then ordered an experiment in image magic. One of the puppets was "set on fire," which prompted the afflicted to scream that "they were burned." Because they "cried out dreadfully," the magistrates ordered that the burning puppet be thrust into water. This caused two of the afflicted to complain that they were "almost choked." The examination of Candy abruptly ended when another of the afflicted raced from the meetinghouse and headed for the river.[34]

As clearly as Candy was a practicing witch, Dorcas Hoar of Beverly had a well-deserved reputation for fortune telling. For several decades, her neighbors knew of her practice. She had read a book of palmistry and enjoyed predicting how peoples' lives would turn out. Joseph Morgan testified that Dorcas Hoar told him that he would precede his wife in death. She also said that his daughter would "never live to be a woman." When Morgan's wife, Deborah, asked how she could know such things, Hoar replied that "she observed some veins about" the girl's eyes "by which she knew."[35] Mary Gage remembered that Hoar had predicted that her child would not live long. Even though the youngster was healthy at the time, "about a month after that time her said child was taken sick & died suddenly." When Gage asked Hoar how she could possibly know when the child would die, Hoar replied that "she had acquaintance with a doctor that taught her to know & had a doctor's book."[36]

Hoar's minister, John Hale, acknowledged her renown as a fortune teller and noted that she had even predicted her husband's death. She had told neighbors that "she should live poorly so long as her husband William Hoar did live, but the said Will should die before her, & after that she should live better." When he died shortly before the witchcraft crisis, county officials felt that an inquest into the sudden death of William was in order. John Richards, who served on the jury of inquest, explained that when the members of the jury assembled in the Hoar home, he argued "that it was necessary that the naked body of the deceased should be viewed." Dorcas, he said, flew into a rage at the suggestion. While stamping her feet and wringing her hands, Hoar asked the jury, "Wicked wretches what do you think I have murdered my husband?"[37] After Hoar's arrest and incarceration, Hale met with her, and she admitted foretelling her husband's death but claimed that "she was told" it would happen "by a shipmaster when she was first married."[38]

So secure had Hoar's reputation as a fortune teller become that neighbors had begun to associate her with witchcraft as well. At least she appeared as a witch in the hallucinations of David Balch. During an illness in 1690, Balch claimed that witches were tormenting him. He identified them as:

Goody Wiles & her daughter & Goody Hoar & one of Marblehead he knew not by name; saying also there was a confederacy of them & they were then whispering together at his bed's feet. And [he] desired Gabriel Hood to strike them & when he did strike at the place where said Balch said they sat said Balch said that he had struck Goody Wiles & she gone presently. . . . At several other times said Balch cried out of Goody Hoar's tormenting him & prayed earnestly to the Lord to bring them out & discover them & farther saith not.[39]

Too many of the accused, however, did not fit neatly into any expected pattern. The accusations against Nehemiah Abbott even puzzled several of the afflicted. A respected church deacon, the aged Abbott was a weaver from Topsfield.[40] Ann Putnam, Jr., Mary Walcott, and Mercy Lewis revealed genuine uncertainty when they confronted this old "hilly faced man" whose long hair "shaded" his features. Initially, Ann Putnam was sure Abbott had hurt her, and Mary Walcott was convinced that "she had seen his shape." Yet when the magistrates pressed them on their identification of Abbot as a wizard, the afflicted felt progressively less sure. Ann Putnam claimed that "it is the same man and then she was taken with a fit. Mary Walcott, is this the man? He is like him, I cannot say it is he. Mercy Lewis said it is not the man."[41] Because of the accusers' indecision, the magistrates ordered Abbott removed for a time. After examining several other suspects, they had him returned. When the afflicted complained that they could not clearly see Abbott because of all the people standing in front of the windows blocking the light, the magistrates told Abbott to walk toward them. "In the presence of the magistrates and many others," the afflicted "discoursed quietly with him." After their singular lengthy exchange with the suspect, every one of the afflicted acquitted him of the charges. As a result, the magistrates told Abbott that he was free to go, the only person who had witchcraft charges dismissed in 1692.[42]

As in the cases of Rebecca Nurse and Sarah Cloyce in March and April, alongside those who admitted practicing witchcraft and those of a contentious character or deviant disposition, were several with a pious reputation. The Reverend Parris spoke of this disturbing development to his congregation. Drawing upon Richard Baxter's *The Certainty of the World of Spirits*, he noted how unlike previous witchcraft outbreaks this one had become, "heretofore some silly ignorant old woman, etc. but now we have known those of both sexes, who professed much knowledge, holiness, & devotion, drawn into this damnable practice."[43]

Mary Bradbury seemed to be one of the most unlikely suspects. Her Salisbury minister, James Allen, testified, "She hath lived according to the rules of the gospel, amongst us, was a constant attender upon the ministry of the word, & all the ordinances of the gospel." Outside of the meetinghouse, Allen recalled her "works of charity & mercy to the sick & poor." In all, he remembered nothing Bradbury had done "unbecoming the profession of the gospel."[44] Salisbury magistrate Robert Pike confirmed the testimony of minister Allen, as did Bradbury's husband, Thomas. Rather than a nefarious threat to her neighbors, Thomas Bradbury described his wife of fifty-five years as "aged & weak & grieved." While the Reverend Allen testified about her public life, Thomas told the court of her contributions to his household. She had raised eleven children and four grandchildren and through it all had been "wonderful laborious diligent & industrious." He characterized his wife as a "prudent, & provident" woman with "a cheerful spirit, liberal, charitable."[45]

Mary Bradbury revealed to the magistrates the traits that caused family and friends to rally to her cause when she submitted to them her response to the charges made against her. She wrote:

I am wholly innocent of any such wickedness through the goodness of God that have kept me hitherto. I am the servant of Jesus Christ & have given myself up to Him as my only Lord & Savior and to the diligent attendance upon Him in all His holy ordinances, in utter contempt & defiance of the Devil, and all his works as horrid & detestable. And accordingly have endeavored to frame my life; & conversation according to the rules of His holy work, & in that faith & practice resolve by the help and assistance of God to continue to my life's end.

For the truth of what I say as to matter of practice I humbly refer myself, to my brethren & neighbors that know me and unto the searcher of all hearts for the truth & uprightness of my heart therein.[46]

Sarah Buckley also had a respectable reputation. The wife of a Salem Village shoemaker, Sarah and her husband, William, had experienced almost no material success. They owned neither land nor a house and had lost much of their personal property in a court case involving their son's debts.[47] Despite her humble circumstances, Sarah had neighbors who respected her godly ways. William Hubbard, who had known her for more than fifty years, noted that Sarah "was bred up by Christian parents" in England and had remained true to her faith ever since. "I never heard from others or observed by myself," he testified, "anything of her that was inconsistent with her profession or unsuitable to Christianity either in word deed or conversation." John Higginson, Sarah's Salem minister, added that in his long association with her, he had "always looked upon her as a serious Godly woman."[48]

Traditionally, the people accused of witchcraft were poor or, at best, of modest means, but the prosperous also faced accusation as witches in

1692. The experiences of Philip and Mary English, John Alden, and Daniel Andrew illustrate how wealth afforded little protection against accusation. The forty-one-year-old English was Salem's most successful merchant.[49] The owner of twenty-one vessels and fourteen commercial buildings, English lived in the town's largest house and employed over a dozen domestic servants. After years of service in various public offices, English had won election as a Salem selectman in March 1692. His wife, Mary, had brought to their marriage a significant portion of the considerable Hollingsworth commercial success, including a tavern, wharf, and warehouse.[50] On April 21, the afflicted cried out against Mary, and the magistrates issued warrants for her arrest. Because of her social position, the Essex County sheriff ordered her detained in a room in the Cat and Wheel Tavern rather than in jail. Nonetheless, witchcraft charges had reached a new social plateau. Nine days later, John Hathorne and Jonathan Corwin issued a warrant for Philip's arrest. On May 2, George Herrick, Essex County marshal, reported that English had fled. Understanding that the fugitive had gone to Boston, the two magistrates issued a second warrant for his arrest in the provincial capital four days later. English successfully evaded capture until May 30 when authorities finally arrested Salem's most prominent merchant and returned him to Salem to answer to charges of his occult actions.[51]

The same day that Philip English faced the magistrates, John Alden of Boston also appeared. The son of the early Plymouth Colony settler of the same name, Alden was a prosperous sea captain and veteran of the Indian wars. His appearance introduced an intriguing element to the proceedings. Not from the immediate Salem area, he was a suspect that none of the afflicted knew personally. Clearly, someone had prompted them to accuse Alden. Their confusion was apparent during the day of his examination. Before the constable brought him forward for questioning, the magistrates asked the afflicted to look about the room and indicate their tormentor. When one of the girls pointed at a Captain Hill, a man standing behind her whispered into her ear and only then could she identify Alden. When asked how she knew that she had picked the right man, the girl said that "the man told her so." Unconvinced, the magistrates ordered the accused and the afflicted to go outside of the meetinghouse where they had several men stand in a circle with Alden. In this seventeenth-century version of a police line-up, the same girl pointed at him and said, "There stands Alden, a bold fellow with his hat on before the judges, he sells powder and shot to the Indians and French, and lies with the Indian squaws, and has Indian papooses."[52]

Back in the meetinghouse, the magistrates ordered Alden to stand on a chair so all could clearly see him. When the afflicted complained that he pinched them, the constable forcibly opened Alden's hands to stop their pain. Astonished at what he saw happening in front of him, Alden asked the magistrates "why they should think that he should come to that village to afflict those persons that he never knew or saw before." Bartholomew Gedney, a friend of Alden's who had joined the panel of examining magistrates, pleaded with Alden to confess. The defiant captain looked at Gedney and challenged anyone who knew him to produce a shred of evidence that he had ever used witchcraft. His appeal to an old friend had no effect. Gedney told Alden that despite knowing him many years, having been "at sea with him," and having always considered him "an honest man," he had witnessed enough that day "to alter his judgment."[53] As had been the case with Mary and Philip English, the magistrates ordered that Alden be held for trial, but the jailer permitted him to remain in his Boston home.

Salem Village's fifth wealthiest resident, Daniel Andrew, also faced accusations. An ambitious man, Andrew had worked his way up from obscure beginnings in Watertown, where he had been born in 1643. After moving to Salem in 1669, Andrew married Sarah, the youngest child of John Porter, and they maintained a school in their home for a time. When John Porter died, he left the couple a sizable inheritance of land. Yet Andrew's rising prosperity did not rest exclusively on this timely marriage. A skilled bricklayer, Andrew was in great demand in Salem. The selectmen hired him to add chimneys to and lath the walls of the townhouse in 1677, and six years later he did some repair work on the Salem meetinghouse. Jonathan Corwin, one of the magistrates in the witchcraft proceedings of 1692, hired Andrew in 1675 to enlarge his impressive home. Andrew dug a cellar and added a kitchen and five fireplaces to a structure that still stands in Salem. Income from his craft, the Porter inheritance, and shrewd land purchases enabled Andrew to become one of the village's most prosperous residents. Moreover, he became more politically active. In addition to serving as a constable in 1677 and on several juries, Andrew won election to the village rate committee four times and as Salem selectman three times. Because of his marriage, Andrew tended to side with the Porter faction in village disputes; notably he was on the village committee that sought to oust the Reverend Parris in the winter of 1692. Like John Alden and Philip English, Daniel Andrew was not a marginal figure in the community; he was a man of consequence and secure status.[54]

The complaints against clergymen, notably former village minister George Burroughs, offered the most dramatic break from conventional witch accusations. Following his stormy departure from the village in 1683, the Harvard-educated Burroughs had lived in Maine, eventually settling into a pastorate in Wells on Casco Bay. The first suspicion of Burroughs's involvement occurred on April 20. That evening, Ann Putnam, Jr., suffered the tortures of a new specter, this time it was "the apparition of a minister." The specter claimed that it was George Burroughs and told young Putnam that he had convinced several to join him in signing the Devil's book. Her reaction to this specter reflects the astonishment many would share: "What are ministers? Witches too?"[55] The following day, Ann's father, Thomas, wrote a letter to magistrates Hathorne and Corwin. He warned them "of what we conceive you have not heard"—that his daughter had identified the wizard who was the leader of the witch conspiracy, "a wheel within a wheel."[56]

Several people had claimed that they had seen a leader of the growing witch cult, but until late April no one had been able to identify that man. This raised more troubling questions than the accusations against church members. The faithful in New England had always assumed that the clergy represented their first line of defense against the machinations of the Devil. Their minister was their premier warrior in the eternal struggle against the prince of darkness. What were the ramifications if the clergy could no longer be trusted? What hope was there if ministers were in league with the Devil? The horror and disgust at such a possibility were obvious in Cotton Mather's account of Burroughs's trial. "Glad should I have been," he wrote, "if I had never known the name of this man; or never had this occasion to mention so much as the letters of his name."[57]

The evidence presented indeed made Burroughs odious in the eyes of many New Englanders. Several acquaintances in Salem Village and in Maine said that he had mistreated his wives. John and Rebecca Putnam recalled that Burroughs "was a very sharp man to his wife" when the couple stayed with them in 1680. The Putnams had shared their home with Salem Village's second minister for about nine months, while the villagers completed construction of the parsonage.[58] In particular, the Putnams remembered "a great difference betwixt said Burroughs & his wife." The minister had demanded that his spouse "give him a written covenant under her hand and seal" that she would not divulge his secrets. The Putnams attempted without success, they claimed, to convince the feuding couple that their marriage covenant had bound "each other to keep their lawful secrets."[59]

Mary Webber, from Casco Bay, testified that she had been a neighbor of the Burroughses in the mid–1680s and recalled Mrs. Burroughs "tell much of her husband's unkindness to her." The minister's wife, Webber contended, had pleaded with her to write to her father, John Ruck of Salem, "to acquaint [him] how it was with her" because Burroughs had forbidden her to communicate with her parent.[60] Hannah Harris, who had lived with the Burroughses in Falmouth, Maine, told the magistrates that the minister often scolded his wife. More serious, once when his wife had been ill about a week, Burroughs "fell out with his wife and kept her by discourse at the door till she fell sick in the place and grew worse at night so that the above said Hannah Harris was afraid she would die."[61] Significantly, these testimonies of ill treatment involved two different wives.[62] Rather than isolated episodes, they suggest a pattern of abuse. Cotton Mather, who was a particularly hostile chronicler of Burroughs's trial, characterized the minister's treatment of his wives as "a strange kind of slavery."[63]

The abuse, according to several of the afflicted, led to murder. Susannah Sheldon, Mary Walcott, Mercy Lewis, Abigail Williams, and Ann Putnam, Jr., all testified that Burroughs had killed his first two wives. Unsure of how Burroughs had committed the crimes, the afflicted offered conflicting versions. Sheldon explained that Burroughs's specter told her that he had smothered his first wife and choked his second. Mary Walcott, on the other hand, said that the specter told her that the clergyman had killed his first wife while she was giving birth to their first child. "He kept her in the kitchen," the specter claimed, "till he gave her death's wound."[64] Young Ann Putnam's more detailed account supported Walcott's version. She said that on the night of May 5, Burroughs's specter tortured her and then told her

that his two first wives would appear to me presently and tell me a great many lies but I should not believe them. Then immediately appeared to me the form of two women in winding sheets and napkins about their heads at which I was greatly affrighted. And they turned their faces towards Mr. Burroughs and looked very red and angry and told him that he had been a cruel man to them and that their blood did cry for vengeance against him and also told him that they should be clothed with white robes in heaven, when he should be cast into hell. And immediately he vanished away. And as soon as he was gone the two women turned their faces towards me and looked as pale as a white wall and told me that they were Mr. Burroughs' two first wives and that he had murdered them. And one told me that she was his first wife and he stabbed her under the left arm and put a piece of sealing wax on the wound and she pulled aside the winding sheet and showed me the place and also told me that she was in the house Mr. Parris now lives when it was done, and the other told me that Mr. Burroughs and that wife which he hath now killed her in the vessel as she was coming to see her friends because they would have one another.[65]

Three of the afflicted also contended that the murderous Burroughs had not limited his crime spree to his household. Goodman Fuller's wife said that "three children at the eastward," and "a great many soldiers" in the Indian wars all died through Burroughs's occult means. Most intriguing, however, was that Ann Putnam, Jr., claimed that Burroughs had murdered Deodat Lawson's daughter, Ann, and his wife, "because she was so unwilling to go from the village."[66]

Other witnesses, acquaintances of the minister in Maine, volunteered evidence of Burroughs's superhuman strength. Thomas Greenslit recalled that during the Indian wars, he saw Burroughs "lift and hold out a gun of six foot barrel or thereabouts putting the forefinger of his right hand into the muzzle of said gun and so held it out at arm's end only with that finger." Greenslit also observed Burroughs pick up a full barrel of molasses with only two fingers.[67] Samuel Webber, who had lived near Burroughs in the mid-1680s, "had heard much of the great strength of him said Burroughs." Once, when the minister dropped by his home, Webber asked him about his reputation. Burroughs proudly confirmed it. He told Webber "that he had put his fingers into the bung of a barrel of molasses and lifted it up, and carried it round him and set it down again."[68]

Most serious in the minds of the magistrates was the testimony about Burroughs's connections with the occult. Casco Bay neighbor Mary Webber recalled Burroughs's wife reporting some inexplicable happenings in their household. She told Webber that a strange noise had awakened the household one night, and her husband and their slave had pursued a specter that had made the noise. When they reached the bottom of the stairs, the specter had taken on the appearance of "a white calf." On another occasion, some force came into her bedroom "and breathed on her, and she being much affrighted at it, would have awakened her husband but could not for a considerable time, but as soon as he did awake it went away."[69]

Webber's insinuation that Burroughs was responsible for the occult tricks that frightened his wife paled in significance to the charge that he was attempting to organize a witch cult in Salem Village. Between late April and early June, Ann Putnam, Jr., Mercy Lewis, Elizabeth Hubbard, Susannah Sheldon, Mary Walcott, Abigail Hobbs and Deliverance Hobbs testified about Burroughs's efforts to recruit a following. In some cases, they said that he tempted them to sign his book. He promised "fine things," good health, and that they "need fear nobody."[70] Burroughs's specter approached Mercy Lewis in a fashion similar to Satan's temptation of Christ. She testified that "Mr. Burroughs carried me up to an exceeding high mountain and showed me all the kingdoms of the earth and told me he would give them all to me if I would write in his book."[71] Threats and torture, however, were Burroughs's more common approach to recruiting. Mary Walcott said that he bit, pinched, and choked her. Susannah Sheldon claimed that he threatened to tear her to pieces, choke her and starve her to death. Mercy Lewis reported that after she spurned Burroughs's offer on the mountain top, he threatened to throw her down and break her neck. Regardless of the approach, Ann Putnam, Jr., Mercy Lewis, and Abigail Williams reported that Burroughs's specter had boasted of converting several in the area to witchcraft.[72]

Not only had he recruited a following but Burroughs had also supplied the means for them to harm their neighbors. According to confessed witch Abigail Hobbs, he brought her images of people or "poppets" and pins to thrust into them to hurt villagers.[73] The afflicted also testified that Burroughs's specter told them that he was mightier than a witch; he was a "conjurer." Their collective assessment of the suspect was best expressed by Elizabeth Hubbard: "I believe in my heart that Mr. George Burroughs is a dreadful wizard."[74]

Abigail Hobbs, along with her mother, Deliverance, and Mary Warren provided vivid accounts of Burroughs's witch meetings in the village. Burroughs, they said, convened the meetings in a field near the Reverend Mr. Parris's house by sounding a trumpet.[75] Many of the previously accused attended—John and Elizabeth Proctor, Rebecca Nurse, Giles and Martha Corey, Bridget Bishop, Sarah Wildes, Sarah Osborne, Sarah Good, John Alden, Ann Pudeator, Alice Parker, and Abigail Soames. At one meeting, Rebecca Nurse and Elizabeth Proctor served as deacons and distributed the sacramental wine of blood and sweet bread. At another, Nurse and Sarah Wildes performed the task. George Burroughs preached at these meetings and, according to Deliverance Hobbs, "pressed them to bewitch all in the village." He had counseled them to rely upon subtlety; "they should do it gradually and not all at once." He assured them that in the end, "they should prevail."

The escalation of stories about the former Salem Village minister compelled magistrates John Hathorne and Jonathan Corwin to issue an order for his arrest on April 30. Officials in Maine cooperated fully and delivered the clergyman to Salem on May 4.[76] Because of the packed jails and his status as a clergyman, the Essex County sheriff held

Burroughs in custody in a second-floor room of Thomas Beadle's home in Salem. During the summer, the magistrates would occasionally use Beadle's house as a place to conduct examinations.[77] Undoubtedly, many in the area crowded about the Beadle house to catch a glimpse of the infamous wizard. Two who got inside, Elizer Keyser and Daniel King, got into an argument over Burroughs. Unconvinced by all the rumors, King argued that the former village minister was "a child of God, a choice child of God, and that God would clear up his innocence." Keyser disagreed. Burroughs was "the chief of all the persons accused for witchcraft or the ring leader of them." Thus, King argued, if Keyser were a Christian, he would go up and discuss his concerns with Burroughs. Reluctant to meddle directly in the affair, Keyser admitted that he would be out of his element discussing matters of religion and the occult with "a learned man" like Burroughs.[78]

Still, Keyser's curiosity drew him up to Burroughs's "chamber." While in the room with this "dreadful wizard," Keyser fell under the spell of his evil eye. "Burroughs," he claimed, "did steadfastly fix [his] eyes upon me." The consequences of the confrontation for Keyser were immediate and chilling. That evening

in my own house, in a room without any light I did see very strange things appear in the chimney. I suppose a dozen of them which seemed to me to be something like jelly that used to be in the water and quaver with a strange motion, and then quickly disappeared. Soon after which I did see a light up in the chimney about the bigness of my hand something above the bar which quivered & shaked and seemed to have a motion upward. Upon which I called the maid, and she looking up into the chimney saw the same, and my wife looking up could not see anything, so I did and do [very certainly] [consider] it was some diabolical apparition.[79]

The magistrates felt obliged to handle the Reverend Burroughs's examination differently than all the others. On May 9, Hathorne and Corwin, joined by William Stoughton and Samuel Sewall, questioned the clergyman in a private session with none of the afflicted present.[80] Because of the numerous stories they had heard about Burroughs's efforts to develop a competing faith in the village, the magistrates first sought to determine Burroughs's commitment to the Christian faith. They discovered that the minister, who was "in full communion at Roxbury," could not remember when he had last participated in the communion sacrament. When he expanded upon his response, Burroughs only made his situation worse. He recalled being at communion meetings in both Boston and Charlestown "yet did not partake of either." Beyond purposely shunning the most important sacrament of the reformed faith, Burroughs also admitted that only his eldest of eight children had been baptized.[81]

The magistrates determined that, at best, Burroughs had been remiss in fulfilling his sacred pastoral and familial obligations. In regard to the accusations against him, Burroughs's responses to the questions suggested a man more interested in non-Christian matters. Drawing from Mary Webber's testimony, the magistrates asked about the alleged occult happenings in Burroughs's home in Casco Bay. He denied "that his house at Casco was haunted." Yet he qualified his denial by admitting that "there were toads," suggesting to the skeptic that he was referring to familiars. Finally, the magistrates inquired about his ill treatment of his wives. Specifically, they wanted to hear his reactions to the accusations made by John and Rebecca Putnam and Mary Webber. Burroughs dismissed their claims. According to the clerk of the proceedings, "he denied that he made his wife swear, that she should not write to her father Ruck without his approbation of her letter to her father."[82]

When the magistrates returned to a public session, a host of witnesses repeated their stories of Burroughs's great strength, treatment of his wives, occult incidents in his home, recruitment of witches, and torture of the afflicted. He denied it all, but the afflicted repeatedly fell to the floor in agony. At one point, the magistrates had to order that some of them be removed, fearing serious injury. When Hathorne asked him what he thought of all that was happening in front of him, Burroughs responded simply that "it was an amazing & humbling providence, but he understood nothing of it."[83]

As the magistrates, ministers, and residents of the Bay Colony considered George Burroughs and the other suspects held in custody by mid-June, they may have agreed with the Maine clergyman. The crisis had become an "amazing & humbling providence." Traditional patterns of accusation and characteristics of the accused failed to explain this intrusion of the occult into their lives. To be sure, women remained the primary suspects. Yet eighteen men stood accused by June 15. The other reliable indicators of an individual's likelihood of being accused as a witch did not apply in the summer of 1692. The wives and daughters of public officeholders, militia officers, church leaders, merchants, artisans, and farmers—in addition to those with little or no status and marginal means of support—had been targets of accusation. The jails held the saints as well as the sinners, the pious as well the irascible. In this unsettling atmosphere, few were sure of exactly what was happening to their communities. Watertown clergyman Henry Gibbs, who watched the examination of Martha Carrier, spoke for many when he confided in his diary: "I spent this day at Salem Village to attend the public examination of criminals (witches), and observe remarkable and prodigious passages therein. Wondered at what I saw, but how to judge and conclude am at a loss."[84] It is no surprise that the judges paused to consider the advice given to them by the clergy and to ponder carefully their next course of action.

NOTES

1. Paul Boyer and Stephen Nissenbaum, eds., *Salem-Village Witchcraft: A Documentary Record of Local Conflict in Colonial New England* (Belmont, CA, 1972), 117–118.

2. Boyer and Nissenbaum, eds., *The Salem Witchcraft Papers* (New York, 1977), I, 209.

3. The judges had consulted the works of several experts. See Chapter 4, 88.

4. Chadwick Hansen, *Witchcraft at Salem* (New York, 1969), 165.

5. Boyer and Nissenbaum, eds., *Salem-Village Witchcraft*, 118.

6. Kenneth Silverman, *The Life and Times of Cotton Mather* (New York, 1984), 101.

7. Ibid., 101–102.

8. Boyer and Nissenbaum, eds., *Salem-Village Witchcraft*, 118.

9. Boyer and Nissenbaum, eds., *Witchcraft Papers*, III, 867.

10. John Hale, "A Modest Inquiry into the Nature of Witchcraft," in George Lincoln Burr, ed., *Narratives of the Witchcraft Cases, 1648–1706* (New York, 1975), reprint, 421.

11. Carol F. Karlsen, *The Devil in the Shape of a Woman, Witchcraft in Colonial New England* (New York, 1987), 89–90.

12. John Demos, *Entertaining Satan, Witchcraft and the Culture of Early New England* (New York, 1982), 74.

13. Lyle Koehler, *A Search for Power, The "Weaker Sex" in Seventeenth-Century New England* (Urbana, IL, 1980), 279.

14. Karlsen, *Devil*, 90–93.

15. Ibid., 91.

16. Boyer and Nissenbaum, eds., *Witchcraft Papers*, II, 558–559.

17. Ibid., 561.

18. Ibid., 572. Mary Andrews and Moses Pike confirmed Downer's testimony, Ibid., 573.

19. Boyer and Nissenbaum, *Witchcraft Papers*, II, 551–552.

20. Cotton Mather, "The Wonders of the Invisible World," in Burr, ed., *Narratives*, 236.

21. The smallpox outbreak claimed the lives of several of Martha's in-laws. Data on Carrier's life drawn from Karlsen, *Devil*, 98–100.

22. Boyer and Nissenbaum, eds., *Witchcraft Papers*, I, 190.

23. Chadwick Hansen, "Andover Witchcraft and the Causes of the Salem Witchcraft Trials," in Howard Kerr and Charles L. Crow, eds., *The Occult in America: New Historical Perspectives* (Urbana, IL, 1983), 42.

24. Boyer and Nissenbaum, eds., *Witchcraft Papers*, I, 190–191.

25. Ibid., 189.

26. Ibid.

27. Ibid., 191–194.

28. Ibid., III, 882.

29. Ibid., I, 185.

30. Ibid.

31. Mather, "Wonders," 244.

32. Boyer and Nissenbaum, eds., *Salem-Village Witchcraft*, 379.

33. Boyer and Nissenbaum, eds., *Witchcraft Papers*, I, 79–80.

34. Ibid., 179.

35. Ibid., II, 400–401.

36. Ibid., 401.

37. Ibid., 394. Joseph Morgan confirmed Richards's testimony, Ibid., 400.

38. Ibid., 399.

39. Ibid., 401.

40. Abbott had received a modest inheritance from his father's estate in 1648. Abbott, who had one son, Nehemiah, Jr., who was also accused, lived until 1707; see James Savage, *A Genealogical Dictionary of the First Settlers of New England* (Baltimore, 1986), reprint, I, 2, and 4; Koehler, *Search*, 480–481; and *Records and Files of the Quarterly Courts of Essex County, Massachusetts* (Salem, 1919), I, 142.

41. Boyer and Nissenbaum, eds., *Witchcraft Papers*, I, 49.

42. Ibid., 49–50. In August, Sarah Bridges, a confessed witch, said that "she had heard of but one innocent man imprisoned yet for witchcraft & that was Abbott of Ipswich." She certainly was referring to Nehemiah; see ibid., 140.

43. Parris, Sermon Book, September 11, 1692, 155.

44. Boyer and Nissenbaum, eds., *Witchcraft Papers*, I, 121.

45. Ibid., 117–118.

46. Ibid., 116–117.

47. Boyer and Nissenbaum, *Salem Possessed, The Social Origins of Witchcraft* (Cambridge, MA, 1974), 202–203.

48. Boyer and Nissenbaum, eds., *Witchcraft Papers*, I, 146–147.

49. Part of English's problem in Salem was the sense that he was an outsider. From the Channel Isle of Jersey, English (he immigrated as Pilippe L'Anglois) brought to Salem several Jerseymen as indentured servants, thereby helping to create a growing French-speaking community. See David Thomas Konig, *Law and Society in Puritan Massachusetts, Essex County, 1629-1692* (Chapel Hill, NC, 1979), 69–74.

50. Bryan F. Le Beau, "Philip English and the Witchcraft Hysteria," *Historical Journal of Massachusetts*, XV (January 1987), 1–2.

51. Boyer and Nissenbaum, eds., *Witchcraft Papers*, II, 313–315.

52. Ibid., I, 52. The afflicted girl's remarks about Alden supplying Indians suggest that someone from the Marblehead area may have prompted the accusations. Two years earlier, Alden had come to that community to requisition cannon for the war against the French and Indians. Fearing that its community would be left defenseless, a crowd "gathered in a riotous and tumultuous manner" and prevented Alden from taking the artillery. It is unlikely that the resentment of Essex County residents had diminished in the intervening two years; see Konig, *Law*, 166 and 183.

53. Boyer and Nissenbaum, eds., *Witchcraft Papers*, I, 53.

54. The material for Andrew's life is drawn from Sidney Perley, *The History of Salem, Massachusetts* (Salem, 1924–1928), II, 8, 93, 161, 307, and 401; III, 42, 71, 72, 76, 160, 173, 176, 238, and 252; *Town Records of Salem, Massachusetts* (Salem, 1913–1934), II, 137, III, 84, 134, and 206; Boyer and Nissenbaum, eds., *Salem-Village Witchcraft*, 353–355; and Boyer and Nissenbaum, *Salem Possessed*, 57, 65, 121, 122, and 130.

55. Boyer and Nissenbaum, eds., *Witchcraft Papers*, I, 164.

56. Ibid., 165. Richard Weisman, among others, has emphasized the significance of the arrest and examination of Burroughs. He said that it confirmed the magistrates' "worst fears about the scope of the conspiracy against New England"; see Richard Weisman, *Witchcraft, Magic, and Religion in 17th Century Massachusetts* (Amherst, MA, 1984), 138.

57. Mather, "Wonders," 215.

58. The villagers agreed to build a parsonage in February 1681, Boyer and Nissenbaum, eds., *Salem-Village Witchcraft*, 320.

59. Boyer and Nissenbaum, eds., *Witchcraft Papers*, I, 176.

60. Ibid., 162–163.

61. Ibid., 163.

62. The dates of his marriages and the name of his first wife are unclear. See Savage, *Dictionary*, I, 310.

63. Mather, "Wonders," 220.

64. Boyer and Nissenbaum, eds., *Witchcraft Papers*, I, 166–172.

65. Ibid., 166.

66. Ibid., 166, 167, and 171. Cotton Mather noted the name of Lawson's daughter, "Wonders," 218.

67. Boyer and Nissenbaum, eds., *Witchcraft Papers*, I, 160–161. Simon Willard and William Wornall confirmed Greenslit's testimony, 161.

68. Ibid., 160.

69. Ibid., 162–163.

70. Ibid., II, 406, and I, 170.

71. Ibid., I, 169.

72. Ibid., 174, 171, 164, and 169.

73. Ibid., II, 411–412.

74. Ibid., I, 164 and 170.

75. This account is drawn from ibid., 172 and 173, and II, 423.

76. Ibid., I, 151–152.

77. See Ibid., III, 706, for mention of the examination of Ann Pudeator.

78. Ibid., I, 176–177.

79. Ibid., 177.

80. Ibid., 153.

81. Several years later, however, his eldest son, Charles, recalled his father's "careful catechizing his children & upholding religion in his family"; see ibid., III, 983.

82. Ibid., I, 153.

83. Ibid.

84. Clifford Shipton, *Sibley's Harvard Graduates* (New York, 1967), reprint, III, 330.

Six

"In a Stinking Gaol": Prison Conditions for the Accused

As the judges on the Court of Oyer and Terminer considered further trials, the jailed accused witches struggled with a host of problems. They worried about how their families could continue to pay their escalating jail expenses. Some faced economic ruin because a zealous sheriff and his deputies confiscated their personal property. Conditions in the small, poorly constructed "gaols" were appalling. Worse, magistrates, fellow prisoners, and even kin, with ever greater urgency, tried to convince them to confess. The cumulative effect of these concerns and conditions, along with the approach of their trial, prompted a few to break out of prison.

Early Americans were unused to seeing large numbers of people in their local jails. Judges, ministers, and the populace agreed that punishment of crime ought to be public to disgrace the offender and to deter future breaches of order. Consequently, they normally resorted to the stocks, pillory, and public whippings. Other than for indebtedness, or for convictions of capital crimes like witchcraft, few colonists ever served jail sentences. Punishment as spectacle also helped to keep the cost of law enforcement low. Town officials spent little money on either the construction or maintenance of jails. The small, cramped, poorly built structures were horribly hot in summer and brutally cold in winter. A 1681 petition from William Morse on behalf of his wife, Elizabeth, provides a clear indication of how suffocating jail conditions could become. Elizabeth had been imprisoned since her conviction a year earlier for practicing witchcraft (see Chapter 1). William sought relief for her, asking that she be permitted "in the daytime to walk in the prison yard . . . and in the night . . . [to] have privilege of a chamber in the common jail, and be freed from the dungeon which is extremely close and hot in this season."[1] To further reduce the demands on the public treasury, prisoners had to supply their "maintenance"—food, drink, clothing, and blankets.[2]

By mid-June, there were nearly seventy accused witches in jail, and before the summer was out, the number reached nearly 150.[3] The explosion of numbers created a crisis for sheriffs, constables, and jailers. Because no single facility could begin to hold them all, authorities placed the prisoners in jails in Salem, Ipswich, Boston, Cambridge, and Charlestown. In addition, courts contracted with individuals to hold several prisoners.[4] Such a dispersal proved time consuming and costly for sheriffs and their deputies who spent many days escorting prisoners to and from Salem for their examination or trial. George Herrick, an Essex County deputy sheriff, declared that meeting his obligations devastated his family's finances. For nine months, Herrick served warrants, apprehended prisoners, delivered them to examinations and sessions of the Court of Oyer and Terminer, and "often conveyed prisoners unto prison & from prison to prison." The judicial proceedings so occupied Herrick's time that he claimed that they left his family impoverished. In December, he complained to Governor Phips that he needed "some supply" to get him through "this hard winter." Herrick feared that his children would be left destitute not only because of his extraordinary service to the province but also because he had "been bred a gentleman & not much used to work."[5]

Most of the accused spent at least several weeks in jails. While the average stay was about four and one half months, some prisoners, like Deliverance and Abigail Hobbs, remained a year.[6] Prisoners never knew how long they would remain in the same facility. Giles and Martha Corey "were removed from one prison to another as from Salem to Ipswich & from Ipswich to Boston and from Boston to Salem again."[7] Regardless of where authorities moved them, the prisoners' kin had to provide food and drink, wood for fires, blankets, and so on. Typically, it cost three to five shillings per week to cover "maintenance" costs for prisoners. In addition, prisoners' families faced payment of several legal fees before their kin could be released (assuming they escaped the gallows). Jail keepers demanded a fee averaging one shilling six pence per week. There was also a uniform court charge of one pound seventeen shillings four pence (although there were a few cases where it was one pound seven shillings four pence). Filing for a bail bond cost six shillings. Given the average stay in jail of four and one half months, a family faced total legal fees of just over four pounds and six shillings.[8] These demands imposed terrific strains upon most families. Ephraim Wildes explained the situation of his family after authorities arrested his mother, Sarah:

My mother was carried to Salem prison some time in April. We were at the cost of it and charge of keeping her there a considerable while and afterwards she was removed to Boston prison. We were at the cost of it and charge of keeping her there about two months and then from Boston she was removed back to Ipswich prison. We were at the cost of that and after a while she was removed to Salem again. We were at all the cost both of caring and providing for her maintenance while in all these prisons. Besides either my father or myself went once a week to see how she did and what she wanted and some times twice a week which was a great cost and damage to our estate.[9]

As time consuming as the trips to supply relatives were, most families faithfully made them. Even Elizabeth How's husband, who was blind, traveled with the aid of his daughters twice a week for over two months to insure that his wife had enough to eat and drink.[10]

For some, the imprisonment of a family member meant more than a strain on the family budget; it led to economic disaster. Because he was arrested in May, John Willard's family had no "opportunity to plant or sow" and so had no crops in the summer of 1692.[11] Abigail Faulkner, arrested and jailed in August, petitioned Governor Phips in early December for her release. In the document, Faulkner argued that gaining her freedom was the only way to keep her family intact. She explained that five years earlier her husband had suffered from "fits which did very much impair his memory and understanding." She had nursed him back to health, but the trauma of her arrest and incarceration had caused a relapse, and her husband was "as bad as ever." Because he was unable to work and she languished in jail, the Faulkner family was "without a head," and Abigail feared for her six children who had "little or nothing to subsist on."[12] Likewise, the arrest of Samuel and Sarah Wardwell left the selectmen of Andover with the problem of providing for their offspring. The Wardwells had several young children "incapable of providing for themselves." Rather than let them become a public charge, the selectmen chose to place them with families and use "their father's estate" to compensate the foster parents.[13]

The arrest of George Burroughs resulted in a particularly poignant case of abandonment. He left behind his third wife and eight children, seven of whom were from his previous marriages. As authorities hustled her husband away, Mrs. Burroughs scrambled to insure financial security for herself and the one child she had borne for the clergyman. As the other children bitterly put it, she "laid hands upon all she could secure." She sold the household goods and Burroughs's considerable library, kept the money, and then "let it out at interest." Burroughs's seven other children, the eldest of whom was just sixteen, were left "to shift for ourselves." Only "the generosity of friends," they later contended, enabled them to survive.[14]

Another pressing financial concern for the accused was the possible seizure of their personal property despite apparent statutory protection against such loss. In seventeenth-century England, penalties for felony convictions could include forfeiture of goods. Worse, descendants of the convicted could not inherit their property. Yet English law exempted the felony of witchcraft from the forfeiture penalty. The 1641 Body of Liberties afforded even greater protection for colonists in Massachusetts by forbidding forfeiture of property for conviction of treason or any felony.[15]

Though seizures of property for witchcraft accusations and convictions were illegal, several families in 1692 found sheriffs or their deputies at their doors, proclaiming that "in their majesty's name" their property "was forfeited to the King."[16] In the cases of Elizabeth Cary, Edward and Sarah Bishop, and Philip English, the seizures followed their escape from custody. After authorities jailed his wife, Nathaniel Cary, a Charlestown shipbuilder, contrived her escape first to Rhode Island and then to New York. Cary left some personal property with a friend, but the sheriff pursuing the couple seized the goods.[17] Following Edward and Sarah Bishop's escape from jail, Essex County sheriff George Corwin, on October 7, proceeded to their farm and told the couple's son, Samuel, that his parents "having been committed for witchcraft and felony, have made their escape; and their goods and chattels were forfeited unto their majesties." Besides household items, Corwin seized the family's livestock—forty-six sheep, six cows, and an undetermined number of swine. Samuel Bishop borrowed ten pounds and paid Sheriff Corwin in return for the household goods but could not recover the livestock.[18]

Sheriff Corwin's biggest haul came from Salem merchant Philip English. When he and his wife fled to New York, English posted a £4000 security bond in Boston to protect his property. Undeterred, Corwin seized English's property in four warehouses, a Salem wharf, and his home. The commercial goods included several hundred bushels of grain; hogsheads of molasses, sugar and wine; thousands of boards, staves, and shingles; and several hundred yards of cloth. Altogether, English calculated the value of the goods at £1183.[19] Despite statutes that prohibited forfeiture of property for witchcraft convictions, Corwin did not act illegally in these cases. English law permitted seizure of the property of individuals fleeing from justice. When Philip English sued Sheriff Corwin two years later, the Massachusetts Superior Court ruled that Corwin had followed the orders of Deputy Governor William Stoughton who was enforcing the statute penalizing those attempting to avoid prosecution.[20]

While Corwin's actions in the Bishop and English cases had judicial sanction, he brazenly violated the law in other seizures. Seven families—those of William Barker, Dorcas Hoar, George Jacobs, Sr., Samuel Wardwell, John Proctor, Giles Corey, and Mary Parker—either had property seized or were threatened with the action. In two of the cases, it is not clear if Corwin was involved, but in the others, he played the major role. He usually proceeded right after the conviction or execution of the accused. No matter when he acted, Corwin did so illegally. Moreover, in dealing with the families of the convicted, he displayed a shocking callousness.[21]

Corwin, if anything, was thorough. After the execution of George Jacobs, Sr., the sheriff and his deputies made a clean sweep of the dead man's house. They took two feather beds, the blankets, sheets, and pillows on them, and the rugs under them. They also seized chairs, brass kettles, pewter, the food in the house, and what little cash they could find. The officers then went outside, rounded up five cows, five pigs, and a mare, and finally hauled away eight loads of hay, twenty-four barrels of cider, and sixty bushels of corn. According to Robert Calef, they even took the widow Jacobs's wedding ring. As he did in other cases, Corwin permitted her to buy some provisions back, but she could afford very little and became dependent on the charity of neighbors.[22] After juries found John and Elizabeth Proctor guilty, Corwin went to their home and took everything. A caustic Robert Calef described the scene:

The sheriff came to his house and seized all the goods, provisions, and cattle that he could come at, and sold some of the cattle at half price, and killed others, and put them up for the West Indies; threw out the beer out of a barrel, and carried away the barrel; emptied a pot of broth, and took away the pot, and left nothing in the house for the support of the children.[23]

Sometimes Corwin resorted to intimidation bordering on extortion. After the death of Giles Corey, he told Corey's sons-in-law John Moulton and William Cleeves that he would seize the old man's estate. A month and a half earlier, Corey had willed all his property to the two men, but they were obviously not aware of the provincial law protecting them. Fearing that Corwin would follow through on his threat, the two men "complied with him and paid him eleven pound six shillings in money."[24]

Corwin's worst injustice involved Mary Parker's sons, John and Joseph. Following her execution on September 22, the sheriff "sent an officer to seize on her estate." The officer, the brothers claimed, told them that their mother's estate "was forfeited to the King." The officer paid no attention when the two men pointed out that she had left no estate. Seizing their "cattle, corn & hay," the officer ordered them "to go down to Salem and make an agreement with the sheriff, otherwise the estate would be exposed to sale." John and Joseph Parker apparently checked the provincial code, because they correctly declared in a petition to the governor: "We know not of any law in force in this province, by which it should be forfeited upon her condemnation; much less can we understand that there is any justice or reason, for the sheriff to seize upon our estate." Nonetheless, because they did not know "what advantage the law might give him against us," the Parkers went to see Sheriff Corwin. He informed them that "he might take away all that was seized if he pleased."[25] There is no evidence that Corwin profited personally from these seizures, nor is it clear why he selected these particular families. Wealth certainly was not the determining factor. Other than Philip English and John Proctor, few of them had much to seize. One of Corwin's deputies took William Barker's cattle, but they were only worth £2 10s and the livestock and household goods taken at Dorcas Hoar's home had a value of about £13.[26] While the motives for the sheriff's actions are unclear, the negative impact on the families involved is not.

Beyond worrying about the drain they caused on limited family budgets and how spouses and children would fare without them, the accused faced the physical and mental challenges of surviving incarceration. Many judges and jailers, particularly after Governor Phips's arrival in May, had worked under the assumption that placing the accused in chains would prevent them from harming the afflicted. It is unclear how many prisoners were manacled, but the many references in jailers' accounts to fetters, shackles, irons, chains, and handcuffs suggest that the practice was typical.[27]

There was little opportunity for privacy during confinement. In the crowded quarters, some of the accused sought to intimidate new arrivals. Rebecca Eames contended that Abigail Hobbs and Mary Lacey had pressured her into a confession. "Closely confined" with the two women in a Salem jail, Eames said that they mocked her, spat in her face, and repeatedly charged her with witchcraft over the course of four days. Hobbs and Lacey argued that if Eames did not confess, she "should very speedily be hanged." Under the intense grilling, Eames broke down and decided to confess.[28] Besides menacing fellow prisoners, the accused had to endure an almost constant stream of visitors, including the curious and the cruel. Mercy Short, a servant girl on an errand to the Boston jail for her mistress, found Sarah Good intriguing. A pipe smoker, Good asked Short if she would give her some tobacco. The young woman responded by picking up a handful of shavings, tossing them at Good, and taunting her: "That's tobacco good enough for you."[29]

Magistrates and ministers also frequented the jails. They often followed up the examinations with visits to further explore questions that had emerged in the public sessions. More important, they tried to force the accused to confess. Two critics of the magistrates, Thomas Brattle and Robert Calef, offered strikingly similar accounts of the pressures that authorities brought to bear on the accused. Brattle claimed that they faced "violent, distracting, and dragooning methods" and "repeated buzzings and chuckings and unreasonable urgings." Calef agreed, arguing that there were many "tedious" interrogations with questioners "taking turns to persuade them" until "the accused were wearied out by being forced to stand so long, or for want of sleep, etc. and so brought to give an assent to what they said."[30]

There is no mistaking the effectiveness of these techniques. Six women from Andover who confessed to practicing witchcraft later explained that it "was no other than what was suggested to us by some gentlemen; they telling us, that we were witches, and they knew it, and we knew it, and that they knew that we knew it, which made us think that it was so." The relentless grilling, the women claimed, caused them to say "any thing and every thing which they desired, and most of what we said, was but in effect a consenting to what they said."[31] In twenty-year-old Sarah Churchill's case, the authorities "told her they would put her into the dungeon and put her along with Mr. Burroughs." Churchill pointed out that the magistrates and clergymen assumed that an accusation indicated guilt. She explained that "if she told Mr. Noyes but once she had set her hand to the Book he would believe her, but if she told the truth and said she had not set her hand to the Book a hundred times he would not believe her."[32]

As threatening as the interrogations often became, rarely did they include physical torture. A letter of John Proctor's, written from the Salem prison, is the only evidence of such abuse. He described the torture of three young men, including his son William. After rigorous questioning produced no confessions from the three, the jailer "tied them neck and heels till the blood was ready to come out of their noses." Only then, according to Proctor, did Richard and Thomas Carrier confess.[33]

Jailers and magistrates were not the only ones to prod the accused into a confession. Family and friends, by late summer, were urging the accused to confess. This curious counsel reflected the attitude that the judges on the Court of Oyer and Terminer adopted. Authorities on witchcraft cases had argued that confession was the best evidence of guilt. During the 1692 Salem outbreak, over fifty people confessed to the crime of witchcraft, but the judges chose to spare them. They may have done so to use the confessors to gain evidence about other suspects. The king's attorney Thomas Newton recommended that approach in the case of two of the accused in late May. He asked that "Tituba the Indian & Mrs. Thatcher's maid may be transferred as evidences but desire they may not come amongst the prisoners but rather by themselves."[34] Newton may have intended to delay prosecution of the confessors only as long as they were useful. Paul Boyer and Stephen Nissenbaum believe that the judges ultimately planned to execute "the confessors in a group when their testimony was no longer needed."[35] Yet the judges' actions suggest another explanation. They seemed to believe that a confession served as the first step toward redemption. For example, when they confronted Mary Lacey, Jr., they said, "You are now in the way to obtain mercy if you will confess and repent. . . . Do not you desire to be saved by Christ?" Her answer: "Yes." "Then you must confess freely what you know in this matter." Similarly, they told John Willard, "If you can therefore find in your heart to repent, it is possible you may obtain mercy."[36]

The best measure of the judges' intent is in their actions. Dorcas Hoar, with five others, was convicted on September 9. The judges scheduled their execution for September 22. On September 21, Hoar, who had proclaimed her innocence all along, confessed to four clergymen who petitioned the judges for a delay in her execution. The ministers explained that Hoar, "out of distress of conscience," had confessed to the crime and had told them "how & when she was taken in the snare of the Devil." The penitent woman now sought "a little longer time of life to realize & perfect her repentance for the salvation of her soul." On Hoar's behalf, the clergymen requested "one month's time or more to prepare for death & eternity." Not only would the postponement give her the opportunity to discover "these mysteries of iniquity" but also it might encourage "others to confess & give glory to God." The judges obliged and ordered "that her execution be respited until further order."[37] The hope they had expressed in the cases of Mary Lacey, Jr., and John Willard had been realized. For Judge Samuel Sewall, Hoar's confession represented a significant breakthrough. Although he made few references to the witchcraft in his diary, on September 21 Sewall noted the order "sent to the sheriff to forbear her execution, notwithstanding her being in the warrant to die tomorrow. This is the first condemned person who has confessed."[38] Whether the judges would have eventually permitted Hoar's execution had not Governor Phips ordered a halt to the trials is unclear. Families of the accused saw little ambiguity, however, in the words and deeds of the judges. The best way to save kin was to convince them to confess. Six confessed witches from Andover admitted as much: "Our nearest and dearest relations . . . apprehending that there was no other way to save our lives . . . but by our confessing . . . they out of tender love and pity persuaded us to confess what we did confess."[39]

When Increase Mather visited Martha Tyler in prison, he discovered how even an individual who believed that "nothing could have made her confess against herself" could be persuaded by a brother to do so. Tyler told Mather that her brother Bridges rode with her when authorities took her from Andover to Salem to be examined. "All along the way," he "kept telling her she must needs be a witch" since the afflicted had accused her and "at her touch were raised out of their fits." Martha told him repeatedly that she was not a witch and "knew nothing of witchcraft." When they finally arrived in Salem, Tyler found herself in a room with her brother and Charlestown schoolmaster John Emerson. The two men continued the effort to persuade her to confess. They even told Martha what to say, that "she was certainly a witch, and . . . she saw the Devil before her eyes at that time (and, accordingly, the said Emerson would attempt with his hand to beat him away from her eyes)." Their entreaties became so intense, Tyler told Mather, that she "wished herself in any dungeon, rather than be so treated." When Emerson gave up, he told Tyler, "Well, I see you will not confess! . . . then you are undone, body and soul, for ever."

Bridges Tyler persisted. He told his sister, "God would not suffer so many good men to be in such an error about it." Apparently no argument would work with her. She protested to her brother, "I shall lie if I confess, and then who shall answer unto God for my lie?" After trying to persuade his sister that she must be a witch because of the actions of the afflicted and the magistrates, Bridges finally explained to her his real reason for demanding that she confess. It was simply that "she would be hanged if she did not confess."

Because of her arrest, trip under guard to Salem, and the prolonged harangue of her brother, Martha Tyler "became so terrified in her mind that she owned . . . almost any thing that they propounded to her." When she appeared before the magistrates on September 17, Martha confessed to practicing witchcraft. However, when Increase Mather saw her in jail afterward, he found a woman suffering from profound guilt for "belying of herself" to save her life. The minister saw in her so much "affection, sorrow, relenting, grief, and mourning, as it exceeds any pen to describe."[40]

The conditions of their incarceration broke the health or spirit of many. Several prisoners and their families complained about the conditions of the jails and the treatment from jailers. Their kin were "dangerously sick"; they suffered "inward grief and trouble."[41] After several months in jail, ten prisoners from Ipswich claimed, "Some of us being aged either about or near four score some though younger yet being with child, and one giving suck to a child not ten weeks old yet, and all of us weak and infirm at the best, and one fettered with irons this half year and all most destroyed with so long an imprisonment."[42] Nicholas Rice explained to the General Court in late October that his wife, Sarah, had "lain in Boston gaol" since June 1. "It is deplorable," he wrote, "that in old age the poor decrepit woman should lie under confinement so long in a stinking gaol when her circumstances rather requires a nurse to attend her."[43] Elizabeth Cary suffered terribly almost from the moment of her incarceration. Her husband later explained that within a day, the jailer put her into leg irons. "These irons and her other afflictions," he wrote, "soon brought her into convulsion fits, so that I thought she would have died that night." He pleaded for the removal of the eight-pound irons, "but all entreaties were in vain."[44]

Some did not survive the wretched conditions. Already ill when she entered jail, Sarah Osborne lingered for a couple of months before dying on May 10.[45] Jailed on May 18, Roger Toothaker, a physician from Billerica, lasted less than one month of incarceration. However, on June 16, a Suffolk County coroner's jury ruled that Toothaker "came to his end by a natural death."[46] Though convicted on September 17, Ann Foster, an old woman from Andover, escaped the executioner because of her confession. She remained in jail for over five months and died in December.[47] Sarah Good, jailed in early March, had a baby apparently on April 5 because the Boston jailer noted in his account book, "2 blankets for Sarah Good's child." The infant died before its mother's execution on July 19.[48]

Prison for people of property and standing, like all of life in the seventeenth century, was less traumatic than for most of the accused. Merchant Philip English and his wife, Mary, for example, enjoyed liberties "suitable to their station." Their jailer permitted them to leave to attend worship services as long as they returned in the evening. In early August, the couple heard a sermon with an unmistakable message by Joshua Moody. A critic of the trials, Moody based his sermon on Matthew 10:23: "If they persecute you in one city, flee to another." The clergyman, joined by Samuel Willard, who had also become an opponent of the trials, accompanied English and his wife back to their prison and urged them to take the sermon text literally. Although English argued that God would "not permit them to touch me," he relented and agreed to flee. With a carriage provided by Boston merchants and a letter of introduction from Governor Phips, Philip and Mary English escaped to New York where Governor Benjamin Fletcher gave them sanctuary.[49]

Surprisingly, only a dozen other accused witches also tried to escape. (There may have been others. If so, the records of their efforts have disappeared.) Charlestown shipbuilder Nathaniel Cary concluded that it was the only way to save his wife, Elizabeth. After she was examined and jailed in late May, Cary convinced authorities to move her to a jail in Cambridge so that he could be nearer to her. Over the next two months, his wife's situation became ever more desperate. Beyond her deteriorating physical condition, Cary believed that there was little hope for the accused. In his mind, the judges' acceptance of specter evidence and "malicious stories" doomed all those awaiting trial. When he failed to persuade the judges to move his wife's trial from Essex County to Middlesex County, Cary began "consulting the means of her escape." On July 30, he got Elizabeth free ("through the goodness of God" was his only explanation), and the couple went to Rhode Island. Because constables were in pursuit, the Carys journeyed on to New York, where they remained safe through the duration of the trials.[50]

Like Philip English, John Alden entered jail confident of acquittal. Moreover, his presence had a salutary effect on Boston jailer John Arnold. He respected Alden and became, according to Robert Calef, "more compassionate to those that were in prison on the like account; and did refrain from such hard things to the prisoners, as before he had used."[51] Yet as he followed the trials, Alden began to agree with Nathaniel Cary's conclusion that there was little hope for the accused. The gravity of his situation is clear from a fast held on his behalf on July 20. In Alden's Boston home, Judge Samuel Sewall read a sermon, and several offered prayers, including Samuel Willard and Cotton Mather.[52]

Desperate by September, Alden broke from jail and fled to the safety of relatives living in Duxbury. "He made his appearance among them late at night," according to a traditional account, "and, on their asking an explanation of his unexpected visit at that hour, replied that he was flying from the Devil, and the Devil was after him."[53]

That only four others broke out of jail is surprising. Though many prisoners were in chains, the jails were not massive structures with tight security. Constables or jailers could not be on duty continuously, and when they were, their scrutiny of prisoners often proved lax. Mary Green, for example, broke out of the jail in Ipswich twice in August.[54] After her early examination in the crisis, Sarah Good was taken into custody by Salem Village constable Joseph Herrick. His testimony at her trial also showed how slack "guards" could be. Herrick explained that at night he "set a guard to watch her at my own house namely Samuel Braybrook, Michael Dunell, Jonathan Baker . . . and the aforenamed persons informed me in the morning that night Sarah Good was gone for some time from them."[55]

Constables only occasionally pursued escapees. This was true whether the person had broken out of jail or had run when informed that magistrates had issued a warrant for his or her arrest. When Constable John Putnam, Jr., could not find John Willard after searching the suspect's home and "several other houses and places," he did not give up. Putnam followed Willard and arrested him in Nashaway, forty miles from Salem Village.[56] Reading constable John Parker contended that he had made a "diligent search" for accused witch Elizabeth Colson but reported that the "best information" he could gather was that she had made it to Boston and intended to depart "to some other country."[57] Parker had taken Reading resident William Arnall to assist him in Colson's arrest. Arnall testified that even using a dog did not enable them to capture a fugitive with occult powers. The following occurred when they reached Sarah Dustin's house (Sarah was Elizabeth Colson's mother):

The constable opening ye out most door, and finding ye inner door fast that he could not get in, called me to him and said he could not get in. And as soon as . . . I came to him we heard ye back door open. Then I ran behind ye house & . . . then I saw said Elizabeth Colson run from ye back door and got over into John Dix's field. And I called to her being not far from her, and asked why she ran away for I would catch her. She said nothing, but run away and . . . quickly fell down and to up again and ran again shaking her hand behind her as it were striking at me, and I ran and seeing I could not gain ground of her, I set my dog at her, and he ran round about her, but would not touch her, and running little further there was a stone wall and on ye other . . . side of it a few bushes that took my sight from her a little, being but little behind her and when I came up to said bushes I looked into them, and . . . could see nothing of her, and running on further there was great cat came running towards me, and stared up in my face, being but a little distance from me, near a fence. I endeavored to set my dog . . . upon her, and ye dog would not mind her but went ye contrary way, and on I offering to strike at her with my stick she seemed to run under ye fence, and so disappeared, and I could get sight of maid nor cat neither any more.[58]

In actuality, there was little evidence of the diligence exhibited by constables Parker and Putnam. In October, Boston merchant Thomas Brattle, who bitterly opposed the legal proceedings against the accused, charged that the Carys, Alden, and Philip and Mary English had not been rigorously pursued because of their status.[59]

Unfortunately, there are no clear patterns among the fugitives that conveniently explain why they, and not all the other accused, bolted. Sex, age, wealth, or place of residence do not offer clues. Seven were men, six were women. The list included the aged Mary Bradbury and sixteen-year-old Elizabeth Colson. John Alden, Philip and Mary English, Daniel Andrew, and Dudley Bradstreet were people of wealth and influence, while Edward and Sarah Bishop, George Jacobs, Jr., and Elizabeth Colson were all of modest means. While five lived in Salem Village, the thirteen escapees came from eight different communities.

Some who stayed behind did so because they knew that they were innocent and believed that they would be vindicated. As Philip English had proclaimed, before being convinced otherwise, "God will not permit them to touch me." Others felt helpless, overwhelmed by the frightening circumstances facing them. If eight Andover petitioners accurately described the situation in October, many in Salem area jails were "a company of poor distressed creatures as full of inward grief and trouble as they are able to bear up in life withall and besides that the aggravation of outward troubles and hardships they undergo."[60] Some believed that running would send the wrong message about their innocence. As magistrates John Hathorne and Jonathan Corwin explained to the captured John Willard, fleeing from arrest "is acknowledgment of guilt."[61] Most important, as the summer wore on, escape became less attractive as it became ever clearer that confession afforded a safer way to avoid execution.

Following the execution of Bridget Bishop on June 10, the increasing number of prisoners had almost three weeks to consider their options before the next trials took place. On June 30, Sarah Good, Susannah

Martin, Elizabeth How, Sarah Wildes, and Rebecca Nurse faced a Court of Oyer and Terminer that had sorted out the questions concerning proper evidence and was ready to deal firmly with the escalating threat of witchcraft.

NOTES

1. John Demos, *Entertaining Satan, Witchcraft and the culture of Early New England* (New York, 1982), 137.

2. David Hawke, *Everyday Life in Early America* (New York, 1988), 105–109; John C. Miller, *The First Frontier: Life in Colonial America* (New York, 1966), 255–259; and Carl Bridenbaugh, *Cities in the Wilderness, Urban Life in America, 1625–1742* (New York, 1964), reprint, 74 and 224–226.

3. Paul Boyer and Stephen Nissenbaum, eds., *Salem-Village Witchcraft: A Documentary Record of Local Conflict in Colonial New England* (Belmont, CA, 1972), 376–378; and Robert Calef, "More Wonders of the Invisible World," in George Lincoln Burr, ed., *Narratives of the Witchcraft Cases, 1648–1706* (New York, 1975), reprint, 373.

4. For example, see the case of John Sawdy held by Walter Wright and Francis Faulkner of Andover in Boyer and Nissenbaum, eds., *The Salem Witchcraft Papers* (New York, 1977), III, 725–726.

5. Ibid., 880. Also see the experience of Middlesex County Sheriff Timothy Phillips who, like many county and town officials, had to pay out of his pocket to transport "the persons then in custody for witchcraft from place to place"; see ibid., 964.

6. This is based on sixty cases noted in ibid., III, 954–959 and 977–1009.

7. Ibid., 985.

8. Ibid., 954–959 and 977–1009.

9. Ibid., 1007. Not only did it place demands upon family budgets but also upon their time. Many were like Isaac Easty, who "went constantly twice a week to provide for her" during the five months of his wife, Mary's imprisonment; see ibid., 988.

10. Ibid., 997.

11. Ibid., 1008.

12. Ibid., I, 334.

13. Ibid., III, 789.

14. Ibid., 983 and 1040–1042.

15. David C. Brown, "The Case of Giles Corey," *Essex Institute Historical Collections*, CXXI (October 1985), 289, 290, 293, and 295. The 1692 provincial charter continued these protections; see ibid., 284–285.

16. Boyer and Nissenbaum, eds., *Witchcraft Papers*, II, 636.

17. Ibid., I, 210.

18. Ibid., III, 979; and Calef, "More Wonders," 370.

19. Boyer and Nissenbaum, eds., *Witchcraft Papers*, III, 989–991.

20. Bryan F. Le Beau, "Philip English and the Witchcraft Hysteria," *Historical Journal of Massachusetts*, XV (January 1987), 6.

21. The sources for these accounts suffer from a clear bias. They include Robert Calef's "More Wonders" and petitions from the families who suffered loss of property. Calef, who opposed the witchcraft prosecutions, portrayed Corwin in the most negative terms possible, and the families of the accused and convicted had no reason to be objective in their description of Corwin's actions. Still, there is no mistaking Corwin's disregard of the law.

22. Boyer and Nissenbaum, eds., *Witchcraft Papers*, III, 997–998; and Calef, "More Wonders," 364.

23. Calef, "More Wonders," 361. In 1710, the Proctor children petitioned the General Court for £ 150, apparently the value of the goods taken; see Boyer and Nissenbaum, eds., *Witchcraft Papers*, III, 1010. To protect his real estate, Proctor wrote a will while in prison, one that his wife contested in 1696; see David Thomas Konig, *Law and Society in Puritan Massachusetts, Essex County, 1629–1692* (Chapel Hill, NC, 1979), 174; and Boyer and Nissenbaum, eds., *Witchcraft Papers*, III, 963.

24. Boyer and Nissenbaum, eds., *Witchcraft Papers*, III, 985; and *New England Historical and Genealogical Register*, X (January 1856), 32.

25. Boyer and Nissenbaum, eds., *Witchcraft Papers*, II, 636–637.

26. Ibid., III, 978, 995–996.

27. Ibid., 796, 881, 950, 951, 953, and 960, for examples.

28. Ibid., I, 284.

29. Cotton Mather, "A Brand Plucked Out of the Burning," in Burr, ed., *Narratives*, 259–260.

30. Thomas Brattle, "Letter of Thomas Brattle," in ibid., 189, and Calef, "More Wonders," 376.

31. Boyer and Nissenbaum, eds., *Witchcraft Papers*, II, 375.

32. Ibid., I, 212.

33. William Proctor, despite several hours of this painful treatment, refused to confess; see ibid., II, 689–690.

34. Ibid., III, 867.

35. Ibid., I, 24. Others agree. Carol F. Karlsen has argued that the delay in executions of confessors "was a temporary expedient, not a permanent change in policy; but because the Salem trials ended before these hangings could take place, it had the effect of a policy change"; see Carol F. Karlsen, *The Devil in the Shape of a Woman, Witchcraft in Colonial New England* (New York, 1987), 278 n. 125. From his reading of the documents, Danvers archivist Richard Trask concluded that "confessed witches had given up their power over their victims and then were not a threat to civil authorities whereas the unconfessed witches were still a danger. Since confessed witches were confessors to capital offenses, they would eventually also be executed and their confession was only a temporary reprise. In practice, however, the question seems ambiguous." Letter to author, December 11, 1984.

36. Boyer and Nissenbaum, eds., *Witchcraft Papers*, II, 532, and III, 828.

37. Ibid., II, 403-404.

38. Mark Van Doren, ed., *Samuel Sewall's Diary*, (New York, 1963), 108.

39. Calef, "More Wonders," 375.

40. Boyer and Nissenbaum, eds., *Witchcraft Papers*, III, 777-778.

41. Ibid., II, 496, and III, 875.

42. Ibid., III, 881.

43. Ibid., 720.

44. Ibid., I, 209.

45. Ibid., III, 954.

46. Ibid., 772 and 774; and Lyle Koehler, *A Search for Power, The "Weaker Sex" in Seventeenth-Century New England* (Urbana, IL, 1980), 488.

47. Boyer and Nissenbaum, eds., *Witchcraft Papers*, III, 992, and Calef, "More Wonders," 366.

48. Boyer and Nissenbaum, eds., *Witchcraft Papers*, III, 953 and 994. Another one of the accused, Sarah Dustin, could not pay her maintenance and died in prison in 1693; see Marion L. Starkey, *The Devil in Massachusetts: A Modern Enquiry into the Salem Witch Trials* (Garden City, NY, 1969), reprint, 229-230.

49. Le Beau, "Philip English," 5.

50. Boyer and Nissenbaum, eds., *Witchcraft Papers*, I, 210.

51. Calef, "More Wonders," 353.

52. Ibid., 355 n. 1.

53. Alden's arrival at a relative's home is described in Charles Upham's *Salem Witchcraft* (Boston, 1867), II, 246. Because Upham is not always reliable, it is difficult to know if Alden's arrival was really that dramatic.

54. Boyer and Nissenbaum, eds., *Witchcraft Papers*, III, 956.

55. Ibid., II, 370. Just three others—Mary Bradbury and Edward and Sarah Bishop—gained their freedom by a jail break; see Calef, "More Wonders," 370, and Chadwick Hansen, *Witchcraft at Salem* (New York, 1969), 194.

56. Boyer and Nissenbaum, eds., *Witchcraft Papers*, III, 819-820.

57. Ibid., I, 237.

58. "Some Documentary Fragments Touching the Witchcraft Episode of 1692," *Publications of the Colonial Society of Massachusetts*, X (1904), 15. Dudley Bradstreet, Daniel Andrew, and George Jacobs, Jr., all fled before a sheriff or constable could find them, and none of them were ever arrested; see Boyer and Nissenbaum, eds., *Witchcraft Papers*, II, 488, and III, 988; and Calef, "More Wonders," 372.

59. Brattle, "Letter of Thomas Brattle," 178.

60. Boyer and Nissenbaum, eds., *Witchcraft Papers*, III, 875.

61. Ibid., 823.

Seven

Crushing the Witch Conspiracy

Between late June and mid–September, a long procession of accused witches filed into court at Salem, and juries found them all guilty. During the June 30, August 5, September 9, and September 17 sessions of the Court of Oyer and Terminer, Sarah Good, Rebecca Nurse, Susannah Martin, Elizabeth How, Sarah Wildes, George Burroughs, John and Elizabeth Proctor, John Willard, George Jacobs, Sr., Martha Carrier, Martha Corey, Mary Easty, Alice Parker, Ann Pudeator, Dorcas Hoar, Mary Bradbury, Margaret Scott, Wilmot Reed, Samuel Wardwell, Mary Parker, Abigail Faulkner, Rebecca Eames, Mary Lacey, Ann Foster, and Abigail Hobbs stood convicted of practicing witchcraft. The residence of the convicted confirms how widespread the outbreak had become. Besides Salem Village, they came from seven communities. Andover, just a few miles northwest of Salem Village suffered the most.

Through the early days of July, only one Andover resident, Martha Carrier, had been named. John Ballard, one of the village's constables, however, concluded that his wife's illness of several months must have been due to witchcraft. She was "sorely afflicted & visited with strange pains and pressures."[1] Neighbors convinced Ballard that he should request the aid of the afflicted girls to determine his spouse's tormentors. According to one contemporary account, "horse and man were sent up to Salem Village, . . . for some of the said afflicted; and more than one or two of them were carried down to see Ballard's wife, and to tell who it was that did afflict her."[2] Once in the presence of Mrs. Ballard or others who were ill, the afflicted fell into fits of pain and accused Andover residents Mary Lacey, Sr., and Mary Lacey, Jr., and the three sons of Martha Carrier.

Quickly, Andover developed its own band of afflicted.[3] Between July 15 and the end of September, they accused over forty villagers.[4] Young and old, male and female, rich and poor faced witchcraft charges. "The overall distribution," Richard Weisman has pointed out, "indicates that the afflicted ignored age and status considerations in Andover just as they had in Salem Village."[5] The Andover experience reveals how much of a crisis atmosphere had developed in Massachusetts. Analysts who argue that witchcraft accusations flourished best in communities in conflict have trouble with Andover. This largely homogeneous farming community was notable for its harmony. Unlike Salem Village, it was a place where "the goals of order, hierarchy, and the closely-knit community" would most likely be met.[6] Yet almost ten percent of the town stood accused by late summer.

Justice, however else it might have been defined in the witchcraft crisis, was swift for the suspects from Andover and elsewhere found guilty. Within days of their convictions, the guilty went to Gallows Hill on the west side of Salem town. Group executions became a monthly event; eighteen faced the hangman on July 19, August 19, and September 22. Eight of the convicted did escape the gallows. Elizabeth Proctor and Abigail Faulkner were pregnant; friends helped Mary Bradbury escape from prison; Ann Foster died in jail; and Dorcas Hoar, Rebecca Eames, Abigail Hobbs, and Mary Lacey confessed.

Yet the executions did little to ease the demands upon prison space. After a lull in June, accusations increased rapidly in July and August. By early September, there were still over 100 people awaiting trial. The escalation in the proceedings against the accused resulted largely from the emerging belief that Massachusetts faced a witch conspiracy of enormous proportions, a terrible divine punishment for a sinful generation.

From its earliest years, the leaders of the Bay colony had described the province as a fragile godly experiment. By mid-century, there was a growing realization that the goals of the founding generation would not be fully achieved because of the shortcomings of the succeeding generations. After 1650, fast day and election day sermons increasingly focused on a people who lacked the commitment of their predecessors and the divine punishment that would accompany their neglect. In 1662, Malden pastor Michael Wigglesworth described it as "God's Controversy with New England":

For think not, O Backsliders, in your heart,
  That I shall still your evil manners bear:
Your sins me press as sheaves do load a cart,
  And therefore I will plague you for this gear
Except you seriously, and soon, repent,
  I'll not delay your pain and heavy punishment.[7]

Wigglesworth had plenty of company. Condemnation of their contemporaries became a ritual for clergymen. "The present generation in
New-England is lamentably degenerate," Increase Mather complained in
a typical "Jeremiad" sermon in 1685. "The first generation of Christians
in New-England," he wrote, "is in a manner gone off the stage, and there
is another and more sinful generation risen up in their stead."[8] Titles of
published sermons increasingly fell into this predictable form: "The Cause
of God and His People in New-England," "New England Pleaded With,"
"The Day of Trouble Is Near," "The Only Sure Way to Prevent Threatened
Calamity," "A Plea for the Life of Dying Religion," "The Possibility of
God's Forsaking a People," and "God's Eye on the Contrite."[9]

Lay leaders, on occasion, joined with clergymen in admonishing their
fellow settlers. In 1652, the General Court called for a fast day, and for the
first time in this solemn ritual, they included the sins of the people along
with external problems as a reason.[10] Most notable, however, was that body's
call for a synod in 1679 to consider, "What are the provoking evils of New
England?" The synod's report was a catalog of the moral failings of the
settlers. There had been a decline in godliness, family discipline, and in the
willingness to embrace reform. At the same time, there had developed an
appalling increase in insubordination of the lower sort to their betters,
contention in congregations, the spread of heretics, swearing, sleeping in
church, violations of the Sabbath, drinking, sexual licentiousness, deception
in the marketplace, speculation in land, and price and wage demands.[11] To
those in religious and secular leadership positions, there never seemed to be
improvement. Introspective gatherings of clergymen became almost as
routine as the fast day sermons. In 1690, Salem Village pastor Samuel Parris
attended such a meeting of ministers at Cambridge.

The Cambridge Association considered a question that illustrates the
fundamental reason for the periodic self-flagellation of the Puritans:
"What shall be done towards the reformation of the miscarriages for
which New England now suffers by the heavy judgments of God?"[12]
They believed that the natural and manmade disasters that befell them
were the warnings or punishments of a righteous God. It became the
standard way to explain personal and collective setbacks.

There certainly was no shortage of catastrophes begging for explanations. Between 1660 and 1690, New England farmers suffered from serious droughts and floods, "blasted" wheat crops, and infestations of worms and caterpillars.[13] Boston endured several devastating fires. In 1676, fire destroyed almost fifty homes and several other structures, including North Meetinghouse and the parsonage of Increase Mather. The town had barely recovered when, three years later, another conflagration consumed much of the commercial sector of the town. Seventy warehouses and several ships at the town dock, in addition to eighty homes, burned. Three more fires between 1683 and 1692 also did considerable damage.[14] The colony also suffered through recurrent outbreaks of measles, dysentery, influenza, and smallpox. Most feared were the smallpox epidemics. Four times between 1649 and 1690, the disease devastated the province. The 1690 outbreak, with its "burning and spotted fevers, shaking agues, dry belly aches, plagues of the guts, and divers other sore distempers," claimed over 150 lives.[15]

Beyond the natural disasters, New England faced manmade challenges. In the early summer of 1675, a conflict with the natives, called King Philip's War, began. By the time the fighting ended over a year later, Indians as well as whites would suffer terribly. Over 1,000 settlers died, and a wave of refugees from the frontier flooded the eastern towns. They left behind burned homes and destroyed crops and livestock. In all, about a dozen frontier villages were abandoned. Increase Mather wrote:

Is it nothing that so many have been cut off by a bloody and barbarous sword? Is it nothing that widows and the fatherless have been multiplied among us? That in a plantation we have heard of eight widows, and twenty fatherless children in one day? And in another of the villages of our Judah, of seven widows and about thirty fatherless children, all at once.[16]

Besides resulting in widespread death and destruction, King Philip's War created a large debt which contributed to huge increases in provincial taxes. The financial crisis was exacerbated by the renewal of warfare in 1688. This time New Englanders faced both the natives and their French allies on the frontier in Maine.[17] Shadows created by this chronic military threat deepened with the loss of the colony charter in 1684, the indignities suffered during the Andros regime, and the uncertainties that accompanied its overthrow.[18]

Reverend Samuel Parris had addressed the issue of a wayward generation only weeks before the outbreak of witchcraft in Salem Village. In

January, he explained that Christ exercises "his Church in spiritual obedience by manifold & various troubles, afflictions, & persecutions in this world." "Christ," Parris said, "hath placed his Church in this world, as in a sea, & suffereth many storms & tempests to threaten its shipwreck, whilst in the meantime he himself seems to be fast asleep."[19] Why would Christ, their mediator with a God angered by their sins, seemingly abandon his congregations of the elect? As so many other ministers of his generation had done, Parris claimed that he did so to "humble his Church for their sins," "make his Church more watchful against sin," and "make us more watchful to duty."[20]

In February, Parris returned to the theme of a righteous punishment for a people who had forgotten the commitment of the founding generation to Christ. "For our slighting of Christ Jesus," he explained, "God is angry & sending forth destroyers."[21] "The present low condition of the Church in the midst of its enemies" was a development that should awaken God's people. They must understand that Christ "governs his Church, not only by his word & spirit, but also by his rod, & afflictions." Yet Parris pointed out that in the end, "he chastens us for our profit."[22]

As he spoke to his congregation, Parris assuredly had in mind the numerous catastrophes vexing the province as well as the contention in his own village (particularly the threats to his position as pastor). Yet by the time of his February 14 sermon, the girls in his household had begun to exhibit the afflictions that would plunge the village into the maelstrom of witch accusations. Perhaps Parris meant the horrifying specters that the girls claimed hurt them when he spoke of God "sending forth destroyers." Maybe they would be the agents of the terrible destruction that so many ministers had predicted for over two decades.

Deodat Lawson suggested as much in his March 24 message, "Christ's Fidelity the Only Shield Against Satan's Malignity." "We all," Lawson charged, "even the best of us, have by sin a hand and share, in provoking God thus to let Satan loose." He told the villagers to look upon the afflictions suffered by an ever larger number of people as a sign that they must reform their lives.[23] Clearly, he knew that there was room for improvement among a people he had spent four difficult years with. As he looked out into the congregation, Lawson made it plain that the members had much to answer for: "And as for you of this place, you may do well seriously to examine, whether the LORD hath not in righteous judgment sent this fire of his Holy displeasure, to put out some fires of contention, that have been amongst you." Lawson reasoned that they were seeing only the opening salvo of a prolonged conflict with Satan for the spiritual allegiance of New Englanders. Reflecting the view held by many religious and civic leaders on both sides of the Atlantic, Lawson worried that a competing cult had begun its assault on the reformed church:

You are therefore to be deeply humbled, and sit in the dust, considering the signal hand of God in singling out this place, this poor village, for the first seat of Satan's tyranny, and to make it (as it were) the rendezvous of devils where they muster their infernal forces appearing to the afflicted as coming armed to carry on their malicious designs against the bodies and if God in mercy prevent not, against the souls of many in this place.[24]

Samuel Parris also warned of a satanically inspired witch cult.[25] Three days after Lawson spoke to his congregation, Parris preached about a conspiracy of witches in Salem Village. They had breached the security of a covenanted congregation of God's elect. Previously, Parris had emphasized the building of a church of true saints, a sanctuary of God's own removed from the contagion of sinners. In microcosm, such a congregation would reflect the founding generation's hope for a pure church separate from the world. Adopting a rigorous test for membership, many thought, had insured such a congregation. But now, Parris told the villagers that there were devils as well as "true saints in the Church."[26] Membership guaranteed nothing, Parris now declared, because there were "hypocrites & dissembling Judas's" among the saints. The extent of infiltration into the congregation was unclear. Parris speculated that it might be worse than anyone imagined. "Why," he said, "so Christ knows how many devils among us: whither one or ten or 20."[27]

By September, after months of accusations, examinations, and trials, Parris no longer characterized the witch crisis as an insidious conspiracy penetrating a single congregation but as an all-out war between the forces of Christ and Satan's minions. He placed the current struggle in the context of the nearly seventeen-hundred-year-old war waged by "the Devil & his instruments" against Christianity. Throughout the life of Jesus, the Devil sought his destruction, from his "manifold temptations of Christ in the wilderness" to his putting "it into the heart of one of Christ's disciples to betray him." In the intervening centuries, the Devil had employed many agents to subvert the church. Now "in our land (in this, & some neighboring places) how many, what multitudes of witches & wizards has the Devil instigated with utmost violence to attempt the overthrow of religion?" Parris felt it essential to speak out on the danger of the Devil's threat "to reprove such as seem to be amazed at the war the Devil has raised amongst us by wizards & witches." "If ever there were witches, men & women in covenant with the Devil," he lectured the skeptics, "here are multitudes in New-England."[28]

This was not an isolated local problem but a transatlantic crisis. Parris cited Richard Baxter's *The Certainty of the World of Spirits* (London 1691) to reveal "the Devil's prevalency in this age." According to Baxter, authorities had discovered hundreds of witches in one English shire:

If fame deceive us not, in a village of 14 houses in the North, are found so many of this damned brood. Heretofore only barbarous deserts had them, but now the civilest & religious parts are frequently pestered with them. Heretofore some silly ignorant old woman, etc. but now we have known those of both sexes, who professed much knowledge, holiness, & devotion, drawn into this damnable practice.[29]

Cotton Mather agreed with Parris's interpretation of events. In a sermon on August 4 that he later expanded in his *Wonders of the Invisible World*, Mather offered an apocalyptic vision of the crisis facing New England. As Parris, Lawson, and others had argued, Mather said that the witchcraft episode was another example of a just divine punishment for a wayward people: "A variety of calamity has long followed this plantation; and we have all the reason imaginable to ascribe it unto the rebuke of heaven upon us for our manifold apostasies."[30] He went beyond Parris in discussing "our *Apocalypse*." His interpretation of scripture led Mather to conclude that the second coming was near and that the Devil was seizing the brief time he had remaining.[31] Given the gravity of the moment, Mather devoted his sermon, in large part, "to countermine the whole PLOT of the Devil, against *New-England*, in every branch of it, as far as one of my *darkness*, can comprehend such a *Work of Darkness*."[32]

Mather and Parris had focused upon the imminent threat of a satanic plot because of the incredible confessions heard in an increasing number of examinations of suspects in late summer. For those who attended the proceedings from mid-July through the first week of September, or for those who heard about them, the enormity of the conspiracy emerged in startling clarity. Dozens of women, men, and children enthralled stunned spectators with details of an extraordinary scheme. They heard how the Devil had recruited a substantial following, called witch meetings, celebrated mock sacraments, and planned to destroy Christendom.

Several of the confessors described the Devil as a cunning black man who had approached them at a vulnerable time in their lives.[33] He knew that some were in financial difficulty. William Barker could not provide for his large family and generally found that "the world went hard with him."[34] Samuel Wardwell worried about the consequences of not applying himself to the task at hand; he "used to be much discontented that he could get no more work done."[35] Individuals with frustrated love lives also attracted the Devil's attention. Mercy Wardwell had been disconsolate because "people told her that she should never hath such a young man who loved her." Convinced that they were right, Mercy did not return the young man's advances, and "he finding no encouragement [from her] threatened to drown himself."[36] Rebecca Eames grew despondent over an adulterous relationship "she was then in such horror of conscience that she took a rope to hang herself and a razor to cut her throat."[37] For Hannah Bromage, the dilemma was a diminished interest in the church. Bromage told the magistrates that "she had been under some deadness with respect to the ordnances for the matter of 6 weeks."[38] Mary Toothaker was terrified by the repeated rumors of Indian attacks. In the spring of 1692, she "was under great discontentedness & troubled with fear about the Indians, & used often to dream of fighting with them."[39]

Whatever their personal problems, the Devil promised to resolve them. The unfaithful Rebecca Eames contended that he had assured her that "she should not be brought out or even discovered" if she would join him.[40] To most, however, the Devil offered material rewards for their allegiance: "fine clothes" for Mary Bridges, Jr., Hannah Post, and Sarah Wardwell; William Barker and Samuel Wardwell could expect to "live comfortably"; and Sarah Hawkes "should have what she wanted."[41] Elizabeth Johnson, Sr., and Mary Marston anticipated "happiness & joy."[42] Mary Toothaker would no longer have to worry about Indian attacks; Stephen Johnson settled for a promised "pair of French fall shoes"; and Mary Lacey, Jr., expected "crowns in Hell."[43]

Whatever the inducement, the confessors testified to the Devil's sustained success in recruiting large numbers to his cause. A few, including Rebecca Eames, Elizabeth Johnson, Sr., and Samuel Wardwell, claimed to have joined the Devil over twenty years earlier.[44] Several indicated that they had been a part of the villainous cult for about three to six years.[45] Most disturbing was the recent effort of this well-established satanic group to attract younger people. Eight-year-old Sarah Carrier and twelve-year-old Mary Bridges, Jr., were among the several children who confessed to joining Satan in the past year.[46]

Joining the Devil, according to the confessors, involved two important rituals—signing his covenant and being baptized by him. The recruits provided their signatures in a variety of ways. Mary Lacey, Jr., and Mary Marston simply signed "with a pen dipped in ink."[47] William Barker and his son dipped their fingers into an inkhorn filled with blood.[48] Hannah Post and Stephen Johnson cut or pricked their fingers enough to make them bleed and, as Johnson explained, "he stamped his finger upon the paper & made a red mark."[49] Sarah Hawkes made "a black scrawl or mark with a stick as a confirmation of the covenant."[50] Once they had signed, the Devil took them either to a pond or a river and baptized them into the cult.[51] While most confessors said that the Devil dipped their faces into the water, Stephen Johnson claimed a more thorough immersion. After a day's work, Johnson said that he stripped off his clothes to take a swim in the Shaw Shim River. At that moment, the Devil "took him up & flung in his whole body over the bank into the water."[52] Mercy Wardwell said that she had experienced the opposite extreme. The Devil baptized her in her home "in a pail of water in which he dipped her face."[53] Regardless of the mode or place of baptism, the confessors agreed to renounce Christ and yield to Satan "soul & body."[54]

Once in the Devil's "Company," the recruits were obligated to attend witch meetings. Several testified that they had met in Salem Village near Samuel Parris's house or in Andover at either "Chandler's Garrison" or at the home of Joseph Ballard.[55] They could afford to be so brazen as to assemble in a minister's pasture because, as Mary Lacey, Jr., explained, the Devil "puts a mist before" the eyes of ordinary people and "will not let them see us."[56] Getting to the meetings proved a novel experience for the witches. Most claimed that they rode upon sticks or poles, a means of transport that took them above the trees.[57] At times the journey could be hazardous. Ann Foster told the magistrates that on one of her trips to a meeting with Martha Carrier, "the stick broke as they were carried in the air above the tops of the trees." Foster said she fell "but she did hang fast about the neck of Goody Carrier & were presently at the village."[58]

The confessors' claims about the number of witches at these gatherings assuredly shocked the magistrates, ministers, and spectators at the examinations. On July 15, Ann Foster said that she saw twenty-five.[59] A week later, Mary Lacey, Jr., testified that there were seventy-seven.[60] On August 10, Elizabeth Johnson, Jr., estimated "about six score."[61] By late August, Sarah Bridges, Hannah Post, and Susannah Post agreed that there had been 200 at meetings they had attended.[62]

Presided over by the Reverend George Burroughs, or more often, the Devil himself, the meetings almost always featured a mock communion and a prophecy of the Devil's triumph over Christianity. There was some disagreement over whether the bread was white or "brownish" and whether the sacramental wine was in "pots" drawn "out of a barrel" or in "earthen cups." Regardless, the confessors regarded the "mock sacrament" as an important prelude to a sermon from Satan.[63]

Elizabeth Johnson, Sr., and Richard Carrier explained to the magistrates that the Devil had convinced them that part of their mission was to afflict their neighbors.[64] Many of the confessors admitted that they had harmed people as a way of weakening Christ's kingdom. They even detailed the various techniques employed. Abigail Faulkner said that she had used "an evil eye" to harm the afflicted.[65] Mary Marston pinched and squeezed her hands to inflict pain.[66] Most often, the confessors stuck pins into or squeezed "poppits."[67] They utilized a variety of materials to make these puppets: "rags or strips of cloth," "birch rhine," a handkerchief, or bedclothes.[68] Mary Lacey, Jr., explained how to make and use the puppets. She would roll up a rag or a piece of cloth "and imagine it to represent such and such a person." Inevitably, the person thus represented would suffer.[69] Richard Carrier testified that "sometimes the Devil stirred me up to hurt the minister's wife." Carrier admitted that he afflicted two in the parsonage, "one of them a grown person the other a child the grown person was the Mrs. of the house."[70]

Beyond imploring his recruits to afflict Christians, the Devil told them of his plans "to pull down the Kingdom of Christ." According to William Barker, the Devil had selected Salem Village to begin his effort because "the peoples being divided & their differing with their ministers." After destroying the village church, he would move next to Salem "and so go through the country."[71] As the campaign against Christianity continued, they would "make as many witches as they could" and eventually establish the Devil's kingdom.[72] The confessors agreed that once that satanic vision became a reality, they would "have happy days."[73] Barker elaborated on this anti-Christian view of utopia. He described a future antithetical to the Puritans' sense of an orderly society. The Devil promised that "all persons should be equal; that there should be no day of resurrection or of judgment, and neither punishment nor shame for sin."[74]

Even more terrifying than Barker's vision was the testimony by several of the confessors about the number of witches in the region. Beyond the ones who had attended meetings, Mary Toothaker and Ann Foster "heard some of the witches say that there were three hundred & five in the whole country."[75] William Barker understood that there were "307 witches," and Susannah Post thought there might be five hundred.[76]

While willing to admit that a few of the confessions may have been little more than the "*delusions* of Satan," Cotton Mather argued that most must be accepted. After all, there were so many "made by intelligent persons of all ages, in sundry towns, at several times," and often there were "harmonious *confessions*." Mather concluded that "the Devil has made a dreadful knot of witches *in the country, and by the help of witches* had dreadfully increased that knot." He had no doubt that the rapidly growing cult was bent on "rooting out the Christian religion from this country."[77] Clearly, Cotton Mather and Samuel Parris were not the only ones convinced by the extraordinary testimony of the confessors. Boston merchant Thomas Brattle, a critic of the trials, acknowledged widespread belief in the confessions. Brattle wrote to a friend on October 8:

The great cry of many of our neighbors now is what, will you not believe the confessors? Will you not believe men and women who confess that they have signed to the Devil's book? that they were baptized by the Devil; and that they were at the mock-sacrament once and again? What! will you not believe that this is witchcraft, and that such and such men are witches.[78]

Equally important, there is no evidence that the judges on the Court of Oyer and Terminer, once Nathaniel Saltonstall left the court, doubted the veracity of the confessors.

Despite the lack of transcripts of the judges' deliberations, there is little indication that they deviated from the approach adopted in the Bridget Bishop trial in early June. Thomas Brattle's summary of the court's mode of operation is helpful. In addition to ordering a physical search of the accused for "a preternatural excrescence," the judges accepted the testimony of the "afflicted persons" against the accused. They also permitted the confessed witches to "declare what they know of the said prisoner." Indeed, according to Brattle, "whoever can be an evidence against the prisoner at the bar is ordered to come into Court."[79]

Defendants under seventeenth-century English law could be tried only if they pleaded in response to an indictment. If they pleaded not guilty, they then had to agree to a trial "by God and my country." Surviving documents from the 1692 witchcraft proceedings reveal that suspects almost always obliged. Bridget Bishop, for example, "pleaded not guilty and for trial thereof put her self upon God and her country."[80] After pleading not guilty to his indictment, Giles Corey, however, refused to "put himself on the country." This prevented the Court of Oyer and Terminer from trying him before a petit jury. Instead, it imposed the sentence of *peine forte et dure*, torture to force him to change his mind. On September 17, Sheriff Corwin ordered great weights, most likely rocks, be placed upon the old man. According to Samuel Sewall, friends and judges tried for hours to persuade Corey to agree to a trial "but all in vain."[81] His ordeal caused at least one of the afflicted to have nightmares that "she should be pressed to death, before Giles Corey."[82] He endured two days of this barbaric treatment before dying around noon on September 19. Traditionally, historians have concluded that Corey "stood mute" on the question of a jury trial to prevent forfeiture of his estate. Yet David C. Brown has offered a convincing argument that Corey did so out of contempt for a court that had convicted all who had come before it.[83]

In the case of two suspects who did agree to a jury trial, it is possible to observe how the judges handled evidence. Fortunately, these brief glimpses concern the two cases that attracted the greatest interest in Salem Village. The revered Rebecca Nurse faced a trial on June 30. In anticipation of her date with the Court of Oyer and Terminer, she petitioned the judges two days earlier to contest the findings of the physical examination she had undergone on June 2. That morning, a panel of nine women and a surgeon reported to the judges that Nurse had "a preternatural excrescence of flesh between the pudendum and anus much like to teats." Yet the same group, only a few hours later, found "instead of that excrescence within mentioned it appears only as a dry skin without sense."[84] On June 28, Rebecca asked the judges for a third physical search to remove any lingering doubts about her having a witch's teat. She explained that the "excrescence of flesh" the women had found in their first examination had a "natural" rather than a "preternatural" explanation. It had resulted "from an overture of nature and difficult exigencies that hath befallen me in the times of my travails [child-birth]."[85] Before her trial two days hence, Nurse requested that women "most grand wise and skillful," primarily midwives, be appointed to confirm her explanation.[86]

While there is no indication that the judges granted Nurse's request, it is clear that her family mounted an extraordinary effort to counter the evidence offered by the afflicted and the depositions submitted by nearly a dozen of Rebecca's neighbors.[87] Led by her husband, Francis, the Nurse clan convinced more than forty people, including leading members of both the Porter and Putnam families, to testify that they had never had cause to suspect Rebecca Nurse of any witchcraft. On the contrary, they found her "life and conversation" consistent with her Christian profession.[88]

The jury found the testimony of Rebecca Nurse's friends persuasive and declared her innocent. Upon announcement of the verdict, according to Robert Calef, the afflicted in and out of the courtroom "made an hideous out-cry," and some on the Court of Oyer and Terminer grumbled their dissatisfaction.[89] The judges asked the jury foreman, Thomas Fisk, if "they let slip the words, which the prisoner at the bar spoke against herself." Specifically, the judges wanted the jury to reconsider Nurse's reaction to the entry of Deliverance Hobbs and her daughter into the courtroom. Rebecca had said, "What, do these persons give in evidence against me now, they used to come among us." Given the judges' concern, Fisk later explained that "several of the jury declared themselves desirous to go out again, and thereupon the honored Court gave leave." Puzzled by the ambiguity of the accused's statement (when Nurse said of Hobbs and her daughter, "They used to come among us," did she mean among a group of witches or among a group of other suspects?), the jury sent Fisk back to seek clarification from Nurse. With the judges' permission, Fisk asked what meaning she had intended to convey, but Nurse "made no reply, nor interpretation of them; whereupon these words were to me a principal evidence against her." The other jurors agreed with Fisk, and they reversed their verdict.[90]

In a futile effort, Nurse sought to explain her statement and failure to respond to Fisk in a petition to the judges. When she had said "that Goodwife Hobbs and her daughter were of our company," Nurse contended that she had meant nothing more than that "they were prisoners with us, and therefore did then, and yet do judge them not legal evidence against their fellow prisoners." When Thomas Fisk had asked her to explain, she failed to respond because she was "hard of hearing, and full of grief." As a consequence, she "had not opportunity to declare what I intended."[91] Nurse's family succeeded in persuading Governor William Phips to grant Rebecca a reprieve. This prompted the afflicted to renew "their dismal outcries against her." Apparently, "some Salem gentlemen prevailed" upon Phips to rescind the reprieve.[92]

While the legal maneuvering continued, the church at Salem passed judgment on Rebecca Nurse. On the Sunday following her trial, the members imposed the ultimate religious sanction on their fellow communicant, "after the sacrament the elders propounded to the Church, and it was by an unanimous vote consented to, that our Sister Nurse being a convicted witch by the Court and condemned to die, should be excommunicated, which was accordingly done in the afternoon, she being present."[93] Rebecca Nurse had lost her case in front of the church, court, and, with Phips's decision to withdraw his reprieve, the provincial government.

If Rebecca Nurse could not convince a jury of her innocence, the Reverend George Burroughs was doomed. Because he had been described by several of the afflicted and confessors as the ringleader of the witch conspiracy, a large crowd sought a place in the courtroom to watch Burroughs face the Court of Oyer and Terminer on August 5.[94] The hopelessness of his situation explains his desperate effort during the trial to convince the jury that there was no witch cult. He submitted to the jury a short paper that, according to Cotton Mather, argued "that there neither are, nor ever were witches." Further, he contended that allegedly signing a "compact with the Devil" did not enable "a Devil to torment other people at a distance." The judges, who had read widely in the literature on witchcraft, recognized that Burroughs had taken the argument from a mid-seventeenth-century skeptic, Thomas Ady. In 1656, when Ady published *A Candle in the Dark*, he gave as the reason for the work: "The grand error of these latter ages is ascribing power to witches, and by foolish imagination of men's brains, without grounds by the scriptures, wrongful killing of the innocent under the name of witches."[95] Burroughs must have known that judges who had demonstrated their fervent belief in a witch conspiracy would not permit the alleged "ringleader" to escape the gallows.

Following his conviction, Burroughs came to terms with the inevitability of his execution. The Reverend John Hale visited with the former Salem Village pastor in the Salem jail. Burroughs denied all the charges made against him and told Hale that he knew he would die because of the evidence presented by the "false witnesses" who had appeared to incriminate him. Still, Burroughs refused to criticize the Court of Oyer and Terminer. "He justified the judges and jury in condemning of him," Hale recalled, "because there were so many positive witnesses against him."[96] He spent his last days thinking of his children back in Maine; in 1710, the children remembered that Burroughs had sent to them "solemn & savory written instructions from prison."[97] On the day prior to his execution, he met with someone who had testified against him. Margaret Jacobs, who had offered evidence at the trials of her grandfather, George Jacobs, and John Willard, as well as of Burroughs, told the minister that she had lied and pleaded for his forgiveness. He "not only forgave her, but also prayed with and for her."[98]

Mary Easty also met her fate with a remarkable equanimity. She submitted a poignant petition to the Court of Oyer and Terminer, not on her own behalf but rather for the others whom she believed innocent.[99] Moreover, Easty did her best to comfort her family. They reported that she was "as serious, religious, distinct, and affectionate as could well be expressed," and her words drew "tears from the eyes of almost all present."[100]

However the condemned prepared for their date with the hangman, the executions became a grim ritual for Salem Villagers in the summer and early fall of 1692. Upon a suspected witch's conviction, William Stoughton issued a death warrant. Excluding Bridget Bishop on June 10, the convicted faced execution in groups. The sheriff took them from jail through the streets of Salem to Gallows Hill in a cart. On September 22, groaning from the weight of condemned witches, the cart could not make it up the hill and "was for some time at a set." The afflicted, always sensitive to departures from the ordinary, claimed that "the Devil hindered it."[101] The public executions attracted large crowds. Judge Samuel Sewall observed that "a very great number of spectators" turned out for George Burroughs's execution.[102]

Once the condemned reached the hill and climbed the ladder beside the hangman, they had an opportunity to speak to the curious awaiting their plunge to death. Some, like Sarah Good, remained defiant to the end. The Reverend Nicholas Noyes implored her to confess what everyone knew to be true, that she was a witch. Good replied, "You are a liar; I am no more a witch than you are a wizard." Further, she taunted, "If you take away my life, God will give you blood to drink."[103] Others faced the rope terrified. John Proctor "pleaded very hard at execution, for a little respite of time." He said that "he was not fit to die."[104]

Despite efforts of clergymen who sought their confessions, most of the condemned remained resolute in their claims of innocence.[105] These protestations were not without incident. While Samuel Wardwell, who had recanted his confession, attempted to speak, the executioner casually smoked his pipe. Some of the smoke curled into Wardwell's face and "interrupted his discourse." Wardwell's accusers immediately claimed that "the Devil hindered him with smoke."[106] The words of the "ring-leader" George Burroughs attracted the greatest interest. He "made a speech for the clearing of his innocency" and concluded with the Lord's Prayer. Burroughs's appeal was "well worded" and delivered with "composedness."[107]

Following their execution, the condemned were quickly buried. Robert Calef claimed an unseemly burial of the Reverend Burroughs and the others executed on August 19.

[Burroughs] was dragged by the halter to a hole, or grave, between the rocks, about two foot deep, his shirt and breeches being pulled off, and an old pair of trousers of one executed, put on his lower parts, he was so put in, together with Willard and Carrier, one of his hands and his chin, and a foot of one [of] them being left uncovered.[108]

NOTES

1. Paul Boyer and Stephen Nissenbaum, eds., *The Salem Witchcraft Papers* (New York, 1977), II, 513. His wife subsequently died from a fever; see Robert Calef, "More Wonders of the Invisible World," in George Lincoln Burr, ed., *Narratives of the Witchcraft Cases, 1648-1706* (New York, 1975), reprint, 371-372.

2. "Letter of Thomas Brattle," in Burr, ed., *Narratives*, 180.

3. Chadwick Hansen, "Andover Witchcraft and the Causes of the Salem Witchcraft Trials," in Howard Kerr and Charles L. Crow, eds., *The Occult in America: New Historical Perspectives* (Urbana, IL, 1983), 46.

4. Hansen found forty-three; see ibid., 46. Richard Weisman found over fifty; see Richard Weisman, *Witchcraft, Magic, and Religion in 17th Century* (Amherst, MA, 1984), 143.

5. Weisman, *Witchcraft*, 143.

6. Philip J. Greven, Jr., quoted in Hansen, "Andover Witchcraft," 40.

7. Alan Heimert and Andrew Delbanco, eds., *The Puritans in America, A Narrative Anthology* (Cambridge, MA, 1985), 233-234.

8. Harry S. Stout, *The New England Soul, Preaching and Religious Culture in Colonial New England* (New York, 1986), 105.

9. Most of these titles are from Perry Miller's classic chapter on the "Jeremiad" sermon in *The New England Mind, From Colony to Province* (Cambridge, MA, 1983), reprint, 30 and 38. Also, see Stout, *New England Soul*, 109. Miller incorrectly argued that "just about all" of the sermon literature after 1660 "dwells on this theme of declension and apostasy"; see Perry Miller "Errand into the Wilderness," *Errand into the Wilderness* (New York, 1964), reprint, 7. Harry Stout has shown that in several printed sermons, particularly those "directed against external enemies," ministers "celebrated the superior piety and unconquerable faith" of New Englanders; see *New England Soul*, 85. Robert Pope has most vigorously challenged the Miller-inspired "myth" of declension; see Robert Pope, "New England Versus the New England Mind: The Myth of Declension," *Journal of Social History*, III (Winter 1970), 95-108. Whether or not there was true declension in New England is not the point; the ministers believed there was, and humans act on what they believe to be true not necessarily what is actually happening.

10. Miller, *Colony to Province*, 28.

11. Ibid., 33-37.

12. The deliberations of the gathered clergymen are in the *Proceedings of the Massachusetts Historical Society*, 1st Ser., XVII (Boston, 1880), 263-264.

13. Stout, *New England Soul*, 75; and John Demos, *Entertaining Satan, Witchcraft and the Culture of Early New England* (New York, 1982), 374-375.

14. "The Diaries of John Hull, Mint-Master and Treasurer of the Colony of Massachusetts Bay," *American Antiquarian Society Transactions and Collections*, III (1857), 242; Arthur B. Tourtellot, *Benjamin Franklin: The*

Shaping of Genius, The Boston Years (Garden City, NY, 1977), 112; and Demos, *Entertaining Satan*, 375.

15. Demos, *Entertaining Satan*, 373; Kenneth Silverman, *The Life and Times of Cotton Mather* (New York, 1984), 56; "Hull Diaries," 244; and Lyle Koehler, *A Search for Power, The "Weaker Sex" in Seventeenth-Century New England* (Urbana, IL, 1980), 385.

16. Koehler, *Search for Power*, 385.

17. Douglas Edward Leach, *The Northern Colonial Frontier, 1607–1763* (New York, 1963), 50–60; T. H. Breen, "War, Taxes, and Political Brokers: The Ordeal of Massachusetts Bay, 1675–1692," in *Puritans and Adventurers, Change and Persistence in Early America* (New York, 1980), 87–105; and Koehler, *Search for Power*, 343.

18. See Chapter 2 for a discussion of the Dominion of New England.

19. Parris, Sermon Book, January 3, 1692, 136–137.

20. Ibid., 137.

21. Ibid., February 14, 1692, 141.

22. Ibid., 141, 144, and 146.

23. Lawson, *Christ's Fidelity the Only Shield Against Satan's Malignity* (Boston, 1693), 48 and 49.

24. Ibid., 54. Richard Weisman has pointed out that the witchcraft outbreak to Lawson was "a providential judgment that bore on the destiny of New England," *Witchcraft*, 127.

25. Weisman is also helpful on this point, *Witchcraft*, 129.

26. Parris, Sermon Book, March 27, 1692, 149.

27. Ibid., 149–150.

28. Ibid., September 11, 1692, 153–154.

29. Ibid., 155.

30. Mather, *Cotton Mather on Witchcraft, Being the Wonders of the Invisible World* (New York, n.d.), reprint, 6.

31. Ibid., 34–37; and Weisman, *Witchcraft*, 130–131.

32. Mather, *Wonders*, 6.

33. The Devil was described as a black man in several documents, Boyer and Nissenbaum, eds., *Witchcraft Papers*, I, 65; II, 503, 509, 545, and 647; and III, 784.

34. Ibid., I, 65.

35. Ibid., III, 783.

36. Ibid., 781. Samuel Wardwell noted that in addition to his inability to work, the Devil had played upon his frustrated infatuation. He said that he had been "in love with a maid named Barker who slighted his love"; see ibid., 783.

37. Ibid., I, 282.

38. Ibid., 143.

39. Ibid., III, 767.

40. Ibid., I, 282.

41. Ibid., I, 65 and 135; II, 387 and 643; and III, 783 and 791.

42. Ibid., II, 502 and 545.

43. Ibid., 509 and 523, and III, 768.
44. Ibid., I, 281; II, 501; and III, 783.
45. For examples, see ibid., I, 65, 73; II, 343, 503, and 647; and III, 791.
46. Ibid., I, 201 and 134.
47. Ibid., II, 525 and 545.
48. Ibid., I, 65 and 74.
49. Ibid., II, 643 and 509.
50. Ibid., 387.
51. Ibid., I, 74; II, 514, 529, 615, and 643; and III, 784.
52. Ibid., II, 509.
53. Ibid., III, 781.
54. Ibid., II, 387.
55. Ibid., I, 66, 135, 140, 143, and 328.
56. Ibid., II, 524.
57. Ibid., I, 135, 140, and II, 514, 521, 546, and 648.
58. Ibid., II, 343.
59. Ibid.
60. Ibid., 523.
61. Ibid., 504.
62. Ibid., I, 140, and II, 643 and 647.
63. Ibid., I, 140, and II, 504, 523, 524, and 647.
64. Ibid., II, 500 and 529.
65. Ibid., I, 328.
66. Ibid., II, 545.
67. Ibid., 342, 343, 504, 505, 514, and 529.
68. Ibid., 504, 505, 514, 529, and 615.
69. Ibid., 514.
70. Ibid., 529.
71. Ibid., I, 66. Also, see Ann Foster's testimony in ibid., II, 343.
72. Ibid., II, 500.
73. Ibid., 522.
74. Ibid., I, 66.
75. Ibid., II, 343, and III, 769.
76. Ibid., I, 66, and II, 648.
77. Mather, *Wonders*, 16.
78. Brattle, "Letter of Thomas Brattle," 174.
79. Ibid., 174–175.
80. Boyer and Nissenbaum, eds., *Witchcraft Papers*, I, 109.
81. Mark Van Doren, ed., *Samuel Sewall's Diary* (New York, 1963), 108.
82. Boyer and Nissenbaum, eds., *Witchcraft Papers*, I, 246.
83. David C. Brown, "The Case of Giles Corey," *Essex Institute Historical Collections*, CXXI (October 1985), 282–299.
84. Boyer and Nissenbaum, eds., *Witchcraft Papers*, I, 107–108.
85. Ibid., II, 606–607.
86. Ibid., 607.

87. Ibid., 595–606.

88. Ibid., 592–594.

89. Calef, "More Wonders," 358.

90. Boyer and Nissenbaum, eds., *Witchcraft Papers*, II, 607–608.

91. Ibid., 608.

92. Calef, "More Wonders," 359.

93. Richard D. Pierce, ed., *The Records of the First Church in Salem, Massachusetts, 1629–1736* (Salem, 1974), 172.

94. *Diary of Cotton Mather* (New York, 1957), I, 142.

95. Burr, ed., *Narratives*, 222 n. 1.

96. Hale, "A Modest Inquiry into the Nature of Witchcraft," in ibid., 421.

97. Boyer and Nissenbaum, eds., *Witchcraft Papers*, III, 1041.

98. Calef, "More Wonders," 364–365.

99. Calef, "More Wonders," 368.

100. Ibid.

101. Ibid., 367.

102. Van Doren, ed., *Sewall Diary*, 108.

103. Calef, "More Wonders," 358.

104. Ibid., 364.

105. Sewall noted that all five said on August 19 that they were innocent; see Van Doren, ed., *Sewall Diary*, 108.

106. Calef, "More Wonders," 367.

107. Ibid., 360. Calef's description of the scene may be a bit suspect, but Samuel Sewall also took particular note of the former Salem Village minister's "speech, prayer, protestation of his innocence"; see Van Doren, ed., *Sewall Diary*, 108.

108. Calef, "More Wonders," 361. Excavations a century later raised some questions about Calef's account. The graves of the condemned "were found of the usual depth, and the remains of the bodies, and of the wood in which they were interred"; see Chadwick Hansen, *Witchcraft at Salem* (New York, 1969), 192.

Eight

The End of the Trials

As the convictions and executions mounted, few in Massachusetts could distance themselves far enough from the evolving crisis to discern the breadth of the emerging opposition to the trials. Several factors contributed to the move to stop the Court of Oyer and Terminer: doubts raised about the integrity of the afflicted; the recantations of several of the confessors; the building public support for many of the accused; the admirable behavior of some of the condemned; and the development of a comprehensive critique of the proceedings capped by Increase Mather's influential *Cases of Conscience*. Collectively, these factors destroyed the consensus that had justified the court's procedures. By early October, only a handful of magistrates and clergymen were willing to defend them.

Throughout the spring and summer, some of the accused had challenged the integrity of the afflicted. Susannah Martin had laughed at their "folly."[1] John Alden had called them "wenches . . . who played their juggling tricks, falling down, crying out, and staring in peoples faces."[2] After his servant Mary Warren began having fits, John Proctor had "kept her close to the wheel & threatened to thrash her," claiming that that eliminated the problem as long as he was around her. If only the magistrates would let him apply a liberal dose of corporal punishment, Proctor said that he could stop what he considered childish pranks.[3] A few of the accused had even stronger words for those who had named them as suspects. John Alden, Martha Carrier, and Sarah Cloyce told their accusers flatly that they lied.[4] One of the more outspoken accused witches, Martha Carrier, even questioned the judgment of the authorities who had eagerly embraced the testimony of the accused. She chided William Hathorne for believing "folks that are out of their wits."[5] After her conviction, Mary Easty told the judges that she could see "plainly the wiles and subtilty" of her accusers. After spending a month in jail under suspicion of practicing witchcraft, Easty temporarily gained her release when some of the afflicted "cleared" her. Yet, "in two days time I was cried out upon by them and have been confined and now am condemned to die."[6]

Besides Martha Carrier, there were suspects who shifted their rejection of the afflicted to a bold defiance of the magistrates. Susannah Martin refused to comply when her inquisitors demanded that she explain her testimony. She made it clear that she could care less what they or her neighbors thought about her. When the afflicted tumbled down at his glance, John Alden turned to magistrate Bartholomew Gedney and asked "what reason there could be given, why Alden's looking upon *him* did not strike *him* down as well."[7]

Old George Jacobs proved particularly difficult for the magistrates. The eighty-year-old Jacobs, who owned a farm about two miles south of the Salem Village meetinghouse, had lived in Salem for over thirty years.[8] He lived modestly, raising a few head of livestock, tilling a few acres of corn, and maintaining a large enough orchard to produce twenty-four barrels of cider in the summer of 1692. When Sheriff Corwin seized his property, it was clear that Jacobs was not a wealthy man; the total value of the confiscated goods was under eighty pounds.[9]

Neighbors knew him as a tough, quick-tempered man. He got into a fight in 1677 that landed him in court. Two witnesses testified that Jacobs, who had gotten into an argument with John Thompkins, struck the man. John Waters and Stephen Small said that if they had not held Jacobs "by the arms, he would have struck him more, he being in such a passion."[10] Jacobs's "passion" was also evident in his treatment of a servant, twenty-year-old Sarah Churchill. Whenever she failed to complete her tasks, he would call her a "bitch witch."[11]

Jacobs was not only a harsh man but he failed to convince magistrates that he was a religious one. He admitted that he rarely prayed with his family but claimed that it was due to his inability to read. Yet when asked to recite the widely used Lord's Prayer, Jacobs "missed in several parts of it, and could not repeat it right after many trials."[12]

Arrested on May 10, Jacobs, like the other suspects, underwent a physical examination, and the outcome was not favorable. Two constables and a jailer found a witch's teat under his right shoulder "about a quarter of an inch long or better with a sharp point drooping downwards." One of the constables thrust a pin into the growth, and, unfortunately for Jacobs, they noted that he "was not in the least sensible" to it. Moreover, "there was neither water blood nor corruption nor any other matter" in the growth.[13]

When the constables brought him into the public examination, the crippled Jacobs hobbled along with the aid of two staves. Hathorne proclaimed, "Here are them that accuse you of acts of witchcraft." An impatient Jacobs replied, "Well, let us hear who are they, and what are they." He laughed when the magistrates said that one of them was Abigail Williams. Incredulous, Jacobs asked, "Your worships all of you do you think this is true?" Their response was to bring forward his servant Sarah Churchill to make their case against the old man. After she had claimed that his shape had both harmed her and offered her the Devil's book, Jacobs sarcastically told Hathorne, "You tax me for a wizard, you may as well tax me for a buzzard I have done no harm." The magistrate persisted, drawing more testimony from Sarah Churchill. Finally, George Jacobs had heard enough. "Well burn me, or hang me," he taunted, "I will stand in the truth of Christ, I know nothing of it."[14]

Since spring, several observers had also expressed doubts about the afflicted. The day after Samuel Parris's powerful witchcraft sermon on March 27, adults assembled in Ingersoll's ordinary challenged the afflicted. When the girls claimed that they had seen Elizabeth Proctor's specter, William Rayment and Hanna Ingersoll told them that they lied because no one else could see the images.[15]

A few weeks later one of the afflicted, Mary Warren, was accused, examined, and jailed. Four other accused witches heard Warren make a damaging admission:

The magistrates might as well examine Keysar's daughter that has been distracted many years and take notice of what she said as well as any of the afflicted persons. For, said Mary Warren, when I was afflicted I thought I saw the apparition of a hundred persons for she said her head was distempered that she could not tell what she said, and the said Mary told us that when she was well again she could not say that she saw any of apparitions at the time aforesaid.[16]

In at least one of the trials, claims by the afflicted proved to be clearly fraudulent. During Sarah Good's trial on June 30, one of the afflicted claimed that Good's specter stabbed her with a knife, and those close by noted "a piece of the blade of a knife." However, a young man attending the trial "produced a haft and part of the blade, which the court having viewed and compared, saw it to be the same." In response to the judges' inquiries, the man explained that the previous day he had broken the knife and had "cast away the upper part, this afflicted person being then present." In the face of this obvious fabrication, the judges surprisingly only bid the young woman "not to tell lies."[17]

Confessions—the driving force behind the numerous August and September examinations and trials—came under increasing scrutiny as ever more suspects recanted. The prospect of an increasingly powerful witch conspiracy dimmed when several witchcraft suspects explained that they had given spurious confessions. After her preliminary examination in June, Sarah Churchill went to Sarah Ingersoll "crying and wringing her hands," claiming that "she had undone herself." When Ingersoll told Churchill that she believed the latter had signed the Devil's book, the distraught young woman "answered crying and said no, no, no, I never, I never."[18] In late August, Margaret Jacobs reported to her father and the judges on the Court of Oyer and Terminer that her confession had no validity. She explained that a combination of bewilderment at the accusations made against her, intimidation by the magistrates, and a desperate hope "to save my life and to have my liberty" led her to falsely incriminate not only herself but also her grandfather, George Jacobs, Sr., and the Reverend George Burroughs.[19] Her explanation would be echoed by several others in succeeding weeks. Thomas Brattle contended that several confessors "soon recanted their confessions, acknowledging, with sorrow and grief, that it was an hour of great temptations with them."[20] When Increase Mather visited several of the confessors in the Salem jail on October 19, he found most eager to renounce their earlier testimonies. Mary Osgood told him that her confession "was wholly false." Eunice Fry said of her confession that "it was all of it false." Deliverance Dane and Mary Barker "said freely, that they had wronged the truth in making their confession." Martha Tyler, Sarah Wilson, Sarah Bridges, and Mary Marston made similar statements.[21]

As the recantations mounted, many also worried about the increasing number of church members among the accused. The Reverend Samuel Parris had argued in late March that membership in a congregation did not insure that an individual was free of complicity with the Devil. Still, as people like Rebecca Nurse, Sarah Buckley, and Mary Bradbury faced legal proceedings, doubts grew. By early October, according to one contemporary, of the twenty-eight condemned, "above a third part were members of some of the churches in N. England, and more than half of them of a good conversation in general."[22] In an account of his wife's prosecution, Nathaniel Cary also noted the many church members and those "unspotted in their conversation" among the accused. This reflected poorly on his generation he thought, "considering what a people for religion, I mean the profession of it, we have been."[23]

The willingness of individuals to offer testimony or to sign a petition on behalf of the accused is the clearest measure of the growing popular unease about the accelerating prosecutions. By early October, almost three hundred people had taken the great risk involved in publicly supporting one or more of the accused. Thirty-five offered testimony before the magistrates, and over two hundred and fifty signed petitions declaring, as in the case of the forty who had signed a petition for Rebecca Nurse, that "we never had any cause or grounds to suspect her of any such thing as she is now accused of."[24] The supporters were family members, neighbors, fellow church members, ministers, and even jailers. They came from Salem Village, Salem, Ipswich, Rowley, Andover, Salisbury, Boston, and Topsfield. One of the great surprises is that several members of both the chronically divided Porter and Putnam families united in support of Rebecca Nurse.[25]

If they doubted the authenticity of the suspects' protestations of innocence before, observers of some of the condemned now openly wondered if serious errors had not been made. Mary Easty's altruistic effort challenged authorities to reevaluate their procedures. After an unsuccessful petition effort to save her own life, Easty drafted one last appeal to the governor and judges on the Court of Oyer and Terminer shortly before her execution on September 22. In the document, Easty acknowledged that she could not save herself. Instead, she poignantly pleaded for the lives of others.

I petition to your Honors not for my own life, for I know I must die, and my appointed time is set; but the Lord he knows it is, if it be possible, that no more innocent blood be shed, which undoubtedly cannot be avoided in the way and course you go in. I question too, but your Honors do to the utmost of your powers in the discovery and detecting witchcraft and witches, and would not be guilty of innocent blood for the world; but by my own innocency I know you are in the wrong way. The Lord in his infinite mercy direct you in this great work, if it be his blessed will, that innocent blood be not shed; I would humbly beg of you, that your Honors would be pleased to examine some of those confessing witches, I being confident there are several of them have belied themselves and others, as will appear, if not in this world, I am sure in the world to come, whither I am going; and I question not, but your selves will see an alteration in these things. They say, my self and others have made a league with the Devil, we cannot confess. I know and the Lord he knows (as will shortly appear) they belie me, and so I question not but they do others; the Lord alone, who is the searcher of all hearts, knows that as I shall answer it at the Tribunal Seat, that I know not the least thing of witchcraft, therefore I cannot, I durst not belie my own soul. I beg your Honors not to deny this my humble petition, from a poor dying innocent person, and I question not but the Lord will give a blessing to your endeavors.[26]

How widely the contents of Easty's petition were known is unclear. The deportment of the condemned at their execution, however, was on display for the large crowds that attended. The conduct of the group executed on August 19 prompted several to note their admiration. "The condemned," Boston merchant Thomas Brattle wrote, "went out of the world not only with as great protestations, but also with as good shows of innocency, as men could do." In the same spirit that Mary Easty would demonstrate a month later in her petition, they "declared their wish, that their blood might be the last innocent blood shed." They asked Cotton Mather to pray with them and, after forgiving their accusers, spoke "without reflection on jury and judges, for bringing them in guilty, and condemning them." In all, the condemned "seemed to be very sincere, upright, and sensible of their circumstances on all accounts." John Proctor and John Willard particularly impressed Brattle. "From the gaol to the gallows, and whilst at the gallows," their words and actions were "very affecting and melting to the hearts of some considerable spectators."[27] Robert Calef argued that George Burroughs had the greatest impact on the crowd. The remarks from the man widely regarded as the ringleader of the witch conspiracy, and particularly his recitation of the Lord's Prayer, "drew tears from many." Judge Samuel Sewall agreed with Calef's assessment of Burroughs's influence. Sewall noted in his diary that the former Salem Village minister's "speech, prayer, protestation of his innocence, did much move unthinking persons."[28]

Samuel Sewall's suggestion that Burroughs's performance at the gallows influenced only "unthinking persons" obscures the growing concern about the trials among "thinking" persons. From late July to early October, a number of individuals raised questions about the procedures employed by the Court of Oyer and Terminer. Prisoners awaiting trial, a Charlestown sea captain, a magistrate from Salisbury, a Boston merchant, and clergymen from Boston to New York all engaged in the debate. Out of these disparate sources, a consensus against a continuation of the trials emerged even though the authors of the arguments were not always aware of the statements being made by others.

John Proctor, Mary Easty, and Sarah Cloyce challenged the judges' handling of the trials in petitions they submitted in late July.[29] Proctor's appeal was on behalf of all the prisoners awaiting trial.[30] In need of influential men sympathetic to his plight (the judges had scheduled his trial for August 5), Proctor addressed his petition to five clergymen—Increase Mather, Samuel Willard, Joshua Moody, John Bailey, and James Allen—whom he believed opposed the proceedings in Salem. Proctor claimed that the juries as well as the judges had "condemned us already before our trials." While he attributed their bias to the "delusion of the Devil," Proctor nonetheless argued that a fair trial in Salem would be impossible. He pleaded with the five clergymen to use their influence with the governor to move the trials to Boston or, failing that, "to have these magistrates changed."[31] Proctor, in part due to an understandable desperation, was one of the few who joined in the critique of the judges, willing to challenge their integrity.

Thomas Brattle was another. He particularly disapproved of the chief judge, William Stoughton. Brattle characterized him as "very zealous in these proceedings" and "very impatient" of criticism. While he had great respect for Stoughton, Brattle charged "that wisdom and counsel are withheld from his honor as to this matter."[32] The Boston merchant also claimed that the judges' class bias prevented them from dispensing justice to all the suspects. The rich often escaped prosecution. Several of the afflicted, according to Brattle, had named sixty-seven-year-old Margaret Thatcher as their tormentor, but the judges had failed to issue a warrant for her arrest. The reason was clear to Brattle; Mrs. Thatcher was Judge Jonathan Corwin's mother-in-law. "I cannot see how, without injustice and violence to conscience," he wrote, "Mrs. Thatcher can escape, when it is well known how much she is, and has been, complained of."[33] An even greater scandal, he believed, was the failure of the judges to pursue prominent escapees. Little had been done to capture Elizabeth Cary, Philip and Mary English, and John Alden, even though the judges knew "where they are gone and entertained." If other justices had been concerned to capture fugitives indicted in other capital cases, "why then is it not practiced in this case, if really judged to be so heinous as is made for?"[34]

Mary Easty and Sarah Cloyce raised two different issues in their petition to the judges, one of which would remain a preeminent concern of the critics of the trials. When the sisters pointed out that they felt helpless in their upcoming trials because no "counsel" had been "allowed to those in our condition," they gave voice to a frustration that most of the accused must have shared. Strangely, they were the only ones ever to broach the subject.[35] Moreover, there is no evidence of lawyers participating on behalf of the accused in any 1692 case.[36] Their other complaint, however, was one that the judges would certainly tire of hearing. Easty and Cloyce argued that the "testimony of witches, or such as are afflicted," particularly against suspects with an "unblemished reputation of Christianity," is insufficient to convict "without other legal evidence concurring." The women reminded the judges that they, and by implication many others, had several people "who have had the longest and best knowledge of us" ready to come forward to testify of their good character.[37] The hundreds willing to sign petitions or submit depositions on behalf of several of the accused are evidence of the strength of their assertion.

Over the next several weeks, others would come forward to endorse the argument of Easty and Cloyce. Salisbury magistrate Robert Pike drafted a letter of criticism to Judge Jonathan Corwin on August 9. Removed from the crisis atmosphere of Salem and Salem Village, Pike had been shocked by the arrest of a highly regarded Salisbury acquaintance, Mary Bradbury. Pike joined dozens of neighbors in petitioning the Court of Oyer and Terminer on her behalf.[38] The magistrate reminded Corwin that he had previously shared his "thoughts of that great case now before you." With Mary Bradbury in mind, he now emphasized the "doubtfulness and unsafety of admitting specter testimony against the life of any that are of blameless conversation, and plead innocent."[39]

Four clergymen from New York echoed Pike's position. Joseph Dudley, New York's chief justice and deputy-governor during the Edmund Andros regime in Massachusetts, still had an interest in his former home. On October 5, he submitted a series of questions on witchcraft to four Dutch and French Calvinist ministers in New York. In one of their responses, they dealt with the issue of charges made against individuals of high repute. Admitting that there could be exceptions, the clergymen nonetheless advised that "an honest and charitable life and conduct, of long continuance, such as meets with universal approbation, probably removes the suspicion of criminal intent from those who are accused of witchcraft by the testimony of the afflicted."[40]

The burden of the New York clergymen's responses, however, resembled that of the other critics. Most had concluded that the evidence the judges had permitted in the preliminary examinations and trials was seriously flawed. Thomas Brattle, for example, condemned the judges for allowing people to introduce evidence that had nothing to do with the accused hurting the afflicted. The prominent Boston merchant had drafted his withering critique on October 8 in response to a letter from a friend. Though not published at the time, Brattle's correspondence demonstrates that people neither connected with the trials nor among the leading religious circles had serious reservations about how the judges conducted the legal proceedings. Since the prisoners stood "indicted for sorcery and witchcraft acted upon the bodies of the afflicted," Brattle contended, ". . . the only pertinent evidences brought in are the evidences of the said afflicted." The judges, to Brattle's astonishment, allowed a bewildering variety of extraneous evidence:

Either that he was at a witch meeting, or that he performed things which could not be done by an ordinary natural power; or that she sold butter to a sailor, which proving bad at sea, and the seamen exclaiming against her, she appeared, and soon after there was a storm, or the like. But what if there were ten thousand evidences of this nature; how do they prove the matter of indictment![41]

Brattle also condemned the tests of touch and sight. Having the accused look at the afflicted during the examinations inevitably led the afflicted to fall into a fit. The judges would then order the prisoner to be blindfolded and to touch the afflicted. At the touch, the afflicted usually came out of the fit, which confirmed for the judges that the prisoners had harmed their accusers. This had served as sufficient proof to commit the suspect "on suspicion of witchcraft."[42] Brattle's incredulity stemmed from the judges' explanation of their acceptance of the touch and sight tests. A mathematician, astronomer, and member of the Royal Society, Brattle rejected the "Salem justices'" contention that they had employed "Cartesian philosophy." Philosopher René Descartes (1596–1650) had accepted as truth only what could be known by observation and reason. The judges, at least according to Brattle, believed that they were following his enlightened path: "By this touch, the venomous and malignant particles, that were ejected from the eye, do, by this means, return to the body whence they came, and so leave the afflicted persons pure and whole." While he was "no small admirer of the Cartesian philosophy," Brattle believed that the reasoning of the judges in no way fit his understanding of Descartes's approach to truth.[43]

Nathaniel Cary, a Charlestown sea captain, also railed against the judges for their easy acceptance of such evidence. Cary, who wrote his account after helping his wife escape from prison on July 30, explained how the judges used the touch test when they questioned his wife in May. As she stood before them, the judges ordered Parris's slave, John Indian, brought in. One of Elizabeth Cary's accusers, the man immediately fell to the floor at her glance. The judges then asked the girls, who afflicted the Indian? They answered she (meaning my wife) and now lay upon him. The justices ordered her to touch him, in order to his cure, but her head must be turned another way, least instead of curing, she should make him worse, by her looking on him, her hand being guided to take hold of his. But the Indian took hold on her hand, and pulled her down on the floor, in a barbarous manner. Then his hand was taken off, and her hand put on his, and the cure was quickly wrought.[44]

Cary recalled making "a hasty speech" to the judges at the time about their permitting such treatment of his wife. Like John Proctor, Cary challenged not only the judges' discretion but also their integrity. He was hopeful that "God would deliver us out of the hands of unmerciful" judges who scandalized the courts by allowing such questionable evidence that led to horrific consequences for the accused.[45]

A Boston clergyman also denounced the touch and sight tests. Samuel Willard dealt with them in his *Some Miscellany Observations On Our Present Debates Respecting Witchcrafts, in a Dialogue Between S. & B.*, which he drafted in early October. According to David Brown, the initials most likely represent Salem and Boston, or perhaps Chief Justice William Stoughton and Thomas Brattle.[46] Whatever the symbolism, *B* reflects Willard's opinions. He has *S* say, "When they have been brought before the afflicted, they have struck them down with their eyes, and raised them again with a touch of their hands." Willard argued variously that the episodes were "illusion," "utterly unlawful," and "exceedingly fallacious." Worse, the test "was borrowed from Popish exorcists." The true meaning of the afflictions remained unclear to Willard, and he was unwilling to accept "men's wild guesses in such an affair," particularly "where life is concerned."[47]

Willard, Robert Pike, and Thomas Brattle all emphatically rejected consulting the afflicted for evidence. They marveled at the afflicted's knowledge of the occult. Pike and Willard reported that the afflicted could name who tormented them, describe faraway events, predict the future, name people they had never heard of, explain things that had happened before their birth, identify people before they arrived on the scene, and communicate with "the dead out of their graves" who demand "to be revenged on the murderers."[48] The three men found it impossible that the afflicted could gain this knowledge, as the Reverend Willard said, "according to the way that is natural for men to know things."[49] The only conceivable source for their profound wisdom was the supernatural. Since, as Robert Pike argued, "none of these actions of theirs have any warrant in God's word," that left only a "diabolical" source.[50]

The disturbing reality to these critics was that the judges had given their "ear to the Devil." The highly educated Brattle would not have been surprised if only "the ruder and more ignorant sort" believed in consulting the afflicted. Although "a very gross evil, a real abomination," such a situation would have been manageable. What had aggravated this evil, making it "heinous and tremendous," was that the "better sort" and "some of our civil leaders, and spiritual teachers" had joined in support of the judges' endorsement of consulting the afflicted.[51]

Willard and Brattle likewise rejected evidence gathered from the growing list of confessed witches, although for different reasons. Brattle had talked to many of the confessors, and those discussions convinced him that "they are deluded, imposed upon, and under the influence of some evil spirit." They were clearly unfit to give evidence against either the accused or themselves. Since the Devil steals their memory and "imposes upon their brain," the confessing witches "very often contradict themselves, as inconsistently as is usual for any crazed, distempered person to do." In Brattle's judgment, over half of the confessors were as "afflicted as the children are."[52] Willard similarly argued that the judges should dismiss the confessors' evidence against the accused because it came from the Devil. Yet where Brattle saw the confessors as possessed, Willard firmly believed that they had entered into a contract with the Devil. They have "abjured God and Christ, and given themselves up to the Devil, the father of lies." As a consequence, Willard had no problem accepting the testimony of the confessors against themselves but argued that no credit should "be given to the testimony of such against the lives of others."[53]

The most compelling argument for stopping the trials was the development of a consensus that opposed the use of specter evidence. Twice in late spring, Cotton Mather had gone on record in opposition to it. On August 17 he did so yet again. John Foster, a member of Governor William Phips's Council, asked Mather to share his thoughts on the issue, and the young clergyman revealed no departure from the advice he had offered earlier. "When there is no further evidence against a person but only this, that a specter in their shape does afflict a neighbor," Mather told Foster, "that evidence is not enough to convict." He pointed out how far opinion had moved since the judges' acceptance of it as the essential form of evidence: "That the devils have a natural power which makes them capable of exhibiting what shape they please I suppose nobody doubts." Still, Mather believed that specter evidence could be useful in "an inquiry into the circumstances of the person accused."[54] In his judgment, the judges had handled the controversial evidence properly.

They had gone far beyond specter evidence and had drawn upon "more human and most convincing testimonies."[55]

Cotton Mather was not alone in his qualified rejection of specter evidence in August. His carefully worded correspondence with an important provincial official reflects the position taken by eight clergymen who considered the use of specter evidence at an August meeting at Cambridge. The group (the only identified participant was Increase Mather) concluded that the Devil could "represent an innocent person." Yet in deference to the august panel of judges hearing the cases, they added, "But such things are rare and extraordinary, especially when such matters come before civil judicature."[56]

Other commentators absolutely rejected specter evidence. They did so because of their understanding of the origin of the specters or images that so terrified the afflicted. Samuel Willard believed that the specters many saw were mere illusions. "The witches themselves," he noted, "do not know when they go in specter, and when in body, and how should they then tell, whether the other be the person bodily or only in specter?"[57] Robert Pike agreed: "Either the organ of the eye is abused and the senses deluded, so as to think they do see or hear some thing or person, when indeed they do not." Pike likened the effect to that created by "common jugglers."[58] Willard and Brattle suggested another possibility. The Devil could be stealing the memory of the afflicted and then deluding them with all kinds of "fancy and imagination."[59] If the afflicted made accusations on the basis of "diabolical visions" from Satan, then the judges must dismiss the evidence. "All that can be rationally or truly said in such a case is this," Robert Pike maintained, "that I did see the shape or likeness of such a person, if my senses or eyesight were not deluded and they can honestly say no more, because they know no more (except the Devil tells them more)."[60]

The most telling criticism leveled by the critics, however, was their conviction that God permitted the Devil, for whatever reason, to take the shape of innocent persons. The French and Dutch Calvinist clergymen in New York explained that God often permitted seemingly inexplicable things to happen to good people. People must accept that reality because God had often demonstrated that he would use "any instrument" to turn "evil into good." He had allowed the Devil "to marvelously vex the holy man, Job," and he had permitted the Devil to tempt Jesus Christ—to "spread before His eyes the idea and image of the empires of the whole world." No one should be surprised then if God allowed "the Devil to abuse the specter of a good man."[61] Robert Pike argued similarly. He drew upon the Old Testament to point out that God permitted the Devil to "appear in the shape of a saint in heaven, namely, in the shape of Samuel (1 Sam. xxviii. 13, 14); therefore he can or may represent the shape of a saint that is upon the earth."[62]

Given this reality, the French and Dutch ministers argued that condemning a suspect on the basis of specter evidence "would be the greatest imprudence." The judges must be aware of the cunning force that they are dealing with. By using the shape of an innocent person to afflict someone, the Devil "may intend two things at once; namely, to vex the one, while he exhibits the specter of the other, and so to bring the latter, whose image he is simulating, into bad repute and danger of his life—for he is a liar as well as a tormentor and murderer."[63]

As the criticism mounted in early autumn, several clergymen asked Increase Mather to draft a treatise on the problems associated with the evidence used in preliminary examinations and trials.[64] Mather read his work entitled *Cases of Conscience Concerning Evil Spirits Personating Men, Witchcrafts, Infallible Proofs of Guilt in Such as Are Accused with That Crime* to a gathering of clergymen on October 3. The ministers were concerned that "men be informed what is evidence, and what is not." They particularly wanted Mather to deal with "specter evidence, and a certain sort of ordeal or trial by the sight and touch."[65] In preparing the manuscript, Mather contributed nothing original to the controversy, yet he lent his considerable prestige to the growing chorus of opposition. Pastor at Boston's North Church and president of Harvard College, Increase Mather had also successfully negotiated with King William for a new provincial charter. He was one of the leading citizens in the Bay colony.[66] Satisfied with his work, the fourteen clergymen, including Samuel Willard, James Allen, and John Bailey, endorsed the manuscript, and Mather circulated it among other associates before sending it to a press for publication.[67]

Increase Mather not only acknowledged that there were bewitched people but also reminded readers of the seemingly unending diversity of the invisible world, occurrences God permitted to afflict his people. He cited learned works, including his own 1684 publication called *An Essay for the Recording of Illustrious Providences* to prove that demons "steal money out of men's pockets, and purses, or wine and cider out of their cellars," and that the Devil has come from Hell and thrown "fire on the tops of houses, and to cause a whole town to be burnt to ashes."[68] God has allowed the Devil "to come and violently carry away persons through the air, several miles from their habitations" and to cause the dead to appear before the living.[69] Mather also reported on voices and specters serving as "harbingers of death."[70] Not only was the Devil an ever present reality in their lives but Mather also emphasized that he was a master of deception: "The father of lies is never to be believed. He will utter twenty great truths to make way for one lie. He will accuse twenty witches, if he can but thereby bring one innocent person into trouble."[71]

Mather believed that the Devil employed the afflicted as instruments to destroy the saints of God. Since the Devil "has perfect skill in optics," he can cause the afflicted to see whatever he wishes, making things "appear far otherwise then they are." If the afflicted saw "things through diabolical mediums," the resourceful prince of darkness also had the power to "impose on the imaginations" of the afflicted. He caused "them to believe that an innocent, yea that a pious person does torment them, when the Devil himself doth it."[72] Most seriously, the Devil could "appear in the shape of an innocent and pious" person. He offered numerous examples of the Devil taking an innocent's shape. Upon the urging of the witch at Endor, he "appeared in the likeness of the prophet Samuel." He appeared before Martin Luther as Christ and has transformed himself into the shape of "eminent ministers of God." The essential point to Mather was that the "Devil is able (by Divine permission) to change himself into what form or figure he pleaseth." The frightening truth was that no one knows when it "may happen to him."[73]

Despite the overwhelming problems with specter evidence, Mather did acknowledge that it had a limited role in the trials. Citing the works of William Perkins and Richard Bernard, particularly Bernard's *A Guide to Grand-Jury-Men in Cases of Witchcraft*, he argued that specter evidence may raise an appropriate suspicion but was not sufficient for conviction.[74] He warned, "To take away the life of anyone, merely because a specter or Devil, in a bewitched or possessed person does accuse them, will bring the guilt of innocent blood on the land, where such a thing shall be done."[75]

Mather also rejected the use of sight and touch tests.[76] First, he pointed out that there was substantial evidence that people fall into fits for a variety of causes. "Some persons," he wrote, "at the sight of bruit-creatures, cats, spiders, . . . at the sight of cheeses, milk, apples, will fall into fits."[77] Second, he contended that no one had the "natural power" to look upon others and bewitch them nor to touch them and cure their affliction.[78] Since a supernatural power was required, those who depended on it for evidence were themselves employing occult techniques, and "we ought not to practice witchcrafts to discover witches." Nor, he added parenthetically, should anyone "make use of a white healing witch" to aid the afflicted.[79]

In conclusion, Mather argued that the judges ought to be as careful in their use of evidence in witchcraft cases as they would be in dealing with any other capital crime:

The word of God does no where intimate, that a less clear evidence, or that fewer or other witnesses may be taken as sufficient to convict a man of sorcery which would not be enough to convict him were he charged with another evil worthy of death. Numb; 35.30 If we may not take the oath of a distracted person or of a possessed person in a case of murder, theft, felony of any sort, then neither may we do it in the case of witchcraft.[80]

Mather called upon the judges and juries to err on the side of mercy. "It were better," he wrote, "that ten suspected witches should escape, than that one innocent person should be condemned."[81]

Mather resisted taking the ultimate step of stating that the judges on the Court of Oyer and Terminer had been wrong in the twenty-eight cases that they had already heard. When discussing the inadvisability of condemning a suspect solely upon the basis of specter evidence, he added as an aside, "And I trust that as it has not, it never will be so in *New-England*."[82] The judges had told Mather that they had "not convicted any one merely on the account of what specters have said, or of what has been represented to the eyes or imaginations of sick bewitched persons." In the only trial that he witnessed, Mather admitted that he would have found the Reverend George Burroughs guilty because so many people testified that "they saw him do such things as no man that has not a Devil to be his familiar could perform." From that experience and the assurances of the judges, Mather concluded, "They are wise and good men, and have acted with all fidelity according to their light, and have out of tenderness declined the doing of some things, which in their own judgments they were satisfied about."[83]

Despite his painful effort not to offend the judges, Increase Mather had submitted a substantial argument to halt the trials and reevaluate the evidence used in any proceedings against the remaining accused. The impact of *Cases of Conscience* was not due to the author's originality; rather, Mather drew upon the arguments of others to reveal a collective sense of how flawed the evidence was. His thoughts on the Devil's use of specters hardly differ from Sarah Cloyce and Mary Easty's petition, Robert Pike's letter to Jonathan Corwin, his son's letters to John Richards in May and John Foster in August, or the Boston clergy's advice to the judges in June. In addition, the Calvinist clergymen in New York were independently reaching similar conclusions in the days following

Mather's presentation of *Cases of Conscience*. In rejecting the tests of sight and touch, he essentially used the arguments of Samuel Willard, Nathaniel Cary, and Thomas Brattle.

Mather's synthesis met with the approval of his colleagues in the clergy, but more important, Governor William Phips found it persuasive. Upon his return from the frontier in which he fought with the French and Indians, Phips "found many persons in a strange ferment of dissatisfaction."[84] Phips sought Mather's counsel in the matter, and certainly the clergyman shared a copy of *Cases of Conscience* with his protégé. Mather's work and the petitions that reached his office convinced the governor that the afflicted had accused people who could not possibly be witches.[85] "The Devil had taken upon him," Phips reported to William Blathwayt, clerk of the Privy Council in London, using words from *Cases of Conscience*, "the name and shape of several persons who were doubtless innocent and to my certain knowledge of good reputation."[86] In a second report to London the following spring, Phips acknowledged Mather's role in reaching a decision to suspend the trials. He noted that the Boston clergyman and "several other divines did give it as their judgment that the Devil might afflict in the shape of an innocent person and that the look and touch of the suspected persons was not sufficient proof against them."[87]

Governor Phips was also responding to a public that had turned against the Court of Oyer and Terminer. On October 8, Thomas Brattle argued that "there are several about the bay, men for understanding, judgment, and piety, inferior to few, (if any,) in N. E. that do utterly condemn the said proceedings, and do freely deliver their judgment in the case to be this, viz. that these methods will utterly ruin and undo poor N. E." Further, Brattle named the people of influence who had taken public positions against the trials:

The honorable Simon Bradstreet, Esq. (our late Governor); the honorable Thomas Danforth, Esq. (our late Deputy Governor); the Reverend Mr. Increase Mather, and the Reverend Mr. Samuel Willard. Major N. Saltonstall, Esq. who was one of the judges, has left the Court, and is very much dissatisfied with the proceedings of it. Excepting Mr. Hale, Mr. Noyes, and Mr. Parris, the Reverend Elders, almost throughout the whole country, are very much dissatisfied. Several of the late justices, viz. Thomas Graves, Esq. N. Byfield, Esq. Francis Foxcroft, Esq. are much dissatisfied; also several of the present justices; and in particular, some of the Boston justices, were resolved rather to throw up their commissions than be active in disturbing the liberty of their Majesties' subjects, merely on the accusations of these afflicted, possessed children.

Finally; the principal gentlemen in Boston, and thereabout, are generally agreed that irregular and dangerous methods have been taken as to these matters.[88]

A week later, Judge Samuel Sewall journeyed to Cambridge to consult with Thomas Danforth, one of the men identified by Brattle as an opponent of the trials. Danforth told Sewall that the court should not continue unless it adopted a procedure that better met with the "consent of ministers and people."[89] On October 20 Cotton Mather agreed. He reported to his uncle, John Cotton, that the "humors of this people now run" against the trials.[90] Given the growing opposition, Governor Phips, on October 29, decided that the Court of Oyer and Terminer "must fall."[91]

NOTES

1. Paul Boyer and Stephen Nissenbaum, eds., *The Salem Witchcraft Papers* (New York, 1977), II, 551.

2. Ibid., I, 52.

3. Ibid., II, 683–684.

4. Ibid., I, 53 and 185, and II, 659.

5. Ibid., I, 185.

6. Ibid., 303–304.

7. The emphasis is Alden's, Ibid., 53.

8. His age is from Sidney Perley, *The History of Salem, Massachusetts* (Salem, 1928), III, 109. His farm location is from Boyer and Nissenbaum, eds., *Salem-Village Witchcraft: A Documentary Record of Local Conflict in Colonial New England* (Belmont, CA, 1972), 395 and 398. That he had lived in Salem thirty-three years is from his examination, Boyer and Nissenbaum, eds., *Salem Witchcraft*, II, 475.

9. Boyer and Nissenbaum, eds., *Witchcraft Papers*, III, 998.

10. *Records and Files of the Quarterly Courts of Essex County, Massachusetts*, (Salem, 1919), VI, 292–293.

11. Boyer and Nissenbaum, eds., *Witchcraft Papers*, I, 211.

12. Ibid., II, 476.

13. Ibid., 480.

14. Ibid., 474–476.

15. Ibid., 665 and 670.

16. Ibid., III, 803.

17. Robert Calef, "More Wonders of the Invisible World," in George Lincoln Burr, ed., *Narratives of the Witchcraft Cases, 1648–1706* (New York, 1975), reprint, 357–358.

18. Boyer and Nissenbaum, eds., *Witchcraft Papers*, I, 211–212.

19. Ibid., II, 490–492.

20. Thomas Brattle, "Letter of Thomas Brattle," in Burr, ed., *Narratives*, 189.

21. Boyer and Nissenbaum, eds., *Witchcraft Papers*, II, 490–492; and *Collections of the Massachusetts Historical Society*, 2d Ser., III (1815), 221–225.

22. Calef, "More Wonders," 373.

23. Boyer and Nissenbaum, eds., *Witchcraft Papers*, I, 210.

24. Ibid., II, 592–593.

25. Ibid., I, 117–121, 126, 146, 211, 212, 293, and 294; II, 383, 384, 403, 404, 440, 444, 592–594, 618–620, 664, 665, 674, 675, and 681–683; and III, 808 and 809.

26. Calef, "More Wonders," 368–369.

27. "Letter of Thomas Brattle," 177.

28. Mark Van Doren, ed., *Samuel Sewall's Diary* (New York, 1963), 108. Although Calef's description of the August 19 executions essentially squares with that of Brattle's and Sewall's, he was the only one to write that some of the spectators tried to "hinder the execution" of Burroughs or that Cotton Mather dissuaded them; see Calef, "More Wonders," 360–361.

29. Proctor sent his on July 23, and the two women submitted theirs no earlier than late July. Had it been sooner, they undoubtedly would have included their sister Rebecca Nurse, who was executed on July 19.

30. Boyer and Nissenbaum, eds., *Witchcraft Papers*, II, 689–690.

31. Ibid.

32. "Letter of Thomas Brattle," 184.

33. Ibid., 177–178.

34. Ibid., 178–179.

35. Boyer and Nissenbaum, eds., *Witchcraft Papers*, I, 302.

36. Sanford Fox, *Science and Justice: The Massachusetts Witchcraft Trials* (Baltimore, 1968), 109. Only since 1686 had lawyers gained professional status. The governor's council had then begun to license attorneys; see John M. Murrin, "The Legal Transformation: The Bench and Bar of Eighteenth-Century Massachusetts," in Stanley N. Katz and Murrin, eds., *Colonial America, Essays in Politics and Social Development* (New York, 1983), 542. There were probably fewer than a dozen lawyers in Massachusetts prior to 1692, and there is little evidence that attorneys "appeared on behalf of defendants"; see Daniel R. Coquillette, ed., *Law in Colonial Massachusetts, 1630–1800* (Boston, 1984), xxxiii–xxxiv and 205.

37. Boyer and Nissenbaum, eds., *Witchcraft Papers*, I, 302–303.

38. Ibid., 119–121.

39. Charles W. Upham, *Salem Witchcraft* (Boston, 1867), II, 538.

40. *Proceedings of the Massachusetts Historical Society*, 2d Ser., I (1884–1885), 357.

41. "Letter of Thomas Brattle," 176.

42. Ibid., 170.

43. Ibid., 171.

44. Boyer and Nissenbaum, eds., *Witchcraft Papers*, I, 209.

45. Ibid.

46. Brown, "The Salem Witchcraft Trials: Samuel Willard's *Some Miscellany Observations*," *Essex Institute Historical Collections*, CXXII (July 1986), 215.

47. Ibid., 234–235.

48. Ibid., 228, and Upham, *Salem*, II, 543.

49. Brown, "Witchcraft Trials," 229.

50. Upham, *Salem*, II, 543.

51. "Letter of Thomas Brattle," 182 and 179.

52. Ibid., 173 and 189.

53. Brown, "Witchcraft Trials," 235.

54. Kenneth Silverman, ed., *Selected Letters of Cotton Mather* (Baton Rouge, LA, 1971), 41.

55. Ibid., 42.

56. Mather, *Cases of Conscience Concerning Evil Spirits* (Boston, 1693), 32.

57. Brown, "Witchcraft Trials," 236.

58. Upham, *Salem*, II, 538.

59. Brown, "Witchcraft Trials," 229; and "Letter of Thomas Brattle," 188.

60. Upham, *Salem*, II, 538.

61. *Proceedings of Massachusetts Historical Society*, 356.

62. Upham, *Salem*, II, 539.

63. *Proceedings of Massachusetts Historical Society*, 357.

64. Cotton Mather, *The Life of Sir William Phips*, edited by Mark Van Doren (New York, 1929), 148.

65. Increase Mather, *Cases of Conscience*, preface. The preface was written by Samuel Willard.

66. The most recent biography of Mather is Michael G. Hall, *The Last American Puritan, The Life of Increase Mather, 1639–1723* (Middletown, CT, 1988).

67. Increase Mather, *Cases of Conscience*, preface; and Paul Boyer and Stephen Nissenbaum, *Salem Possessed, The Social Origins of Witchcraft* (Cambridge, MA, 1974), 10 n. 24.

68. Increase Mather, *Cases of Conscience*, 17 and 18.

69. Ibid., 19–20.

70. Ibid., 23–24.

71. Ibid., 40.

72. Ibid., 1.

73. Ibid., 1, 2, 7, and 33.

74. Ibid., 31–32.

75. Ibid., 34.

76. Strangely, Mather did not comment on the searches for witchs' teats; see Boyer and Nissenbaum, *Salem Possessed*, 13 n. 32.

77. Increase Mather, *Cases of Conscience*, 51.

78. Ibid.

79. Ibid., 45–46.

80. Ibid., 52.

81. Ibid., 66.

82. Ibid., 34.

83. Ibid., postscript.

84. Boyer and Nissenbaum, eds., *Witchcraft Papers*, III, 861.

85. There is a petition from nine Andover residents on behalf of their family members dated October 12, the day that Phips composed his letter to London officials; see ibid., 875–876.

86. Ibid., 861–862.

87. Ibid., 864.

88. "Letter of Thomas Brattle," 184–185.

89. Van Doren, ed., *Sewall Diary*, 109.

90. Silverman, ed., *Selected Letters*, 45.

91. Van Doren, ed., *Sewall Diary*, 110.

Nine

"Through the Clouds of Human Weakness"

Governor William Phips understood that news of the long summer of witchcraft trials would soon reach his superiors in London, so on October 12, he dispatched a letter to William Blathwayt, clerk of the Privy Council. Phips not only sought advice on how to proceed but also, and more important, offered a defense of his actions.[1] After ordering an end to the proceedings of the Court of Oyer and Terminer, Phips forbade the publication of "any discourses one way or other, that may increase the needless disputes of people upon this occasion, because I saw a likelihood of kindling an inextinguishable flame."[2] Several dozen people remained in prison awaiting trial, and many of them, or their relatives, had begun to petition him for release upon posting bond.[3] Persuaded by their arguments about the cold and privation they endured, Phips "caused some of them to be let out upon bail and put the judges upon considering of a way to relieve others and prevent them from perishing in prison."[4]

The governor then appointed five judges to sit on the Superior Court of Judicature.[5] Holdovers from the summer trials included William Stoughton, Samuel Sewall, Wait Winthrop, and John Richards. He added a notable critic of the Court of Oyer and Terminer's procedures, Thomas Danforth. These men acknowledged that "their former proceedings were too violent and not grounded upon a right foundation."[6] The judges assured Phips that they would not place the same emphasis as before upon specter evidence or the tests of sight and touch.[7] Although the judges did not indicate what specific evidence they would now employ, it is likely that they followed the advice of Increase Mather, Samuel

Willard, and Robert Pike. All three of these critics of the summer trials argued that there were only two reliable grounds for conviction in witchcraft cases. They believed a confession sufficient proof as long as the accused was "in his right mind, and not frighted or forced into it."[8] They also accepted, as Mather explained, the sworn testimony of "two credible persons" who had "seen the party accused speaking such words, or doing things which none but such as have familiarity with the Devil ever did or can do."[9]

Following these guidelines, the judges apparently used specter evidence only as presumptive evidence against the accused, and, true to their word, they did not lay the "same stress" on it as before. In the new trials, even the confessions carried little weight. John Hale explained that "the confessors generally fell off from their confessions; some saying, they remembered nothing of what they said; others said they had belied themselves."[10]

On December 23, the new court issued warrants to eleven Essex County towns to select jurors who were to assemble in Salem on January 3.[11] On that day, the Superior Court handed over indictments against fifty-two of the accused to a newly impaneled grand jury and adjourned. The trials took place in four locales: in Salem from January 4 to 13; in Charlestown on January 31; in Boston on April 25, and in Ipswich in May. In all but three of the trials, the juries voted to acquit, or the judges dismissed the case. Sarah Wardwell, Elizabeth Johnson, Jr., and Mary Post, who had confessed in 1692 to practicing witchcraft, were convicted.[12] William Stoughton, still functioning as the chief justice, signed warrants for their deaths as well as for five who had been condemned by the Court of Oyer and Terminer. Governor Phips, however, consulted with the king's attorney general who pointed out "that some of the cleared and the condemned were under the same circumstances or that there was the same reason to clear the three condemned as the rest."[13] As a consequence, Phips issued a reprieve for the eight until he received advice from the Privy Council on how best to proceed. Stoughton, who was in Charlestown when he received word of the governor's action on January 31, was, according to Phips, so "enraged and filled with passionate anger" that he "refused to sit upon the bench."[14] According to Robert Calef, as Stoughton left, someone overheard him sharply criticize the governor: "We were in a way to have cleared the land of these, etc., who it is obstructs the course of justice I know not; the Lord be merciful to the country."[15]

The speed with which they dispatched the cases reveals how earnestly the four judges, other than Stoughton, sought to end the episode. Between

January 4 and 12, they handled twenty cases.[16] Perhaps the best indication of the judges' eagerness was their handling of the Lydia Dustin case on January 31.[17] Her thirty-year-old reputation as a witch brought a large crowd from Boston to observe the Charlestown trial of the elderly Reading resident. "A multitude of witness" came forward to testify about their quarrels with Dustin and all the "accidents, illness, etc., befalling them" afterward. At one point, Judge Thomas Danforth told Dustin, "Woman, woman, repent, there are shrewd things come in against you." At the conclusion of Dustin's trial, one of the judges admitted that the prosecution had offered more evidence against Dustin than against those who had been tried in Salem. Still, the jury found her not guilty because the judges instructed them no longer to accord specter evidence any significant weight.[18]

The long-awaited reply to William Phips's October letter to the Privy Council asking for help did not arrive until early summer.[19] Fortunately for the Massachusetts Bay governor, resolution of the crisis was not dependent on the instructions of the imperial government. Drafted by the Earl of Nottingham and signed by Queen Mary, the council noted its approval of the governor's "care and circumspection" in ending the crisis. Then, in a master stroke of bureaucratic obfuscation, it added:

We do hereby will and require you to give all necessary directions that in all proceedings against persons accused for witchcraft or being possessed by the Devil the greatest moderation and all due circumspection be used, so far as the same may be without impediment to the ordinary course of justice within Our said Province.[20]

Eventually, Phips released all prisoners who had paid their fees and issued a pardon to the condemned who had escaped the executioners.[21]

The residents of Massachusetts found it difficult to put the year of afflictions, accusations, examinations, incarcerations, convictions, confiscations, and executions behind them as easily as the governor and judges ended the legal proceedings. Bitterness and outrage prevented a rapid reconciliation of those divided by the events of 1692. Most of the individuals whose actions contributed to the incarceration and conviction of the accused—the afflicted, clergymen, judges, and jurors—could never bring themselves to admit publicly that they could have been mistaken in their campaign to destroy the forces of evil. Yet over time, some came forward and admitted error. In so doing, they began a process of healing. Between 1694 and 1706, the minister who led the crusade against the witches, a judge from the Court of Oyer and Terminer, twelve of the jurors, and one of the leading accusers acknowledged that their actions contributed to the sorrow suffered by many families in the province.

The Reverend Samuel Parris was the first. In the midst of a vicious struggle to save his job in Salem Village, Parris made a public overture to those seeking his dismissal. During a special gathering of his supporters and opponents on November 26, 1694, Parris offered his "Meditations for Peace." That "the late horrid calamity" had begun in his household Parris acknowledged as "a very sore rebuke." Not only had there been "accusers and accused" in his family but also servants who sought "to raise spirits and create apparitions in a no better than diabolical way." Parris intended in his presentation to do more than concede that "God has been righteously spitting in my face." His primary aim was "to own any errors" he had made in his conduct during the witchcraft crisis. In his sermons during that "sore hour of distress and darkness," he had "always intended but due justice." "Through weakness or sore exercise," he now admitted, "I might sometimes, yea and possibly sundry times, unadvisedly expressed myself." When he had served as a clerk during the examinations of several of the accused, Parris contended he had "been very careful to avoid the wronging of any." Most significantly, he indicated his belated change of position on the validity of specter evidence. "I question not," he said, "but God sometimes suffers the Devil (as of late) to afflict in the shape of not only innocent but pious persons."[22]

To the families that had "unduly suffered in these matters," Parris offered his sympathy. To the community, he offered an apology and a plea for peace:

In fine, the matter being so dark and perplexed as that there is no present appearance that all God's servants should be altogether of one mind, in all circumstances touching the same, I do most heartily, fervently, and humbly beseech pardon of the merciful God through the blood of Christ, of all my mistakes and trespasses in so weighty a matter; and also all your forgiveness of every offense in this or other affairs, wherein you see or conceive I have erred and offended. Professing, in the presence of the Almighty God that what I have done has been, as for substance, as I apprehended was duty,—however through weakness, ignorance, &c., I may have been mistaken. I also, through grace, promising each of you the like of me. And so again, I beg, entreat, and beseech you, that Satan, the devil, the roaring lion, the old dragon, the enemy of all righteousness, may no longer be served by us, by our envy and strifes (where very evil work prevails whilst these bear sway, . . . ; but that all from this day forward, may be covered with the mantle of love, and we may on all hands forgive each other heartily, sincerely, and thoroughly, as we do hope and pray that God, for Christ's sake, would forgive each of ourselves. . . . Put on therefore, as the elect of God, holy and beloved, bowels of mercies, kindness, humbleness of mind, meekness, long-suffering, forbearing one another, and forgiving one another. If any man have a quarrel against any, even as Christ forgave you so also do ye. . . . Let all bitterness and wrath and anger and clamor and evil-speaking be put away from you, with all malice; and be ye kind to one another, tenderhearted, forgiving one another, even as God, for Christ's sake, hath forgiven you.[23]

In his extended appeal, Samuel Parris was not altogether contrite. He carefully qualified his admissions of error. In the campaign to discover the Devil's plot against New England, he had been too zealous. Yet a concern to do what was right and not malice had prompted his action. In a sense, Parris argued, he, too, had become a victim, a target of "Satan's wiles and sophistry." He also reminded the villagers that he was not the only one to blame for the excesses of 1692; God "has suffered the evil angels to delude us on both hands."[24]

Two years after Parris's effort at reconciliation, the significance of the witchcraft episode remained on the mind of Samuel Sewall. By the latter months of 1696, he could not escape reminders of it. In August, a Boston acquaintance, Jacob Melyen, "upon a slight occasion, spoke to me very smartly about the Salem witchcraft."[25] Melyen apparently had challenged Sewall's acceptance of evidence used in the case of George Burroughs. Several people had come forward to testify about Burroughs's herculean strength. Melyen told Sewall, "If a man should take Beacon Hill on's back, carry it away; and then bring it and set it in its place again, he should not make any thing of that."[26] The following month, during a day of prayer, Sewall heard the Reverend Samuel Willard challenge the governor and other provincial leaders "about the Salem witchcrafts." Willard wondered why "no order had been suffered to come forth by authority to ask God's pardon."[27]

Willard's chastisement prompted the General Court to debate a call for a day of fasting, an act of penance for the collective sins of the province. The lower house, the Deputies, had approved a proclamation drafted by Cotton Mather. In the list of provincial sins and God's punishment for them, he focused on the "wicked sorceries . . . practiced in the land"; "the late inexplicable storms from the invisible world"; and the consequent "hardships . . . brought upon innocent persons."[28] The upper house, the Council, rejected Mather's document, because, traditionally, it had initiated such orders for proclamations in conjunction with the governor. Samuel Sewall submitted a substitute bill that all parties accepted on December 17. His version likewise called for a day of fasting and prayer in light of the "many sins prevailing in the midst of us." In particular, Sewall called upon his fellow citizens to remember "the late tragedy raised among us by Satan and his instruments."29

As he pondered his role in the Salem trials, Sewall also worried about his two-year-old daughter, Sarah, who was gravely ill. Despite public and private prayers for her by Samuel Willard and Increase Mather, the child died on December 23. In his mourning, Sewall reflected on how he had failed his child—he felt that he "had not been so thoroughly tender" of her "nor so effectually careful of her defense and preservation" as he should. The next day, the melancholy Sewall listened to his son, Sam, read from Matthew 12. As he heard verse seven, "But if ye had known what this meaneth, I will have mercy, and not sacrifice, ye would not have condemned the guiltless," the elder Sewall admitted that it "did awfully bring to mind the Salem tragedy."30

Out of his grief, Samuel Sewall resolved to use the fast day to admit his guilt. During the afternoon worship at Boston's South Church, as the Reverend Samuel Willard walked by his pew, Sewall handed the clergyman his confession and stood while Willard read:

Samuel Sewall, sensible of the reiterated strokes by God upon himself and family; and being sensible, that as to the guilt contracted upon the opening of the late commission of Oyer and Terminer at Salem (to which the order for this day relates) he is, upon many accounts, more concerned than any that he knows of, desires to take the blame and shame of it, asking pardon of men, and especially desiring prayers that God, who has an unlimited authority, would pardon that sin and all other his sins; personal and relative and according to His infinite benignity, and sovereignty, not visit the sin of him, or of any other, upon himself or any of his, nor upon the land. But that He would powerfully defend him against all temptations to sin, for the future; and vouchsafe him the efficacious, saving conduct of His word and Spirit.31

When Willard completed the statement, Sewall bowed and sat down, his conscience partially assuaged.

Judge Sewall was not the only one who saw the occasion as an opportunity to purge nagging doubts. Twelve individuals who served on several juries during the witchcraft trials also publicly asked for forgiveness.32 Noting that they were "much disquieted and distressed," the twelve sought to explain why they had been so quick to convict. In 1692, they "were not capable to understand, nor able to withstand the mysterious delusions of the powers of darkness." Consequently, they had been willing to accept evidence that "we justly fear was insufficient for the touching the lives of any." The result of their ill-advised decision was to bring upon themselves and "this people of the Lord, the guilt of innocent blood." Speaking directly to the survivors of the trials and family members of the deceased, the jurors asked "forgiveness of you all, whom we have justly offended, and do declare according to our present minds, we would none of us do such things again on such grounds for the whole world; praying you to accept of this in way of satisfaction for our offense."

The last, and the most significant to offer a public confession, was Ann Putnam. She had been the leading accuser among the afflicted, naming twenty-one people as witches.[33] Still living in Salem Village in 1706, the twenty-seven-year-old woman decided to make peace with neighbors who had suffered from her actions fourteen years earlier. Putnam was seeking acceptance into the congregation, and Pastor Joseph Green had advised that she confront the central event of her life, her role in the witchcraft episode, if she hoped to gain the favor of the congregation. In the tradition established by the Reverend Samuel Parris seventeen years earlier, Ann had drafted a profession of faith in consultation with the pastor.[34] While she stood, Reverend Green read her statement. When he began, "I desire to be humbled before God for that sad and humbling providence that befell my father's family in the year about '92," the congregation understood that Ann Putnam's profession of faith would really be a confession of the great evil that she had helped trigger as a thirteen-year-old.

Through her pastor, she continued:

I then being in my childhood, should, by such a providence of God, be made an instrument for the accusing of several persons of a grievous crime, whereby their lives were taken away from them, whom now I have just grounds and good reason to believe they were innocent persons; and that it was a great delusion of Satan that deceived me in that sad time, whereby I justly fear I have been instrumental, with others though ignorantly and unwittingly, to bring upon myself and this land the guilt of innocent blood. Though what was said or done by me against any person I can truly and uprightly say, before God and man, I did it nor out of any anger, malice, or ill-will to any person, for I had no such thing against one of them; but what I did was ignorantly, being deluded by Satan. And particularly, as I was a chief instrument of accusing Goodwife Nurse and her two sisters, I desire to lie in the dust, and to be humbled for it, in that I was a cause, with others, of so sad a calamity to them and their families; for which cause I desire to lie in the dust, and earnestly beg forgiveness of God, and from all those unto whom I have given just cause of sorrow and offense, whose relations were taken away or accused.[35]

In these public confessions, Samuel Sewall's seems the most genuine. He blamed no one or nothing else for his actions in 1692. In assuming full responsibility for decisions that cost several people their lives, Sewall was willing to take the "blame and shame." This candor is not evident in the words of Samuel Parris, the jurors, and Ann Putnam. Their explanations, though separated by twelve years, fell into a predictable pattern. They admitted making errors, and they acknowledged that their mistakes had caused considerable suffering. Yet their motives had been beyond reproach. They accused or convicted people partly because of a sense of duty, or ignorance, or weakness. Most important, as Ann Putnam and the jurors complained, they had no control over their actions because they had been deluded. Their interpretation of what happened, along with the 1697 fast day proclamation, fit the long-developing notion of a divine punishment for a wayward people. God had permitted the Devil to use these people as instruments to wreak havoc on the province. Perhaps, as Samuel Sewall had written, "through the awful judgment of God," the people of Massachusetts would be properly humbled, that they would gain a pardon for their collective sins. God, he hoped, "would remove the rod of the wicked from off the lot of the righteous; that he would bring the American heathen, and cause them to hear and obey His voice."[36]

These confessions, then, no matter how qualified, supplied a framework for the colony to make sense out of what had happened in 1692. Over the next twenty-five years, references to the episode scarcely deviated. In the consensual view, the witchcraft crisis had been a dark time, a time of delusion, a time when good people were led astray and shed innocent blood. A sampling of references from a variety of sources illustrates this: "This delusion of the Devil," "that sad time of darkness," "the time of the great trouble by witchcraft," "the dark and doleful times that past over this province in the year 1692," "that gloomy day," "the late sorrowful time of the witchcraft," "that hour of darkness and temptation," "hour of sore tribulation and temptation," and "the dark time of the confusions."[37]

This interpretation of the witchcraft episode also convinced many of the necessity of offering justice to the innocent victims of its excesses. Notably, a movement developed to reverse the convictions and compensate the victims or surviving family members. The dilemma faced by those convicted but not executed surfaced when Elizabeth Proctor petitioned the General Court in 1696.[38] She explained that her husband, John, had signed a will shortly before his execution and left her out, despite "a contract in writing made with me before marriage with him." Those who had received Proctor's estate claimed that she could not contest the will, not even claim her dower right, because her conviction made her "dead in the law." Governor Phips's pardon had saved her life but had not restored her legal standing. As a consequence, Proctor asked the General Court to place "me into a capacity to make use of the law to recover that which of right by law I ought to have for my necessary supply and support."[39] Unfortunately for Elizabeth Proctor, she submitted her petition prior to the round of confessions and proclamations of guilt. Thus, it would be several years before the provincial government would move to respond.

In his *Modest Inquiry into the Nature of Witchcraft* of 1702, John Hale argued "for clearing the good name and reputation of some that have suffered."[40] In that same year and the following one, Abigail Faulkner and Sarah Wardwell, along with family members of some of the accused, joined with Elizabeth Proctor in petitioning the General Court. They asked for action to remove the "infamy from the names, and memory of those who have suffered" and so "their posterity" would not "suffer reproach upon that account."[41] The provincial government finally obliged in July 1703. So that the "infamy and reproach" suffered by the petitioners and families "may in some measure be rolled away," the members of the General Court voted to acquit the condemned of the "penalties" resulting from their convictions.[42] The General Court's action only reversed the attainder against Elizabeth Proctor, Abigail Faulkner, and Sarah Wardwell. This partial response did nothing for the other surviving convicted witches or the family members of the executed.

The Reverend Michael Wigglesworth worried about God's controversy with New England over its failure to atone for the shedding of innocent blood. In a letter to Increase Mather in 1704, Wigglesworth said that he felt it imperative that more who had "been actors" in the affair should admit guilt. That would be the only way "to turn away" God's "judgments from the land, and to prevent his wrath from falling upon the persons and families of such as have been most concerned." Moreover, the governor and General Court must take action to aid "the families of such as were condemned" who had been "ruined by taking away and making havoc of their estates, & leaving them nothing for their relief."[43]

Yet the General Court moved slowly. A petition from Philip English, John Tarbell, and three members of the Easty family, along with twelve others, in the spring of 1709 brought the issue to public attention. The petitioners requested legislation to "restore the reputations to the posterity of the sufferers & remunerate them as to what they have been damnified in their estates."[44] The petitioners gained an important ally when Cotton Mather addressed the Deputies in November. Since they had already declared that errors had been made in 1692, Mather urged the provincial legislators to comply with the petitioners' request. They had taken an essential first step in 1697 when they had called for a "General Day of Humiliation . . . to bewail the errors of our dark time." Now they must make reparations to the suffering innocent.[45]

Finally, the General Court took action. In May 1710, it appointed a committee to evaluate all the claims from accused witches or their survivors. Claimants requested compensation for court costs, jail expenses, travel costs to attend court sessions, and confiscated property. By November of the following year, the committee had received requests for £796 18s.[46] After sorting through the documentation, the General Court, on December 17, approved payment of £578 12s to claimants.[47] As they awaited the committee's recommendations for compensation, the General Court voted in October that the conviction and attainders of George Burroughs, John Proctor, George Jacobs, John Willard, Giles Corey, Martha Corey, Rebecca Nurse, Sarah Good, Elizabeth How, Mary Easty, Sarah Wildes, Abigail Hobbs, Samuel Wardwell, Mary Parker, Martha Carrier, Abigail Faulkner, Anne Foster, Rebecca Eames, Mary Post, Mary Lacey, Mary Bradbury, and Dorcas Hoar be reversed.[48] Along with their action in 1703, they had restored the good names of all but seven of the convicted. Apparently, no one stepped forward as an advocate for Bridget Bishop, Elizabeth Johnson, Susannah Martin, Alice Parker, Ann Pudeator, Wilmot Redd, or Margaret Scott because their convictions and attainders have never been reversed.

Not everyone was satisfied with the provincial government's belated effort to repair the damage done two decades earlier. The most important malcontent was Philip English. The Salem merchant had initiated his campaign for compensation in 1694. He sued Essex County sheriff George Corwin for confiscating his property. The provincial Superior Court ruled, however, that Corwin had acted within the law in taking the property of fugitives. Undaunted, English pursued the sheriff even after his death. He attached Corwin's estate in 1697 for just over £60 for debts owed him by the sheriff.[49] In the 1711 distribution of money to claimants, the General Court awarded English nothing. He returned to the legislators again in June 1717 with a claim "for a great part of his estate taken from him . . . in the late sorrowful time of the witchcraft." After a year and a half of negotiation and deliberation, a committee appointed to investigate his claim recommended compensation of two hundred pounds, a figure that the proud merchant promptly refused.[50]

English lived out his life believing that his good name as well as his property had been wrongfully taken from him. Others sought to remove completely the reproach connected to the names of those executed. Following the General Court's reversal of attainder in late 1711, Samuel Nurse successfully appealed to the church in Salem to remove the excommunication of his mother, Rebecca. At a private meeting in March 1712, church members noted that "the testimony on which she was convicted" was no longer "satisfactory to ourselves, and others." As a consequence, they voted to blot out of the church record her excommunication, "that it may no longer be a reproach to her memory, and an occasion of grief to her children." While they were at it, the church members decided to reverse their excommunication of Giles Corey. Some had supplied testimony "that before his death he did bitterly repent of his obstinate refusal to plead in defense of his life."[51]

The Bay colony struggled for years with the issue of justice and compensation for those who suffered in the witchcraft crisis. Assigning blame for it, however, began almost immediately. The letters from Governor Phips and most public confessions were often tortuous efforts at shifting the responsibility for the excesses of 1692. That was not satisfactory for those who believed that someone should be held accountable. Strangely, the justices on the Court of Oyer and Terminer did not suffer politically. In 1693, all of them were selected to the Governor's Council. Indeed, the judge who had the greatest difficulty following the trials was the one who quit the tribunal in protest, Nathaniel Saltonstall. Rumors reached the Haverhill judge that he would lose his place on the Council and that the governor intended to replace him as head of the North Essex militia. Worse, word spread that some were afflicted by his specter.[52] The troubled Saltonstall began to drink heavily, and the effects of it were obvious in the Council chamber. Samuel Sewall saw that he "had drunk to excess" and that his "head and hand were rendered less useful than at other times."[53]

The provincial clergy, because it had consistently though not forcefully opposed specter evidence, escaped essentially unscathed. The notable exceptions were Cotton Mather and Samuel Parris. Mather engaged in an eight-year struggle with Boston merchant Robert Calef to defend his actions in 1692. Calef's criticism began with the publication of Mather's *Wonders of the Invisible World*. While Mather had repeatedly advised the judges to use caution in handling specter evidence, he firmly believed that clergymen and jurists in Massachusetts had uncovered a diabolic plot against reformed Christianity. In his "zeal to assist" the judges destroy "as wonderful a piece of devilism as has been seen in the world," Mather wrote to William Stoughton, chief judge on the Court of Oyer and Terminer, in early September.

In this offer to help, Mather explained that he believed that the provincial clergy had an obligation "to do some singular thing in a way of testimony against those evils." His proposed contribution would be an essay "on the prodigious occasion that is now before us." Always properly deferential, Mather asked Stoughton if he could include an "account of the trials." He promised to submit the manuscript to the judge for approval and asked for an endorsement of the proposed work.[54] Mather then approached Governor Phips for his blessing, and Phips apparently suggested that the young clergyman contact Stephen Sewall, who served as the Court of Oyer and Terminer's clerk, for narratives of sample trials.[55] Sewall not only obliged but also met with Mather, Stoughton, John Hathorne, Salem minister John Higginson, and Samuel Sewall at the latter's house on September 22 to discuss "publishing some trials of the witches."[56]

Eager to get the work into print, Cotton Mather rapidly wrote a book that left him open to innumerable criticisms. Printed by mid–October, *Wonders of the Invisible World* is an eclectic collection of trial narratives, sermons, extracts of other works on witchcraft, and a liberal sprinkling of Mather's efforts to defend the judges' actions.[57] As his leading biographer, Kenneth Silverman, has observed, Mather created "an effect of endless jerky beginnings, obscured by tedious verbosity and an insuperable difficulty in getting to the point."[58] More important, he made his opposition to specter evidence a minor theme in the book and emerged as an advocate of the trials.[59] His timing could not have been worse. As he completed his book, his father was circulating his critique of the trials, *Cases of Conscience*. While over a dozen leading clergymen endorsed the elder Mather's work, Cotton could not. He worried because people were saying that "I run against my own father and all the ministers in the country." Yet, as he explained to his uncle, John Cotton, in an October 20 letter, Mather feared that opponents of the trials would use *Cases of Conscience* to condemn the judges:

I did, in *my* conscience, think that as the humors of this people now run, such a discourse going alone would not only enable our witch-advocates very learnedly to cavil and nibble at the late proceedings against the witches, considered in parcels, while things as they lay in bulk, with their whole dependencies, were not exposed; but also everlastingly stifle any further proceedings of justice, and more than so, produce a public and open contest with the judges, who would (though beyond the intention of the worthy author and subscribers) find themselves brought unto the bar before the rashest *Mobile*.[60]

Sensitive to the rumors that he had repudiated his son's rash defense of the judges, the elder Mather included a disclaimer in his postscript: "I perused and approved of that book before it was printed. And nothing but my relation to him hindered me from recommending it to the world."[61]

The elder Mather's statement had no impact on Robert Calef. He conducted a remarkably successful campaign to destroy Cotton Mather's credibility. Until recently, Mather has been vilified as a leading promoter of the witchcraft crisis. As Samuel Eliot Morison so colorfully put it, Robert Calef "tied a tin can to him after the frenzy was over; and it has rattled and banged through the pages of superficial and popular historians."[62] Calling his work *More Wonders of the Invisible World*, Calef not only attacked Mather's 1692 publication but also the minister's reports on two other cases of afflicted individuals. The circulation of his manuscript, and its eventual publication in 1700, contributed to a backlash against the Boston clergyman.

During the immediate aftermath of the Salem trials, the occult experiences of Mercy Short and Margaret Rule had attracted Mather's interest. Short began suffering afflictions following her visit in the spring of 1692 to the Boston jails holding accused witches. While there, Short had taunted Sarah Good. In response, Good "bestowed some ill words upon her." Soon afterward, the young servant woman began to suffer "fits as those which held the bewitched people then tormented by invisible furies in the county of Essex."[63] Unable to attend the proceedings in Salem because of illness, Mather seized this opportunity to counter the Devil's effort to expand his influence. As he prayed with Short, she seemed to recover. In November, however, she fell into fits again, which continued until March. Margaret Rule began to suffer her afflictions in September 1693, and her case drew Mather and others to her bedside on numerous days and nights. The two young women had similar extraordinary bouts with the occult world. They had confrontations with specters, suffered hallucinations, conversed with demonic voices, lost their appetites, endured horrid burning sensations, and developed skin lesions. A particularly frightening episode in Margaret Rule's case, according to Mather and several others who witnessed the scene, was the night her tormentor levitated her to the ceiling. Equally disturbing to Mather was Rule's claim that *his* specter had harmed her.[64]

Mather wrote an account of each case—"A Brand Plucked Out of the Burning" and "Another Brand Plucked Out of the Burning"—but did not seek a printer for either. Since the public mood had shifted so decisively against the trials, he correctly concluded that few would be receptive to a new account. Mather also worried that in her afflictions, Short had supplied new evidence against some of the accused in Salem, and she offered support for the validity of the now maligned specter evidence.[65] Finally, Mather certainly had no desire to give ammunition to his new antagonist, Robert Calef.

The Boston merchant had been outraged by the witchcraft episode and denounced the "zeal governed by blindness and passion" that he believed had characterized the actions of the clergy in 1692.[66] Calef ridiculed the contradictory role of Cotton Mather. Because the minister had defended the judges and preached about a massive Devil's plot, while at the same time advising caution in the use of specter evidence, Calef saw him as one who had carried "both fire to increase, and water, to quench, the conflagration."[67] Carefully monitoring Mather's actions in 1693 and fascinated by the Margaret Rule case, Calef attended one of the young woman's bouts with her occult oppressors, making sure that Mather would also be there. Joining over thirty other spectators in Rule's home, Calef said that Cotton, joined by his father, Increase, asked leading questions of Rule, drawing from her the answers that he wanted. He explained that the two Mathers also attempted to console Rule, whenever she suffered from fits, by the laying on of hands. Calef charged that the younger Mather went beyond comforting the young woman; he wantonly massaged her. "He laid his hand upon her face and nose," Calef wrote, "but, as he said, without perceiving breath; then he brushed her on the face with his glove, and rubbed her stomach (her breast not covered with the bed-cloths) and bid others do so too, and said it eased her, then she revived." When Rule once again fell into a fit, Mather "again rubbed her breast." When a woman in the room attempted to assist, according to Calef, Rule pushed her away, preferring the touch of the clergyman.[68]

When Calef circulated his version of the evening's events, Mather reacted with a stinging letter of denunciation. He told Calef that in reading his account of the episode, "I do scarcely find any one thing . . . either fairly or truly represented." Mather was particularly outraged that Calef had written that he rubbed Rule's stomach, "her breast not being covered." This lie, he said, had damaged his reputation. Now the people of Boston "believe a smutty thing of me."[69] Getting no retraction from Calef, Mather denounced him from the pulpit and filed suit against him for "scandalous libel." Even though Mather dropped the suit, he engaged in an extended exchange of angry letters with Calef, in which they debated a range of occult issues in addition to Mather's actions in the Margaret Rule case.[70] In 1698, Mather learned that Calef's book of "invented and notorious lies" would be published in England. When a copy of *More Wonders of the Invisible World* (which included "Another Brand Plucked from the Burning") reached Massachusetts, Increase Mather displayed his family's contempt by ordering a copy of it burned in the yard at Harvard College.[71]

The controversy with Calef took its toll on the sensitive clergyman. In the evening after Samuel Sewall's remarkable fast day confession of January 1697, he pondered "the Divine displeasure" with his family "for my not appearing with vigor enough to stop the proceedings of the judges, when the inextricable storm from the invisible world assaulted the country."[72]

Samuel Parris also could not escape denunciation for his role in the witchcraft affair. Renewed opposition to his ministry surfaced by mid-August of 1692. He called a special church meeting because "our brother Peter Cloyce, and Samuel Nurse and his wife, and John Tarbell and his wife have absented from communion with us at the Lord's Table, yea have very rarely (except our brother Samuel Nurse) been with us in common public worship."[73] Their absence represented a protest against Parris's March 27 sermon that implicated Rebecca Nurse, Samuel and Mary Tarbell's mother, in the witch plot. Peter Cloyce's wife, Sarah, had stormed from the meetinghouse and subsequently faced witchcraft charges. Rebecca Nurse had been executed on July 19, and Sarah Cloyce awaited trial in an Ipswich jail.[74] Parris could neither persuade the wayward to return nor reduce the ever widening breach in the village. Those who wanted him out before the witchcraft crisis joined with these dissenters over the next five years in pursuing his removal as Salem Village's pastor.

Occasionally, the two sides clashed over Parris's control of the parsonage or his back pay, but most often they returned to his actions in 1692. In the struggle, the minister's supporters and opponents fought each other with all the weapons available to them: election to the village tax committee, lawsuits, appeals to provincial authorities, and requests that outside clergymen intervene. Initially, Parris attempted to use persuasion. He met with the dissenters in his study almost a dozen times by July 1693 but made no progress. He sought reconciliation through the pulpit. In an October 1692 sermon, when explaining a verse from the Song of Solomon on allegorical kisses, Parris emphasized, "Kisses are exceeding sweet among friends that have been long absent. Why, so Christ's manifestation of his love after a long-seeming absence is exceeding sweet."[75] In his 1694 "Meditations for Peace," Parris even admitted making errors two years earlier and expressed his sorrow for the families that had suffered.[76] One of his antagonists, John Tarbell, told Parris frankly that his remorse was far too late. "If half so much had been said formerly," he explained, "it had never come to this."[77]

Unable to produce a consensus by persuasion, Parris worked closely with his supporters as they maneuvered to gain control of the village's only governmental body, the rate committee. That accomplished by March 1694, pro-Parris activists also successfully pursued former committee members for failing to levy a tax for their pastor's salary and won court orders for the village constables "to make distress on such persons as neglect or refuse to pay their respective rates." As they lost influence in the village and cases in court, Parris's opponents sought the aid of outside clergymen. Early in their confrontation, the dissenters had asked Parris to agree to an arbitration of their differences by a council of clergymen. Their repeated demands and consultations with neighboring ministers who contacted Parris on their behalf finally wore the Salem Village minister down. He agreed to lay before a panel of the province's leading clergymen and laymen the differences between himself and his opponents. Notable among the group were three ministers who had played critical roles in the witchcraft crisis: Increase Mather, Samuel Willard, and Cotton Mather.[78]

The seventeen men journeyed to Salem Village on April 3, 1695, and listened to the positions of both sides. Most likely, Parris's opponents submitted a document that they had given their pastor in late November 1694. In it, they explained that they had withdrawn from worship because of the "tumults and noises made by the persons under diabolical power and delusions" and because they feared "being accused as the Devil's instruments to molest and afflict the persons complaining." More important, they disapproved of the "principles and practices" of their pastor during and since the witchcraft crisis. His sermons on "our molestation from the invisible world" too often differed from "the generality of the orthodox ministers of the whole country." He too readily accepted the words of the afflicted and displayed too little "charity towards his neighbors, and especially towards those of his church." They believed that Parris gave "unsafe and unaccountable" testimony against several of the accused and failed to enter a fair account of the examinations when he served as a clerk for the court. Finally, he had persisted in his unsound principles and had rendered no "satisfaction to us when regularly desired, but rather farther offending and dissatisfying ourselves."[79] What people like John Tarbell and Samuel Nurse wanted from Parris was quite simple. In a private conversation with the pastor, the two men had made it clear that they desired him to admit that he had been "the great prosecutor" in the witchcraft crisis. They pointed out that "others wise and learned who had been as forward . . . were sorry for what they had done." Until Parris made as clear an admission, they could not return to worship with him.[80] Parris's "Meditations for Peace" speech in November 1694 had been insufficient; the only possible solution now was his dismissal.

For his part, Parris had a lengthy indictment against the dissenters that he had drafted in late 1693. The seventeen charges dealt largely with the dissenters failing to proceed in an acceptable way to resolve the conflict. They had repeatedly appealed to outsiders, delayed in responding to inquiries from the church, scandalized the church in their treatment of negotiators, and withdrawn "their purses . . . from upholding the Lord's Table and ministry." The most serious offense was their issuing "factious and seditious" libels about their pastor.[81]

The extraordinary council had the almost impossible task of trying to reconcile this bitterly divided community. Increase Mather, who served as moderator, issued the council's recommendation on April 4. The council acknowledged that during "the dark time of the confusions," Parris had taken "unwarrantable and uncomfortable steps." Yet the council pointed out that he had "tendered in his Christian acknowledgments of the errors therein committed." Moreover, Parris had "with much fidelity and integrity acquitted himself in the main course of his ministry since he hath been pastor to the church in Salem Village." Consequently, the council advised that Parris "be accordingly respected, honored, and supported."[82]

"Utterly frustrated" by the council's endorsement of Parris, village dissenters sent another petition to Increase Mather. They implored the Boston clergyman to "advise Mr. Parris . . . that he cannot with comfort or profit to himself or others abide in the work of the ministry among us." At the very least, they asked that Mather reconvene the council and consider the evidence anew. Most persuasive to Mather was that the dissenters had eighty-four signatures on their petition.[83] After consulting with his colleagues, Mather wrote to Parris explaining that such opposition made his "removal necessary."[84] Although Parris's supporters gathered 105 signatures on a petition to retain him "in his present station," it was clear that the embattled minister would have to leave.[85] The following spring he tendered his resignation.[86] The two factions in the village agreed to resolve the nagging issues of the pastor's back pay and his control of the parsonage by placing them before a panel of arbitrators. Appropriately, two of the three men that they agreed on brought back memories of the year of witch trials. Samuel Sewall and Wait Winthrop had served on the Court of Oyer and Terminer. (Elisha Cook was the third member.) In July 1697, the arbitrators ordered the village to pay Parris just over seventy-nine pounds and that he return the deed to the parsonage to the villagers.[87]

Only with Parris's departure could Salem Village begin to heal its long festering wounds. After an extensive search, the village had the great good fortune to hire twenty-two-year-old Joseph Green as their new pastor. He moved quickly to bring the dissenters back into the congregation. In November 1698, Green indicated to the members that the leading dissenters, John Tarbell, Samuel Nurse, and Thomas Wilkins (Peter and Sarah Cloyce had moved to Marlborough, Massachusetts), "were heartily desirous that they would join with us in all ordinances."[88] The members demonstrated the hope that all could "live lovingly together" by their unanimous consent. Six weeks later, the three families joined their brethren "in the Lord's Supper." Green called it a moment of "thankfulness, seeing they have for a long time been so offended as that they could not comfortably join with us."

Three years later, Green supported the request of friends and neighbors of Martha Corey to reverse her excommunication. With Green presiding, the congregation voted to grant their wish on February 14, 1703. In so doing, the church members in Salem Village chose, like some others who had admitted making mistakes in 1692, to take no responsibility for the excommunication of Corey. "We were at that dark day," they voted, "under the power of those errors which then prevailed in the land; and we are sensible that we had not sufficient grounds to think her guilty of that crime for which she was condemned and executed; and that her excommunication was not according to the mind of God."[89]

When the Salem Village congregation noted that they were "under the power of those errors which then prevailed in the land," the members did not mean that they erred in believing in witchcraft. They, along with virtually all their contemporaries, continued to believe in the invisible world. They still accepted the proposition that some individuals had occult powers. Even the critics of the trials conducted by the Court of Oyer and Terminer had been careful to note their firm belief in witches. After all, if an individual accepted the reality of God, he or she necessarily had to accept the idea that there was a Devil and his handmaidens, witches.[90] The available evidence indicates that few would question that belief. Judge Samuel Sewall, who anguished over his role in the deaths of the convicted witches, noted in his diary in early 1694: "This day Mrs. Prout dies after sore conflicts of mind, not without suspicion of witchcraft."[91]

In addition to his inquiry into the cases of Mercy Short and Margaret Rule, Cotton Mather returned to Salem in September 1693 for material to write a "complete *History* of the late *Witchcrafts and Possessions.* During his visit, Mather met a woman who predicted "a *new Storm of Witchcraft.*" It would "chastise the iniquity that was used in the willful smothering and covering of *the Last*; and that many fierce opposites to the discovery of that *Witchcraft* would bee thereby convinced." He had planned to give three sermons while in Salem, but his notes for the discourses disappeared. The circumstances convinced him that "specters, or agents in the *invisible world*, were the *robbers.*"[92]

There were also new indictments of witchcraft. In the summer of 1697, for example, Winifred Benham of Wallingford, Connecticut, went on trial following accusations by several neighborhood children. After failed searches for witches' teats and "the experiment of casting her into the water," the Superior Court at Hartford acquitted her because the only evidence against her was spectral.[93] That was the rub. Without specter evidence, it became almost impossible to convict witches. The Massachusetts General Court essentially closed the possibility of any future convictions in 1703 when it ruled that "no specter evidence may hereafter be accounted valid, or sufficient to take away the life, or good name, of any person or persons within this province."[94]

Charges of occult practices circulated in Salem Village again in 1746, but with this new perspective, no one suffered any legal penalties. Indeed, it became a matter exclusively of the church. Reverend Peter Clark reported to the congregation that he had information that "several persons in this parish" had "resorted to a woman of a very ill reputation, pretending to the art of divination and fortune-telling." First, the members approved a statement condemning such practices. They said that it was "highly impious and scandalous" for "Christians, especially church-members, to seek and consult reputed witches or fortune-tellers." Second, and most significant, the church members did not recommend a legal solution. Rather, they said that such a practice rendered "the persons guilty of it subject to the just censure of the church." Finding proof remained the difficulty, and when that was not forthcoming, the pastor's only recourse was a public admonition against

this infamous and ungodly practice of consulting witches or fortune-tellers, or any that are reputed such; exhorting all under their watch, who may have been guilty of it, to an hearty repentance and returning to God, earnestly seeking forgiveness in the blood of Christ, and warning all against the like practice for the time to come.[95]

New Englanders had decided, as had most authorities in Europe, that there were no reliable methods of detecting witches. As Eric Midelfort pointed out in his study of witchcraft in Germany, "It would seem that witch hunters in many regions stopped hunting and executing witches not because they no longer believed in them, but because they no longer knew how to find them."[96] As Samuel Willard had explained in 1692, "God never intended to bring to light all hidden works or workers of darkness in this world."[97]

The most compelling contemporary effort to that end came from the pen of Reverend John Hale, the pastor at Beverly, barely two miles from Salem. Although he had urged caution upon men like Samuel Parris, Hale, from the earliest days of the outbreak, had supported the 1692 assault on the witches. Since the end of the trials, he had worried about his role in the tragedy. He hoped in vain that one of the leading clergymen in the province would come forward with a treatise on the meaning of it. After considerable soul searching, he decided to offer his view of what had gone wrong and what lessons could be learned from the events of that awful year.[98] He revealed his interest in the project to Samuel Sewall in November 1697, and the judge, at a time when so many were bemoaning the evils caused by a zealous acceptance in 1692 of a belief in the power of witches, worried "lest he go into the other extreme."[99]

Within a month, Hale had finished the work, and early the next year, he persuaded the aged Salem pastor John Higginson to write an introduction. Higginson believed it an essential and timely work. He hoped that it would serve as a "warning and caution to those that come after us, that they may not fall into the like."[100] The manuscript did not find a publisher until 1702, two years after Hale's death. Perhaps he wanted it to serve as a posthumous confession; if so, *A Modest Inquiry into the Nature of Witchcraft* became a fitting testament to his concern for justice.

Hale saw no human villains in this tragedy, only people who made flawed decisions. The "justices, judges and others concerned" displayed "a conscientious endeavor to do the thing that was right."[101] Their actions, and his, however, had led to the shedding of innocent blood. Hale contended that there were plausible reasons for the course adopted by the esteemed judges and the initial support for the Court of Oyer and Terminer. They simply followed widely accepted principles from past cases. Chief among them was the notion that "the Devil could not assume the shape of an innocent person in doing mischief unto mankind." Additionally, they accepted the search for witches' teats or Devil's marks and testimony from accusers of mischief who had followed "anger between neighbors."[102] Support for the trials grew with the mounting accusations from the afflicted and the numerous confessions.[103]

"The numbers and quality" of people accused, however, challenged authorities to question their earlier convictions about their war against the forces of Satan. Several factors led Hale to reevaluate his position. Once the number of accused reached one hundred, he came to believe it unlikely that "so many in so small a compass of land should so abominably leap into the Devil's lap at once." He worried that too many of the accused were people of "blameless and holy lives." Particularly telling for him was the denial of guilt uttered by all who were executed. Out of that number, he would expect some "to seek mercy for their souls in the way of confession."[104] Belatedly, Hale concluded that he and the authorities, since the first case in the 1640s, had depended on flawed principles: "I do not say that all those were innocent that suffered in those times upon this account. But that such grounds were then laid down to proceed upon, which were too slender to evidence the crime they were brought to prove; and thereby a foundation laid to lead into error those that came after." As he pondered why so many decent people had been willing to condemn on the basis of "slender" evidence, Hale decided that Satan had manipulated them.

John Hale ultimately saw the tragedy of Salem as God's punishment for a profligate people. When He saw that His chosen people had departed from the founding generation's sense of divine mission, God had released Satan from his chains and permitted them to devour each other in a furious, futile struggle against witches:

The errand of our fathers into this wilderness, was to sacrifice to the Lord; that is, to worship God in purity of heart and life, and to wait upon the Lord, walking in the faith and order of the gospel in church fellowship; that they might enjoy Christ in all his ordinances. But these things have been greatly neglected and despised by many born, or bred up in the land. We have much forgotten what our fathers came into the wilderness to see. The sealing ordinances of the Covenant of Grace in church-communion have been much slighted and neglected; and the fury of this storm raised by Satan hath fallen very heavily upon many that lived under these neglects. The Lord sends evil angels to awaken and punish our negligence.[105]

His generation had made a choice. They could have followed the path of their revered predecessors. Unfortunately, they neglected their divine errand and pursued their own ends.

Hale was left with this remarkably telling explanation for the disaster of 1692: "But such was the darkness of that day, the tortures and lamentations of the afflicted, and the power of former precedents, that we walked in the clouds, and could not see our way."[106]

NOTES

1. Phips concluded the letter with an appeal: "Sir I beg pardon for giving you all this trouble, the reason is because I know my enemies are seeking to turn it all upon me and I take this liberty because I depend upon your friendship, and desire you will please to give a true understanding of the matter if anything of this kind be urged or made use of against me. Because the justness of my proceeding herein will be a sufficient defense"; see Paul Boyer and Stephen Nissenbaum, eds., *The Salem Witchcraft Papers* (New York, 1977), III, 861–863. He dispatched a second letter on February 21, 1693; see ibid., 863–865.

2. Ibid., 862.

3. See the petition from Andover residents, ibid., 875–876.

4. Ibid., 864.

5. Samuel Sewall reported that the judges received their commissions on December 22; see Mark Van Doren, ed., *Samuel Sewall's Diary* (New York, 1963), 110.

6. Boyer and Nissenbaum, eds., *Witchcraft Papers*, III, 864.

7. Ibid.

8. For this, they drew upon verses in Second Samuel and Joshua. See David C. Brown, "The Salem Witchcraft Trials: Samuel Willard's *Some Miscellany Observation*," *Essex Institute Historical Collections*, CXXII (July 1986), 223; Charles W. Upham, *Salem Witchcraft* (Boston, 1867), II, 540; and Increase Mather, *Cases of Conscience Concerning Evil Spirits* (Boston, 1693), 59.

9. Here, they followed verses in Deuteronomy and Matthew. See Mather, *Cases*, 65–66; Brown, "Witchcraft Trials," 225; and Upham, *Salem*, II, 540.

10. Hale, "A Modest Inquiry into the Nature of Witchcraft," in George Lincoln Burr, ed., *Narratives of the Witchcraft Cases, 1648–1706* (New York, 1975), reprint, 422.

11. Boyer and Nissenbaum, eds., *Witchcraft Papers*, III, 887–901.

12. Ibid., 904–950.

13. Ibid., 865.

14. In his dispatches to England, Phips did his best to shift the blame for the excesses of the crisis to someone else, usually William Stoughton. In his

October letter, Phips emphasized, "I was almost the whole time of the proceeding abroad in the service of Their Majesties in the eastern part of the country and depended upon the judgment of the Court as to a right method of proceeding in cases of witchcraft." He openly blamed Stoughton for the colony's misery in the February dispatch: "The Lieut. Gov. . . . hath from the beginning hurried on these matters with great precipitancy and by his warrant hath caused the estates, goods, and chattels of the executed to be seized and disposed of without my knowledge or consent." See Boyer and Nissenbaum, eds., *Witchcraft Papers*, III, 861 and 865.

15. Robert Calef, "More Wonders of the Invisible World," in Burr, ed., *Narratives*, 382–383.

16. Boyer and Nissenbaum, eds., *Witchcraft Papers*, III, 904–930.

17. In Robert Calef's account, he spelled her name as Dastin. Calef confused thirty-nine-year-old Sarah Dustin with her mother, Lydia; see "More Wonders," 383.

18. Ibid.

19. His second letter, composed in February 1693, did not arrive at Whitehall until May 24, 1693; see Boyer and Nissenbaum, eds., *Witchcraft Papers*, III, 863–865.

20. *Essex Institute Historical Collections*, IX (1868), 88–90.

21. Calef, "More Wonders," 384.

22. Boyer and Nissenbaum, eds., *Salem-Village Witchcraft: A Documentary Record of Local Conflict in Colonial New England* (Belmont, CA, 1972), 297–298. The following year, upon the prodding of other clergymen, Parris confessed, "I fear that in and through the throng of many things written by me, in the late confusions, there has not been a due exactness always used; and, as I now see the inconveniency of my writing so much on those difficult occasions, so I would lament every error of such writings"; see ibid., 298.

23. Ibid., 299.

24. Ibid.

25. Melyen was a leather seller and Boston constable; see James Savage, *A Genealogical Dictionary of the First Settlers of New England* (Baltimore, 1986), reprint, III, 196.

26. Van Doren, ed., *Sewall Diary*, 134.

27. Ibid., 135.

28. Chadwick Hansen, *Witchcraft at Salem* (New York, 1969), 264.

29. Van Doren, ed., *Sewall Diary*, 136; and Calef, "More Wonders," 386.

30. Van Doren, ed., *Sewall Diary*, 137–138.

31. Ibid., 140.

32. Calef, "More Wonders," 387–388.

33. Boyer and Nissenbaum, eds., *Salem-Village Witchcraft*, 379.

34. Ibid., 270.

35. Upham, *Salem*, II, 510.

36. Calef, "More Wonders," 386.

37. Boyer and Nissenbaum, eds., *Witchcraft Papers*, III, 865, 963, 964, 972, and 1043; Richard D. Pierce, ed., *The Records of the First Church in Salem, Massachusetts, 1629-1736* (Salem, 1974), 219; and Boyer and Nissenbaum, eds., *Salem-Village Witchcraft*, 255 and 306.

38. Boyer and Nissenbaum, eds., *Witchcraft Papers*, III, 963-964.

39. Ibid., 963-964.

40. Hale, "Modest Inquiry," 427.

41. Boyer and Nissenbaum, eds., *Witchcraft Papers*, III, 966-969.

42. Ibid., 970.

43. *Massachusetts Historical Society Collections*, 4th Ser., VIII, (Boston, 1868), 646.

44. Boyer and Nissenbaum, eds., *Witchcraft Papers*, III, 973.

45. Hansen, *Witchcraft*, 274-275.

46. Boyer and Nissenbaum, eds., *Witchcraft Papers*, III, 1012. This total did not include any of Philip English's requests for £1183.

47. Ibid., 1017-1018.

48. Ibid., 1015-1017.

49. Bryan F. Le Beau, "Philip English and the Witchcraft Hysteria," *Historical Journal of Massachusetts*, XV (January 1987), 6 and 17 n. 35.

50. Ibid., 7 and 8; and Boyer and Nissenbaum, eds., *Witchcraft Papers*, III, 1043-1045.

51. Pierce, ed., *Salem Church Records*, 219.

52. Robert E. Moody, ed., *The Saltonstall Papers, 1607-1815* (Boston, 1972), I, 53 and 211.

53. Ibid., 211-212.

54. Kenneth Silverman, ed., *Selected Letters of Cotton Mather* (Baton Rouge, LA, 1971), 44.

55. Ibid., 45.

56. Van Doren, ed., *Sewall Diary*, 108.

57. He barely beat the governor's order forbidding any further publications on the subject of witchcraft. See the first page of this chapter.

58. Silverman, *The Life and Times of Cotton Mather* (New York, 1984), 115.

59. See the discussion in ibid., 114-118; and Hansen, *Witchcraft*, 216-221.

60. Silverman, ed., *Letters*, 45.

61. Increase Mather, *Cases*, postscript.

62. Morison, *The Intellectual Life of Colonial New England* (Ithaca, NY, 1970), reprint, 259. Beginning with Chadwick Hansen and continuing with the work of David Levin and Kenneth Silverman, Mather's reputation has been partially restored, *Witchcraft at Salem*; *Cotton Mather, The Young Life of the Lord's Remembrancer, 1663-1703* (Cambridge, MA, 1978); and *The Life and Times of Cotton Mather*. Critics remain, however. Russell K. Osgood has recently argued that Mather lost influence in New England "because he was a hypocrite and a windbag"; see "John Clark, Esq., Justice of the Peace,

1667–1728," in Daniel R. Coquillette, ed., *Law in Colonial Massachusetts, 1630–1800* (Boston, 1984), 108 n. 1.

63. Mather, "A Brand Plucked Out of the Burning," in Burr, ed., *Narratives*, 259–260.

64. Ibid., 259–287; and Calef, "More Wonders," 308–323. Also, see Hansen's account of the Short and Rule cases, *Witchcraft*, 221–237, and Silverman's, *Life and Times*, 120–135.

65. Silverman, *Life and Times*, 121.

66. Calef, "More Wonders," 299.

67. Silverman, *Life and Times*, 130.

68. Calef, "More Wonders," 325.

69. Silverman, ed., *Letters*, 50–51.

70. Silverman, *Life and Times*, 132–134.

71. Calef, "More Wonders," 293.

72. *Diary of Cotton Mather* (New York, 1957), I, 216.

73. Boyer and Nissenbaum, eds., *Salem-Village Witchcraft*, 279.

74. Larry Gragg, *A Quest for Security, The Life of Samuel Parris, 1653–1720* (Westport, CT, 1990), 153.

75. Parris, Sermon Book, October 23, 1692, 162.

76. Boyer and Nissenbaum, eds., *Salem-Village Witchcraft*, 297–299.

77. Ibid., 295.

78. This protracted struggle can be followed in Gragg, *Quest*, 153–167.

79. Boyer and Nissenbaum, eds., *Salem-Village Witchcraft*, 296–297.

80. Ibid., 282–283.

81. Ibid., 302–303.

82. Ibid., 306–308.

83. Ibid., 260–262.

84. Ibid., 308.

85. Ibid., 262–263.

86. Ibid., 311.

87. Ibid., 265–268.

88. Upham, *Salem*, II, 506–507.

89. Ibid., 507.

90. *Proceedings of the Massachusetts Historical Society*, 2d Ser., III (1884–1885), 354–355; and Increase Mather, *Cases*, preface.

91. Van Doren, ed., *Sewall Diary*, 115.

92. *Mather Diary*, 171–172.

93. Calef, "More Wonders," 385; and John M. Taylor, *The Witchcraft Delusion in Colonial Connecticut, 1647–1697* (New York, 1908), 155.

94. Boyer and Nissenbaum, eds., *Witchcraft Papers*, III, 970.

95. Upham, *Salem*, II, 513.

96. Midelfort, *Witch Hunting in Southwestern Germany, 1562–1684* (Stanford, 1972), 6. Also, see Joseph Klaits, *Servants of Satan, The Age of the Witch Hunts* (Bloomington, IN, 1985); and G. R. Quaife, *Godly Zeal and Furious Rage: The Witch in Early Modern Europe* (New York, 1987).

97. Brown, "Witchcraft Trials," 232.

98. Hale's ruminations can be seen in his preface to "Modest Inquiry," 402–405.

99. Van Doren, ed., *Sewall Diary*, 146.

100. Hale, "Modest Inquiry," 401–402.

101. Ibid., 415.

102. Ibid., 411.

103. Ibid., 421.

104. Ibid., 412, 423, and 424.

105. Ibid., 429.

106. Ibid., 427.

Ten

Afterword: Interpretations

"It is faintly embarrassing for a historian to summon his colleagues to still another consideration of early New England witchcraft." That is the way that John Demos began an article on Salem witchcraft in 1970.[1] He quoted two venerable scholars of New England Puritans, Samuel Eliot Morison and Perry Miller, who had argued that the episode represented little more than "a small incident in the history of a great superstition."[2] Demos's apologetic introduction to his important article suggested that there remained little interest among scholars in analyzing the events in Salem. To the contrary, Demos's work inaugurated a flood of major studies that continued unabated in the following two decades.[3] The output demonstrates the continuing fascination that scholars and laymen alike have retained with this early American encounter with the occult.

Beginning with the works of Cotton Mather, Robert Calef, and John Hale, authors have attempted to explain how the outbreak of witchcraft in Salem almost overwhelmed the province in a wave of accusations. Beginning with those who lived through the events, the concern of most analysts was to assign blame. Contemporaries grappled with Satan's role in the affair. Embracing the reality of witchcraft, many wondered if the Devil had not manipulated the people of New England into an orgy of destructive accusations.

With the passing of the participants, writers began to discount a satanic role and sought instead to assign blame to human agents for the tragedy. By the mid-eighteenth century, Thomas Hutchinson, in his history of Massachusetts, was certain that he understood what had happened.

Anyone who still believed that there was anything preternatural in the afflictions of the accusers was being overly "kind and charitable." Such a notion, he argued, was "winking the truth out of sight." Hutchinson believed that the events in Salem had been caused by "fraud and imposture." Begun "by young girls, who at first perhaps thought of nothing more than being pitied and indulged," it had been "continued by adult persons, who were afraid of being accused themselves." The two groups, "rather than confess their fraud, suffered the lives of so many innocents to be taken away, through the credulity of judges and juries."[4]

This argument remained persuasive well into the nineteenth century and reached full development in the writings of Charles Upham. A clergyman and mayor of Salem, Upham published a two-volume account of the witchcraft episode in 1867. The accusing girls, he argued, "had acquired consummate boldness and tact." They had no equals "in simulation of passions, sufferings and physical affections; in sleight of hand, and in the management of voice and feature and attitude." He concluded, "There has seldom been better acting in a theatre than displayed in the presence of the astonished and horror-stricken rulers."[5] Marion L. Starkey, in her 1949 work *The Devil in Massachusetts*, likewise challenged the integrity of the accusers. She believed that the afflicted (whom she called "bobbysoxers") participated in an "emotional orgy" of accusations because they were "depressed by the lack of any legitimate outlet for their natural high spirit."[6]

Upham joined several authors who also blamed the clergy for the excesses of Salem. One of the most popular historians of the nineteenth century, George Bancroft, argued that New England's ministers played upon the superstitious beliefs of the masses to regain lost influence. He was particularly harsh with Cotton Mather, charging that the Boston clergyman "staked his own reputation for veracity on the reality of witchcraft."[7] For Bancroft, Mather was an "example how far selfishness, under the form of vanity and ambition, can blind the faculties, stupefy the judgment, and dupe consciousness itself."[8] That characterization is also evident among the influential "progressive" historians of the twentieth century, notably Vernon Louis Parrington. In his *Main Currents in American Thought*, Parrington described the Salem witchcraft episode as a "common seventeenth-century delusion." Cotton Mather's role was clear; he "not only ran with the mob, but he came near to outdistancing the most credulous. His speech and writings dripped with devil-talk."[9]

In addition to Mather, critics targeted Samuel Parris for part of the blame. Upham contended that the Salem Village pastor supported the campaign against the witches to bolster his faltering religious authority.[10] George Bancroft believed that Parris acted out of "personal malice" and "blind zeal."[11] Brooks Adams, in an 1887 book that was sharply critical of Puritan culture, argued that Parris was "a madman" who not only preached "inflammatory sermons," but also:

. . . conducted the examinations, and his questions were such that the evidence was in truth nothing but what he put in the mouths of the witnesses; yet he seems to have been guilty of a darker crime, for there is reason to suppose he garbled the testimony it was his sacred duty to truly record.[12]

Marion Starkey echoed this view of Parris, characterizing him as a man of "credulity and pitiless zeal," eager to prosecute suspected witches.[13]

Chadwick Hansen has argued that clergymen, including Cotton Mather, actually sought to restrain the excesses of the witchcraft crisis. He chose to blame, in part, the individuals who were accused of practicing witchcraft. He made the case that Goody Glover, Bridget Bishop, Candy, and Wilmot Reed used black magic to harm people and said that it is likely that George Burroughs, Sarah Good, Samuel Wardwell, and Roger Toothaker also practiced witchcraft.[14] Asserting that witchcraft works in a society that believes in the power of the occult, Hansen argued that these individuals' efforts to work black magic lent credence to the fears of the people of Salem. In that sense, they contributed to the crisis atmosphere.[15]

In the past two decades, scholars have been less interested in the debate over blame than in exploring the psychological, social, and economic dimensions of the witchcraft crisis. Many have employed a number of social scientific techniques from a variety of disciplines, notably sociology, anthropology, and psychology. The resulting body of work has led to both enlightenment and confusion.

Some authors have argued that the afflicted used witchcraft to resist authority, but they cannot agree on the motives that inspired the challenges. In a 1972 article called "Salem Revisited," Roger Thompson argued that the Salem episode had a "liberating effect" on the afflicted; it was an "exhilarating shattering of conventions of respect for age and visible sainthood."[16] John Demos agreed that participants in the Salem episode, particularly the afflicted, exploited it to challenge "conventional standards and received authority." Yet he saw something else involved. In *Entertaining Satan*, Demos contended that "attention-seeking or outright exhibitionism" was another aspect of the afflicted's behavior. They hoped to gain some fame in their villages through their actions.[17]

Lyle Koehler believed that gender relationships were the preeminent concerns in these challenges of authority. Witchcraft presented an "avenue for female resistance and for the assertion of female power."[18] David Konig contended, in his *Law and Society in Puritan Massachusetts*, that focusing on one factor was missing the point. "The people of Essex," he wrote, understood that witchcraft was "a social tool to be used by anyone—regardless of economic factors—for the purpose of overstepping or challenging established authority patterns."[19]

This "inner" dimension of seventeenth-century witchcraft has been particularly attractive to recent scholars. John Demos has emerged as the leading practitioner of the psychohistorical analysis of witchcraft. Of special interest to Demos is the theme of "projection." In his influential 1970 article, he explained its role in the behavior of the afflicted:

The seizures themselves have the essential character of attacks: in one sense, physical attacks by the witches on the persons of the accusers and in another sense, verbal attacks by the accusers on the reputations and indeed the very lives of the witches. This points directly toward one of the most important inner processes involved in witchcraft, the process psychologists call "projection," defined roughly as "escape from repressed conflict by attributing . . . emotional drives to the external world." In short, the dynamic core of belief in witchcraft in early New England was the difficulty experienced by many individuals in finding ways to handle their own aggressive impulses. Witchcraft accusation provided one of the few approved outlets for such impulses in Puritan culture. Aggression was thus denied in the self and attributed directly to others. The accuser says, in effect: "I am not attacking you; you are attacking me!" In reality, however, the accuser is attacking the witch, and in an extremely dangerous manner, too. Witchcraft enables him to have it both ways; the impulse is denied and gratified at the same time.[20]

In *Salem Possessed*, Paul Boyer and Stephen Nissenbaum agreed that the afflicted projected onto the accused "unacknowledged impulses which lay within themselves." Yet where Demos saw them as "aggressive impulses," Boyer and Nissenbaum identified them as attractions to the material world. In their analysis of Salem witchcraft, they argued that the accusations could best be understood as part of "the resistance of back-country farmers to the pressures of commercial capitalism and the social style that accompanied it."[21] The village farmers' resentment of their more cosmopolitan Salem neighbors led the farmers to accuse them of witchcraft. The authors reasoned, however, that some accusers saw "that they were themselves being transformed by the forces of change that were buffeting Salem Village" and projected their guilt onto the accused.[22]

This confusion over the "inner" dimension of witchcraft episodes can best be seen in the dissimilar meanings that three historians have read into the experiences of Elizabeth Knapp.[23]

Carol Karlsen saw in the Knapp case support for Lyle Koehler's argument concerning gender resistance. In the young Groton maiden's possession, Karlsen detected a challenge to her master and minister, Samuel Willard:

He was a young, well-off Harvard-educated minister whose life was full of promise; she was a young woman with little schooling and little prospect of anything but service to others, whether as a servant, daughter, or wife. He spent most of his time reading, writing, and traveling; she had never been taught to write, seldom left Groton, and spent her time sweeping his house, caring for his children, carrying his wood, keeping his fires burning—all so he could continue his work in peace and comfort.[24]

John Demos, however, found a sixteen-year-old who had regressed to episodes of her infancy and childhood. From a troubled family—her father was prosecuted for adultery, her mother apparently went insane, and her only sibling died at four months—Knapp was quite ill. As Demos diagnosed her situation, she "missed those forms of parenting that are most essential to inner development. Her budding self never achieved secure 'cohesion' because she was not adequately *recognized*, or *affirmed*, or *empowered*, by the people closest around her." "Her 'grandiose' yearnings, . . . were ignored or rebuffed; driven underground, they survived in archaic form to present her developing ego with a constant threat of disruptive intrusion." The death of her "little brother froze her infantile rage so as to make it inaccessible to the influence of subsequent experience." As she grew older, Knapp "looked in vain for someone new to idealize. Her relation to the Rev. Willard proved especially hopeful in prospect—and bitterly disappointing in actual result." Her possession, in Demos's words, "wove together all these threads of narcissistic imbalance: rage, archaic grandiosity and the demand for mirroring, attachment to a figure of eminence."[25]

When David Hall read the evidence from the Knapp case, he saw a young woman on "the threshold of conversion." In her discussions with the Reverend Willard, she had admitted that she had not been a good Christian. She confessed to a multitude of sins. Not only had she neglected the ordinances of the church but she had also disobeyed her parents and had attempted to commit suicide and murder. "Resisting even as she confessed," Hall explained, "she acted out her resistance in the form of her alter-ego, the devil-voice that saucily defied the minister." To Hall, the significance of the episode lay in Knapp's effort to reconcile herself with the church.[26]

The most provocative recent effort to explain the witchcraft accusations of the seventeenth century is that of Carol Karlsen. In *The Devil in the Shape of a Woman*, Karlsen developed a collective portrait not only of the accused but also of the people who accused them of practicing witchcraft. She concluded that "most witches in New England were middle-aged or old women eligible for inheritances because they had no brothers or sons."[27] As such, "they stood in the way of the orderly transmission of property from one generation of males to another."[28] As land became more scarce in the more settled communities, men began to resent these women who had access to it through a demographic accident. The resentment was expressed in witchcraft accusations. "Whether as actual or potential inheritors of property, as healers or tavern-keepers or merchants," Karlsen argued, "most accused witches were women who symbolized the obstacles to property and prosperity."[29]

It is easy to give up in this often bewildering search for "the ideological and socio-economic origins of witchcraft."[30] Were the accusers attempting to rid their communities of capitalists or women who controlled property that should belong to men? Were they resentful? Were they simply projecting "unacknowledged impulses"? Most important, where are the witches in these analyses? As critics of Boyer and Nissenbaum's *Salem Possessed* have pointed out, "They never suggest that there might have been a witch in New England, or any sound evidence of witchcraft."[31] The most persistent questions have concerned the use of psychoanalytic "models" in witchcraft studies. Which theoretical model is best? Can concepts such as "narcissistic rage," which are useful in modern psychoanalysis, be applied to people of a different age?[32] Is there a danger, as one reviewer of John Demos's work has asked, in concentrating on "explaining away witchcraft beliefs and practices by revealing their latent psychological and social meanings"?[33] Most important, is there too little evidence to employ psychoanalytic techniques? As Lyle Koehler has argued, "At best, all analyses of causation are speculative, since we have no live Puritans before us—Puritans whose mentalities we can probe in elaborate detail."[34]

Despite these serious reservations about some of their work, the scholars of the past twenty years have provided a clearer understanding of seventeenth-century demographic patterns; of class structure in Massachusetts villages; of clashes between the agricultural and commercial elements of the population; and of the relationships between men and women, and between adults and children. More to the point, they have expanded our understanding of seventeenth-century witchcraft. In a recent judicious review of the literature, David Hall has shown that a consensus has emerged on a number of fundamental points. "We may safely conclude," he wrote, "that witchcraft accusations originated in local conflict and personal misfortune." Most of the participants in the episodes not only knew each other but also lived close together. Usually, witches were "older women, many of them marginal or deviant in some respect: in social or economic position, sexual behavior, or possibly religious attitude. Anyone who practiced folk healing or fortune-telling became vulnerable to accusations of witchcraft." Further, it is evident that "belief in witchcraft is not 'irrational' . . . accusations of witchcraft were a constant feature of the village community."[35]

Hall was careful to point out, however, that much of the above does not apply to witch panics like the one in Salem Village in 1692.[36] Indeed, that is the greatest weakness of the scholarship of the past two decades. As engaging and helpful as it has been, it does not adequately explain why Salem Village's outbreak of accusations, unlike those that had come before, turned into a thorough witch hunt. I have tried to show that the best way to appreciate the unique experience of Salem Village is to explore the particular decisions made by the individuals involved and their consequences. The diagnosis of the afflicted by physicians; Samuel Parris's furious attack upon witchcraft from the pulpit; and the judges' acceptance and the clergy's qualified support of specter evidence all contributed to the rapid expansion of the witch crisis.

Individuals' decisions also played a paramount role in the end of the witch hunt. When it became clear that a confession would enable them to escape the gallows, several of the accused chose execution rather than renouncing their innocence, a courageous decision that caused many observers to reconsider their faith in the judicial proceedings. When nearly 300 individuals decided to testify or sign petitions on behalf of the accused, they contributed to a shift in public opinion on the advisability of continuing the trials. As an increasing number of articulate and vocal critics voiced their outrage against the examinations and trials, provincial officials began to consider an end to the proceedings. Finally, the courage of Samuel Sewall, Ann Putnam, and several of the jurors to admit error in the aftermath of the trials helped promote reconciliation.

These were not just "obscure and inarticulate men and women" whose "lives were being shaped by powerful forces of historical change."[37]

Rather, they were individuals whose decisions had a significant impact on the outcome of events in Salem Village. Their actions remind us that people are not passive victims of historical change but active participants who exercise some control over their lives and who help shape the past.

NOTES

1. John Demos, "Underlying Themes in the Witchcraft of Seventeenth-Century New England," *American Historical Review*, LXXV (June 1970), 1311.

2. Ibid.

3. Paul Boyer and Stephen Nissenbaum, *Salem Possessed, The Social Origins of Witchcraft* (Cambridge, MA, 1974); David C. Brown, "The Case of Giles Corey," *Essex Institute Historical Collections*, CXXI (October 1985), 282–299; David C. Brown, "The Salem Witchcraft Trials: Samuel Willard's *Some Miscellany Observations*," *Essex Institute Historical Collections*, CXXII (July 1986), 207–236; Jon Butler, "Magic, Astrology, and the Early American Religious Heritage, 1600–1760," *American Historical Review*, LXXXIV (April 1979), 317–346; John Demos, *Entertaining Satan, Witchcraft and the Culture of Early New England* (New York, 1982); John Demos, "John Godfrey and His Neighbors: Witchcraft and the Social Web in Colonial Massachusetts," *William and Mary Quarterly*, 3d Ser., XXXIII (April 1976), 242–265; Richard Gildrie, "Visions of Evil: Popular Culture, Puritanism and the Massachusetts Witchcraft Crisis of 1692," *Journal of American Culture*, VIII (Winter 1985), 17–33; Larry Gragg, *A Quest for Security, The Life of Samuel Parris, 1653–1720* (Westport, CT, 1990); David D. Hall, "Witchcraft and the Limits of Interpretation," *New England Quarterly*, LVIII (June 1985), 253–281; David D. Hall, *Worlds of Wonder, Days of Judgment, Popular Religious Belief in Early New England* (New York, 1989); Chadwick Hansen, "Andover Witchcraft and the Causes of the Salem Witchcraft Trials," in Howard Kerr and Charles L. Crow, eds., *The Occult in America: New Historical Perspectives* (Urbana, IL, 1983), 38–57; Christine Heyrman, "Spectres of Subversion, Societies of Friends: Dissent and the Devil in Provincial Essex County, Massachusetts," in David D. Hall, et al., eds., *Saints and Revolutionaries: Essays on Early American History* (New York, 1984); Carol F. Karlsen, *The Devil in the Shape of a Woman, Witchcraft in Colonial New England* (New York, 1987); James Kenses, "Some Unexplored Relationships of Essex County Witchcraft to the Indian Wars of 1675 and 1689," *Essex Institute Historical Collections*, CXX (July 1984), 179–212; Ann Kibbey, "Mutations of the Supernatural: Witchcraft, Remarkable Providences, and the Power of Puritan Men," *American Quarterly*, XXXIV (September 1982), 125–148; Lyle Koehler, *A Search for Power, The "Weaker Sex" in Seventeenth-Century New England* (Urbana, IL, 1980); David Thomas Konig, *Law and Society in Puritan Massachusetts,*

Essex County, 1629-1692 (Chapel Hill, NC, 1979); Bryan F. Le Beau, "Philip English and the Witchcraft Hysteria," *Historical Journal of Massachusetts*, XV (January 1987), 1-20; Marilynne K. Roach, "'That Child, Betty Parris': Elizabeth (Parris) Barron and the People in Her Life," *Essex Institute Historical Collections*, CXXIV (January 1988), 1-26; Marshall W. S. Swan, "The Bedevilment of Cape Ann (1692)," *Essex Institute Historical Collections*, CXVII (July 1981), 153-177; Roger Thompson, "Salem Revisited," *American Studies*, VI (December 1972), 317-346; Richard Weisman, *Witchcraft, Magic, and Religion in 17th Century Massachusetts* (Amherst, MA, 1984); and Richard Werking, "'Reformation Is Our Only Preservation': Cotton Mather and Salem Witchcraft," *William and Mary Quarterly*, 3d Ser., XXIX (April 1972), 281-290.

4. Hutchinson, *The History of the Colony and Province of Massachusetts-Bay*, edited by Lawrence Shaw Mayo, (New York, 1970), reprint, II, 47.

5. Upham quoted in James West Davidson and Mark Hamilton Lytle, *After the Fact, The Art of Historical Detection* (New York, 1982), I, 36.

6. Starkey, *The Devil in Massachusetts, A Modern Enquiry into the Salem Witch Trials* (Garden City, NY, 1969), reprint, 14.

7. Bancroft, *History of the United States of America from the Discovery of the Continent* (Boston, 1879), II, 256.

8. Ibid., 266.

9. Parrington, *Main Currents in American Thought* (New York, 1954), reprint, I, 116.

10. Upham, *Salem Witchcraft* (Boston, 1867), I, 300-312.

11. Bancroft, *History of United States*, II, 257.

12. Adams, *The Emancipation of Massachusetts, The Dream and the Reality* (Boston, 1962), reprint, 394-395.

13. Starkey, *Devil*, 214.

14. Hansen, "Salem Witches and DeForest's *Witching Times*," *Essex Institute Historical Collections* CIV (April 1968), 89-108; and *Witchcraft at Salem* (New York, 1969), 93-120.

15. Carol Karlsen has complained that this argument is tantamount to blaming the victim; see Karlson, *Devil*, 117-118 and 309 n. 1. David D. Hall, however, thinks that there is something to Hansen's argument. "Certainly some of the accused in the Salem panic," he has written, "were fortune-tellers in the manner of cunning folk"; see Hall, "Limits of Interpretation," 265.

16. Thompson, "Salem Revisited," 325.

17. Demos, *Entertaining Satan*, 159-160.

18. Koehler, *Search for Power*, 294.

19. Konig, *Law and Society*, 178.

20. Demos, "Underlying Themes," 1322.

21. Boyer and Nissenbaum, *Salem Possessed*, 180.

22. Ibid., 215-216.

23. See Chapter 1.

24. Karlsen, *Devil*, 246-247.

25. Demos, *Entertaining Satan*, 128.

26. Hall, "Limits of Interpretation," 278–279.

27. Karlsen, *Devil*, 117.

28. Ibid., 116.

29. Ibid., 217.

30. Ibid., 222.

31. *Virginia Quarterly Review*, L (Autumn 1974), CXXXVIII and CXXXIX.

32. David Hall raised this question, "Limits of Interpretation," 271.

33. Michael McDonald, "New England's Inner Demons," *Reviews in American History*, XI (September 1983), 324.

34. Koehler, *Search for Power*, 276. John Demos contends that there is sufficient evidence. He cited Samuel Willard's carefully kept account of Elizabeth Knapp's possession, Cotton Mather's writings in the Goody Glover case, and the numerous court records; see Demos, "Underlying Themes," 1320.

35. Hall, "Limits of Interpretation," 279–280.

36. Ibid., 280.

37. Boyer and Nissenbaum, "Salem Possessed: The Social Origins of Witchcraft," in Stanley N. Katz and John M. Murrin, eds., *Colonial America, Essays in Politics and Social Development* (New York, 1983), 344.

Select Bibliography

This list of sources is not a comprehensive one. Rather, it includes the most useful printed primary materials on witchcraft in the English colonies and secondary works on witchcraft on both sides of the Atlantic. Whenever possible, the latest edition of a work is included.

PUBLISHED PRIMARY SOURCES

Boyer, Paul, and Nissenbaum, Stephen, eds. *Salem-Village Witchcraft: A Documentary Record of Local Conflict in Colonial New England.* Belmont, CA: Wadsworth, 1972.

———. *The Salem Witchcraft Papers.* 3 vols. New York: Da Capo Press, 1977.

Burr, George Lincoln, ed. *Narratives of the Witchcraft Cases: 1648–1706.* New York: Barnes and Noble, 1975. Reprint.

Dow, George Francis, ed. *Records And Files of The Quarterly Courts of Essex County, Massachusetts.* 8 vols. Salem, MA: Essex Institute, 1911–1921.

Drake, Samuel G. *Annals of Witchcraft in New England.* New York: Benjamin Blom, 1967. Reprint.

Hall, David D., ed. *Witch-Hunting in Seventeenth-Century New England: A Documentary History, 1638–1692.* Boston: Northeastern University Press, 1991.

Woodward, W. Elliot, ed. *Records of Salem Witchcraft Copied from the Original Documents.* 2 vols. New York: Da Capo Press, 1969. Reprint.

BOOKS

Bever, Edward. "Old Age and Witchcraft in Early Modern Europe." In *Old Age in Preindustrial Society*, ed. Peter N. Stearns, 173–180. New York: Holmes and Meier, 1982.

Boyer, Paul, and Nissenbaum, Stephen. *Salem Possessed: The Social Origins of Witchcraft*. Cambridge, MA: Harvard University Press, 1974.

Cohn, Norman. *Europe's Inner Demons: An Enquiry Inspired by the Great Witch-Hunt*. New York: New American Library, 1975.

Demos, John. *Entertaining Satan: Witchcraft and the Culture of Early New England*. New York: Oxford University Press, 1982.

Easlea, Brian. *Witch Hunting, Magic, and the New Philosophy: An Introduction to Debates of the Scientific Revolution, 1450–1750*. Atlantic Highlands, NJ: Humanities Press, 1980.

Erikson, Kai T. *Wayward Puritans: A Study in the Sociology of Deviance*. New York: Wiley, 1966.

Fox, Sanford, J. *Science and Justice: The Massachusetts Witchcraft Trials*. Baltimore: Johns Hopkins Press, 1968.

Ginzburg, Carlo. *The Night Battles: Witchcraft and Agrarian Cults in the 16th and 17th Centuries*. New York: Penguin Books, 1985. Reprint.

Gragg, Larry. *A Quest for Security: The Life of Samuel Parris, 1653–1720*. Westport, CT: Greenwood Press, 1990.

Hall, David D. *Worlds of Wonder, Days of Judgment: Popular Religious Belief in Early New England*. New York: Knopf, 1989.

Hansen, Chadwick. "Andover Witchcraft and the Causes of the Salem Witchcraft Trials." In *The Occult in America: New Historical Perspectives*, eds. Howard Kerr and Charles L. Crow, 38–57. Urbana, IL: University of Illinois Press, 1983.

———. *Witchcraft at Salem*. New York: Braziller, 1969.

Henningsen, Gustav. *The Witches' Advocate: Basque Witchcraft and the Spanish Inquisition*. Reno, NV: University of Nevada Press, 1980.

Karlsen, Carol F. *The Devil in the Shape of a Woman: Witchcraft in Colonial New England*. New York: Norton, 1987.

Kieckhefer, Richard. *European Witch Trials: Their Foundations in Popular and Learned Cultures, 1300–1500*. Berkeley, CA: University of California Press, 1976.

Kittredge, George Lyman. *Witchcraft in Old and New England*. New York: Atheneum, 1972. Reprint.

Klaits, Joseph. *Servants of Satan: The Age of the Witch Hunts*. Bloomington, IN: Indiana University Press, 1985.

Koehler, Lyle. *A Search for Power: The "Weaker Sex" in Seventeenth-Century New England*. Urbana, IL: University of Illinois Press, 1980.

Konig, David Thomas. *Law and Society in Puritan Massachusetts: Essex County, 1629–1692*. Chapel Hill, NC: University of North Carolina Press, 1979.

Kunze, Michael. *Highroad to the Stake: A Tale of Witchcraft*, trans. by William E. Yuill. Chicago: University of Chicago Press, 1987.

Larner, Christina. *Enemies of God: The Witch-Hunt in Scotland*. Baltimore: Johns Hopkins University Press, 1981.

Levack, Bryan P. *The Witch-Hunt in Early Modern Europe*. London: Longman, 1987.

MacFarlane, Alan. *Witchcraft in Tudor and Stuart England: A Regional and Comparative Study*. London: Routledge and Kegan Paul, 1970.

Mappen, Marc. *Witches & Historians: Interpretations of Salem*. Huntington, NY: Krieger Publishing, 1980.

Midelfort, H. C. Erik. *Witch Hunting in Southwestern Germany, 1562–1684*. Stanford, CA: Stanford University Press, 1972.

Monter, E. William. *Witchcraft in France and Switzerland: The Borderlands During the Reformation*. Ithaca, NY: Cornell University Press, 1976.

Nelson, Mary. "Why Witches Were Women." In *Women: A Feminist Perspective*, ed. Jo Freeman, 451–468. Palo Alto, CA: Mayfield Publishing, 1979, 2nd ed.

Peters, Edward. *The Magician, the Witch, and the Law*. Philadelphia: University of Pennsylvania Press, 1978.

Quaife, G. R. *Godly Zeal and Furious Rage: The Witch in Early Modern Europe*. New York: St. Martin's Press, 1987.

Russell, Jeffrey Burton. *Witchcraft in the Middle Ages*. Ithaca, NY: Cornell University Press, 1972.

Starkey, Marion L. *The Devil in Massachusetts: A Modern Inquiry into the Salem Witch Trials*. Garden City, NY: Doubleday, 1969. Reprint.

Taylor, John M. *The Witchcraft Delusion in Colonial Connecticut, 1647–1697*. New York: Grafton Press, 1908.

Thomas, Keith. *Religion and the Decline of Magic*. New York: Scribner's, 1971.

Trevor-Roper, H. R. *The European Witch-Craze of the Sixteenth and Seventeenth Centuries and Other Essays*. New York: Harper and Row, 1969. Reprint.

Upham, Charles W. *Salem Witchcraft*. 2 vols. Williamstown, MA: Corner House, 1971. Reprint.

Weisman, Richard. *Witchcraft, Magic, and Religion in 17th Century Massachusetts*. Amherst, MA: University of Massachusetts Press, 1984.

ARTICLES

Ardiff, William. "Bridget Bishop: Salem Witch." *Danvers Historical Society, Historical Collections*, XLII (1964): 37–50.

Ben-Yehuda, Nachman. "The European Witch Craze of the 14th to 17th Centuries: A Sociologist's Perspective." *American Journal of Sociology*, LXXXVI (July 1980): 1–32.

Brown, David C. "The Case of Giles Corey." *Essex Institute Historical Collections*, CXXI (October 1985): 282–299.

———. "The Salem Witchcraft Trials: Samuel Willard's *Some Miscellany Observations.*" *Essex Institute Historical Collections*, CXXII (July 1986): 207–236.

Butler, Jon. "Magic, Astrology, and the Early American Religious Heritage, 1600–1760." *American Historical Review*, LXXXIV (April 1979): 317–346.

Caporael, Linnda R. "Ergotism: The Satan Loosed in Salem?" *Science*, CXCII (April 2, 1976): 21–26.

Clark, Stuart. "Inversion, Misrule and the Meaning of Witchcraft." *Past & Present*, LXXXVII (May 1980): 98–127.

Cohn, Norman. "Was There Ever a Society of Witches?" *Encounter*, XLIII (December 1974): 26–41.

Demos, John. "Entertaining Satan." *American Heritage*, XXIX (August/September 1978): 14–23.

———. "John Godfrey and His Neighbors: Witchcraft and the Social Web in Colonial Massachusetts." *William & Mary Quarterly*, 3d Ser., XXXIII (April 1976): 242–265.

———. "Underlying Themes in the Witchcraft of Seventeenth-Century New England." *American Historical Review*, LXXV (June 1970): 1311–1326.

Drake, Frederick C. "Witchcraft in the American Colonies, 1647–1662." *American Quarterly*, XX (Winter 1968): 695–725.

Gildrie, Richard P. "Visions of Evil: Popular Culture, Puritanism and the Massachusetts Witchcraft Crisis of 1692." *Journal of American Culture*, VIII (Winter 1985): 17–33.

Gragg, Larry. "Samuel Parris: Portrait of a Puritan Clergyman." *Essex Institute, Historical Collections*, CXIX (October 1983): 209–237.

Hall, David D. "Witchcraft and the Limits of Interpretations." *New England Quarterly*, LVIII (June 1985): 253–281.

Henningsen, Gustav. "The Greatest Witch-Trial of All, Navarre, 1609–1614." *History Today*, XXX (November 1980): 36–39.

Hoak, Dale. "The Great European Witch-Hunts: A Historical Perspective." *American Journal of Sociology*, LXXXVIII (May 1983): 1270–1274.

———. "Witch-Hunting and Women in the Art of the Renaissance." *History Today*, XXXI (February 1981): 22–26.

Horsley, Richard A. "Who Were the Witches? The Social Roles of the Accused in the European Witch Trials." *Journal of Interdisciplinary History*, IX (Spring 1979): 689–715.

Kenses, James. "Some Unexplored Relationships of Essex County Witchcraft to the Indian Wars of 1675 and 1689." *Essex Institute Historical Collections*, CXX (July 1984): 179–212.

Kibbey, Ann. "Mutations of the Supernatural: Witchcraft, Remarkable Providences, and the Power of Puritan Men." *American Quarterly*, XXXIV (September 1982): 125–148.

Larner, Christina. "Witch Beliefs and Witch-Hunting in England and Scotland." *History Today*, XXXI (February 1981): 32–36.

Le Beau, Bryan F. "Philip English and the Witchcraft Hysteria." *Historical Journal of Massachusetts*, XV (January 1987): 1–20.

Monter, William. "French and Italian Witchcraft." *History Today*, XXX (November 1980): 31–35.

Nicholls, David. "The Devil in Renaissance France." *History Today*, XXX (November 1980): 25–30.

Roach, Marilynne K. "'That Child, Betty Parris': Elizabeth (Parris) Barron and the People in Her Life." *Essex Institute, Historical Collections*, CXXIV (January 1988): 1–27.

Robbins, Peggy. "The Devil in Salem." *American History Illustrated*, VI (December 1971): 4–9 and 44–48.

Spanos, Nicholas P., and Gottlieb, Jack. "Ergotism and the Salem Village Trials." *Science*, CXCIV (December 24, 1976): 1390–1394.

Thompson, Roger. "Salem Revisited." *American Studies*, VI (December 1972): 317–346.

Trask, Richard B. "Raising the Devil." *Yankee*, XXXVI (May 1972): 74–77 and 190–201.

Werking, Richard H. "'Reformation Is Our Only Preservation': Cotton Mather and Salem Witchcraft." *William and Mary Quarterly*, 3d Ser., XXIX (April 1972): 281–290.

Zguta, Russell. "Witchcraft Trials in Seventeenth-Century Russia." *American Historical Review*, LXXXII (December 1977): 1187–1207.

Index

ABOUT THE AUTHOR

LARRY GRAGG is Professor of History at the University of Missouri-Rolla. He has published two other books, *Migration in Early America* and *A Quest for Security: The Life of Samuel Parris, 1653–1720* (Greenwood Press, 1990).

ISBN 0-275-94189-2

HARDCOVER BAR CODE